The Quest for Statehood

THE QUEST FOR STATEHOOD

Korean Immigrant Nationalism and U.S. Sovereignty, 1905–45

Richard S. Kim

UNIVERSITY PRESS

Oxford University Press, Inc., publishes works that further
Oxford University's objective of excellence
in research, scholarship, and education.

Oxford New York
Auckland   Cape Town   Dar es Salaam   Hong Kong   Karachi
Kuala Lumpur   Madrid   Melbourne   Mexico City   Nairobi
New Delhi   Shanghai   Taipei   Toronto

With offices in
Argentina   Austria   Brazil   Chile   Czech Republic   France   Greece
Guatemala   Hungary   Italy   Japan Poland   Portugal   Singapore
South Korea   Switzerland   Thailand   Turkey   Ukraine   Vietnam

Copyright © 2011 by Oxford University Press, Inc.

Published by Oxford University Press, Inc.
198 Madison Avenue, New York, NY 10016

www.oup.com

Oxford is a registered trademark of Oxford University Press

All rights reserved. No part of this publication may be reproduced,
stored in a retrieval system, or transmitted, in any form or by any means,
electronic, mechanical, photocopying, recording, or otherwise,
without the prior permission of Oxford University Press.

Portions of this book are adapted from articles previously published in:
Richard S. Kim. "Inaugurating the American Century: The 1919 Philadelphia Korean Congress, Korean Diasporic Nationalism, and American Protestant Missionaries," *Journal of American Ethnic History* 26, no. 1 (Fall 2006): 50–76. Copyright by the Immigration and Ethnic History Society. Reprinted by permission.
"Local Struggles and Diasporic Politics: The 1931 Court Cases of the Korean National Association of Hawai'i," in *From the Land of Hibiscus: Koreans in Hawai'I*, edited by Yŏng-ho Ch'oe. © University of Hawai'i Press. Reprinted with permission.
"Managing the 'Foreign' and 'Domestic': Kilsoo Haan, Korean Diasporic Nationalism, and the U.S. Liberal State, 1931-1945," *Seoul Journal of Korean Studies* 19, no. 1 (2006), 15–59. Copyright by Kyujanggak Institute for Korean Studies. Reprinted with permission.
"Diasporic Politics and the Globalizing of America: Korean Immigrant Nationalism and the 1919 Philadelphia Korean Congress," in *Diasporas: New Conceptions, New Frameworks*, edited by Rhacel Salazar Parreñas and Lok Siu. Copyright © 2008 by the Board of Trustees of the Leland Stanford Jr. University All rights reserved. Used with the permission of Stanford University Press, www.sup.org.

Library of Congress Cataloging-in-Publication Data
Kim, Richard S., 1967–
The quest for statehood : Korean immigrant nationalism and U.S. sovereignty, 1905–1945 / Richard S. Kim.
    p. cm.
Includes bibliographical references.
ISBN 978-0-19-536999-1 (acid-free paper) — ISBN 978-0-19-537000-3 (acid-free paper) (pbk.) 1. Korean resistance movements, 1905–1945. 2. Koreans—United States—History—20th century. 3. Koreans—United States—Politics and government. 4. Nationalism—Korea—History—20th century. 5. Korea—History—Japanese occupation, 1910-1945. I. Title.
DS916.594.U6K46   2011
320.54095190973—dc22   2010037525

For Darius, Olivia, and Sylvia
who have sustained me

CONTENTS

Acknowledgments   *ix*
List of Abbreviations   *xiii*
Note on Transliteration   *xv*

Introduction   3
Chapter 1: Mapping the Geopolitical Terrain of the Korean Diaspora   15
Chapter 2: Becoming Diasporic: From Labor Migrants to Political Wanderers, 1905–19   26
Chapter 3: Inaugurating a "New Korea": The March First Movement and the Korean Provisional Government   46
Chapter 4: Contesting Issues of State Power in the Diaspora   66
Chapter 5: Local Struggles and Diasporic Politics: The 1931 Court Cases of the Korean National Association of Hawaii   92
Chapter 6: Kilsoo Haan and "Constructive Americanism": The Ethnicization of Korean Immigrant Nationalism, 1931–45   109
Chapter 7: "In Due Course": Diasporic Nationalism, the United Korean Committee in America, and U.S. Sovereignty   135
Conclusion   158

Notes   165
Bibliography   191
Index   215

ACKNOWLEDGMENTS

This book would not have been possible without the help and support of so many individuals and institutions. I am deeply grateful to all of them. The book originated as a doctoral dissertation. With his incredible breadth of historical knowledge, my dissertation chair, Richard Cándida Smith, guided me in useful and, at times, unexpected directions that always led to productive analytical insights. His unwavering support, especially during critical times, will always be appreciated. Terry McDonald introduced me to the complexities and contradictions of U.S. liberalism. His intellectual influence profoundly shaped the fundamental arguments of this book. Silvia Pedraza was tremendously supportive from the beginning. She helped me navigate the voluminous sociological literature on migration and immigration, which allowed me to see the possibilities and limits of the concept of diaspora. Gail Nomura's support and guidance were indispensable as well. Her incisive questions and comments always pushed me to sharpen my ideas and to strive for clarity. While at the University of Michigan, I had the good fortune of working with other amazing scholars who have directly and indirectly contributed to the writing of this book. I wish to especially thank Fred Cooper, Henry Em, Susan L. Johnson, Robin D. G. Kelley, Earl Lewis, Susan Najita, George Sánchez, Steve Sumida, Penny Von Eschen, and Ernie Young.

Many individuals provided invaluable assistance during my research trips to archives around the country. Special thanks to Yong-ho Ch'oe, Ned Schultz, Michael Macmillan, James Cartwright, Kyungmi Chun, Amy Fine, and Joan Hori at the University of Hawai'i, Manoa. I am also deeply indebted to Roberta Chang of Honolulu for sharing valuable archival materials and her expansive knowledge of Korean American history in Hawaii. In Washington, D.C., Carolyn Chung's extraordinary generosity and hospitality enabled my research at the National Archives, for which I am eternally grateful. Ken Klein at the University of Southern California graciously allowed me open access to archival materials while they were being prepared for digitization. Since my ability to travel to South Korea was limited, Do Hyung Kim at the Independence Hall of Korea and Hae Kyung Chung at Hoseo University laboriously packed and shipped numerous boxes of books and other source materials to me in California. My heartfelt thanks to the Haan family, particularly Stanley and Dorothea, for their unwavering support and trust in my research on their father, Kilsoo Haan. I will always remember with great fondness their generosity and enthusiasm in sharing their extraordinary family history with me.

At UC Davis, I have been lucky to be surrounded by so many wonderful individuals who have helped in the process of revising my dissertation into a book manuscript. As department chair, Wendy Ho ensured a supportive institutional environment. She has cheerfully provided valuable assistance every step of the way and extended herself far beyond the call of duty. My colleagues in the Department of Asian American Studies have been steadfast in their helpful advice and encouragement. Two colleagues deserve special mention. Over the last six years, Susette Min has been a close and trusted friend and ally as we have passed through life's major moments during our time at UC Davis. Rhacel Parreñas has patiently guided me through the world of academic publishing. In spite of her incredibly hectic life, she has been extraordinarily generous with her time and advice. I have benefited greatly from her mentorship and friendship. Other colleagues at UC Davis also have offered valuable encouragement and intellectual stimulation, including Miroslava Chavez-Garcia, Bill Hing, Mark Jerng, Caren Kaplan, Ari Kelman, Kyu Hyun Kim, Sunaina Maira, Lisa Materson, Kimberly Nettles, Bettina Ng'weno, Dina Okamoto, Carolyn de la peña, Ron Saufley, Karen Shimakawa, Stanley Sue, Julie Sze, Cecilia Tsu, Georges Van Den Abbeele, Grace Wang, and Nolan Zane. I would like to thank Jieun Lee, Su Lee, Gowoon Noh, and Jee-Eun Song for their assistance with research and translations. Kathy Entao, Billie Gabriel, Jennifer Mattheis, Karen Nofziger, Tina Tansey, and Connie Zeiller each helped me navigate the perplexing bureaucracies of the university system. My deans at the Division of Humanities, Arts, and Cultural Studies—Elizabeth Langland, Jessie Ann Owens, and Pat Turner—provided crucial financial assistance over the years. The research and writing of this project were also partially supported by funding from the President's Research Fellowships in the Humanities, University of California. My undergraduate students deserve special thanks for serving as the test audience for some of my ideas and arguments that were still in progress. Their humor and frankness always kept me grounded and constantly reminded me why my scholarship should matter. During my very first visit to the Davis campus, I had the good fortune of meeting longtime local residents K. W. Lee and Grace and Luke Kim. Over the years, they have been treasured sources of inspiration, ideas, information, and encouragement.

I am extremely grateful to Sucheng Chan, Henry Em, Donna Gabaccia, Mae Ngai, Gary Okihiro, Rhacel Parreñas, and Cecilia Tsu for reading early incarnations of the manuscript. Their helpful feedback was instrumental in its overall development, and many of their insightful suggestions have made their way into the book. I am also indebted to the two anonymous reviewers for Oxford University Press. Their closely engaged feedback and thoughtful critiques helped sharpen my conceptualization and arguments in substantial ways. In the long course of researching and writing this book, I have been graced by the advice, feedback, support, and good cheer of many colleagues, friends, and family members. Special thanks to Henry Ahn, Kimberly Alidio, Eichiro Azuma, John Byun, John Cheng, John Chun, Cary Cordova, Arleen de Vera, Arif Dirlik, Gisele Fong, Tom Guglielmo, Brian Hayashi, Stacey Hirose, Alice Hom, Madeline Hsu, David Hyun, Yuji Ichioka, Tom Im, Moon-Ho Jung, Barbara Kim, Elaine Kim, Lili Kim, Michael Kim, Steve Kim, Scott Kurashige, Simona Kwon, Erika Lee, Marjorie Lee, Russell Leong, John Lie, Anthony Macias, Daryl Maeda, Linda Maram, Valerie Matsumoto, Aims McGuiness, John McKiernan Gonzalez, Nancy Mirabal, Don Nakanishi, Brian Niiya, Wayne Patterson, Jeffrey Rangel, Lok Siu, Willie Song, Nicole Stanton, Dean Toji, K. Scott Wong, Eun Sik Yang, Meredith Woo Cumings, David Yoo, Grace Yoo, Ji-Yeon Yuh, and Judy Yung. Liz Lee, Judy Han, and Jennifer Giang provided invaluable cartographic assistance. Many thanks also to Emily Han Zimmerman, who meticulously proofread every page during the very last stages of production and expertly compiled the index.

Portions of this book were previously published in the *Journal of American Ethnic History*, the *Seoul Journal of Korean Studies*, and edited collections by the University of Hawai'i Press and Stanford University Press. They are reprinted here in revised form with permission of the respective editors and publishers. Special thanks to Ken Klein, K. W. Lee, and the University of Hawai'i Press for permission to use the photos in this book.

Working with Susan Ferber, my editor at Oxford, has been an extraordinary experience. She patiently guided me through the process of scholarly publication, providing valuable advice at every stage. She also magnanimously accommodated my irregular schedule for which I am extremely grateful. Under great time constraints, Susan meticulously read through my entire manuscript and gave thoughtful comments and suggestions on nearly every page. Her expert editing helped sharpen my ideas and writing throughout the manuscript, making this a much better book.

Lastly, I would like to thank my family. My parents, Yoon and Hyun Kim, have never questioned my long and winding career path and have supported me unconditionally along the entire way. My in-laws, Kang and Haeja Kwon, have given me so much. I will always remember and appreciate their loving care and support, especially during difficult times. The stars of my life, Olivia and Darius, came into this world during the writing of this book. They have brought so much love and happiness into my life. They have enriched both my life and this book in immeasurable ways. Finally, I would like to thank Sylvia Kwon. She has been present from the very start of this project. Throughout this time, she has been my sharpest critic and strongest supporter. Her faith in me has never wavered. Her feedback, advice, love, and encouragement have been unceasing sources of sustenance and inspiration. Without her, this book would not have been possible.

LIST OF ABBREVIATIONS

HONUKC	Honolulu United Korean Committee
HSPA	Hawaiian Sugar Planters' Association
KNA	Korean National Association
KOPOGO	Korean Provisional Government
KORIC	Korean Commission
KPG	Korean Provisional Government
LAUKC	Los Angeles United Korean Committee
MID	Military Intelligence Division
ONI	Office of Navy Intelligence
UKC	United Korean Committee

A NOTE ON TRANSLITERATION

Wherever possible, I have adhered to the McCune-Reischauer system of transliteration for Korean names, organizations, and other terms. For personal names, I have placed surnames before given names, as is the practice in East Asia, except in cases where individuals used alternative spellings of their name and included their surname last, such as Syngman Rhee, Kiusic, Kimm, Philip Jaisohn, Henry Chung (DeYoung), Kilsoo Haan, and Jacob Dunn. Moreover, the original source materials often use transliterations of personal names, organizations, and places that do not always conform to the McCune-Reischauer system. In such cases, I choose to use a consistent spelling of the name as contained in the original sources.

The Quest for Statehood

Introduction

On June 26, 1913, eleven Korean laborers arrived in the small rural town of Hemet, California. Local ranchers Joseph Simpson and William Wilson had hired the Korean men to pick apricots at their orchard during what was expected to be a record harvest season. They and their fellow ranchers were frustrated to find a shortage of available labor from the local area. According to grower estimates, over 600 laborers would be required for the harvest, but the region could supply only 350 workers. Remembering the previous year's hardships when a large portion of their crops went unharvested due to similar labor shortages, many ranchers believed they had no choice but to hire laborers from outside areas to avoid major financial losses.[1] Under the circumstances, Simpson and Wilson had contracted Korean laborers from nearby Riverside to pick their apricot crops.

Upon arriving in Hemet by train around midnight, the Korean workers contacted Simpson for transportation to his orchard and in the meantime they made their way to a recreation hall near the railroad station. News of the arrival of a group of "Asiatics" quickly spread throughout the small town. When they left the building, the Korean laborers suddenly found themselves surrounded by an angry mob of over 100 white men, who had been gathering in front of the recreation hall.[2] The strong presence of Japanese tenant farmers in California agriculture had been igniting virulent anti-Asian sentiments among white workers throughout the state. In May, the California legislature, responding to the powerful anti-Japanese movement, almost unanimously passed the Alien Land Law of 1913 that prohibited Japanese, as well as other Asians, from owning land and greatly limited the length of tenure for leasing land. Consequently, anti-Asian, particularly anti-Japanese, sentiment was running high in Hemet when the Korean laborers arrived.

The angry crowd, who assumed the Koreans were Japanese, threatened them with physical violence and ordered them to leave town immediately. Greatly outnumbered and fearing for their lives, the Koreans rushed back to the train station. The large mob followed them and continued to harass them until the next train arrived at around 1:30 a.m. As soon as it pulled into the depot, the Korean men hastily jumped aboard leaving behind their baggage and camping gear. As the train pulled away, the crowd cheered and defiantly threw in the laborers' cargo.[3] Soon thereafter, orchard owners Simpson and Wilson arrived at the scene and informed the crowd that the expelled men were actually Korean. In response, a member of the mob exclaimed that the difference did not matter because Hemet was "a white man's valley."[4]

The incident received widespread press coverage. The Japanese Association of Southern California quickly gathered information from local Japanese residents and provided the Japanese consulate in San Francisco with details of the Koreans' expulsion. Representatives urged the consular-general to investigate the matter, claiming that the Korean victims, as colonial subjects of Japan, were entitled to protection from the Japanese government, as was any Japanese citizen.[5]

News of the Hemet incident also reached government officials in Washington, D.C., who were greatly disturbed by the event. The Japanese ambassador in Washington directed the consular-general in San Francisco to investigate the matter promptly. Without waiting for any complaints from the Japanese ambassador, U.S. Secretary of State William Jennings Bryan immediately ordered his own investigation through the Department of Justice.[6] Suddenly, the small farm town of Hemet had become a hot spot for a potential international crisis.

Bryan was particularly concerned that the incident could exacerbate already tense diplomatic relations between the two nations. In the preceding months, Japanese Ambassador Viscount Sutemi Chinda had vehemently protested the passage of the Alien Land Law, arguing that it violated international treaty agreements in which citizens of either nation had the right to own land and property in the nation of the other.[7] To ease tensions with the Japanese government, Secretary of State Bryan assured Ambassador Chinda that he had personally ordered an official inquiry into the incident and that the U.S. government would prosecute the perpetrators. Relieved that no physical harm had been inflicted on the Korean laborers, Bryan hoped that his office's swift action would prevent similar incidents against Japanese nationals in California that could easily escalate into violence.⁸

While federal officials from Washington were making their way to Hemet, the Japanese vice-consul from San Francisco and a representative of the Japanese Association of Southern California met with the expelled Korean men in Riverside on June 27. Explaining that Koreans in the United States had no official diplomatic relations with the American government, the Japanese officials offered to help the Korean laborers receive compensation for the incident. The Koreans adamantly refused Japanese assistance for what they considered to be a "purely Korean problem," emphatically asserting that Koreans in America were capable of handling their own problems. Incensed at what they perceived to be Japan's attempt to interfere in the internal affairs of the Korean community, the Korean laborers reported the Japanese diplomatic overtures to the Korean National Association (KNA) headquarters in San Francisco, which had been formed in 1909 to provide social services to Korean immigrants and promote the cause of Korean independence.⁹

Greatly disturbed by Japanese intervention, KNA President David Lee sent a telegram to Secretary of State Bryan informing him that the incident in Hemet had been resolved and requesting that the State Department cease its dealings with the Japanese government in matters pertaining to Koreans. Lee asserted that Koreans in the United States were not Japanese subjects because they had left Korea before Japan's annexation in 1910. As a result, Japan had no jurisdiction over Koreans in America. Lee added that Koreans would never submit to Japanese rule "as long as the sun remains in the sky," and that the American government should deal directly with the Korean National Association on all matters involving Koreans in the United States.¹⁰

To address the situation, the KNA sought to establish its own diplomatic relations with the U.S. State Department. The KNA informed Bryan that Koreans in the United States were a separate and autonomous diplomatic entity, capable of attending to their own affairs without Japanese assistance. They continued to assert that Japan's annexation of Korea violated international treaties and the U.S. government should officially distinguish Koreans from the Japanese.¹¹

The self-declared autonomy of the Koreans from the Japanese would help Bryan deflect any criticisms from the Japanese government concerning the expulsion of the Korean laborers. He promptly issued a press release explaining that the matter at Hemet had been resolved and the government's investigation would be discontinued immediately.[12] Though he avoided direct contact with the Koreans, Bryan's decision to close the case represented a de facto recognition by the U.S. government that Koreans were not Japanese subjects and thus Japan had no jurisdiction over Koreans in the United States. Moreover, the KNA was indirectly acknowledged as a quasi-diplomatic representative for Koreans residing in America.[13]

Despite the response of the State Department, the case was not altogether over for the Koreans. The Japanese Association of Southern California continued to make public statements that the Korean laborers still intended to pursue Japanese diplomatic channels to gain financial indemnity from the U.S. government for losses suffered as a result of their expulsion from Hemet.[14] Outraged by the ongoing diplomatic gestures from the Japanese, one of the Korean men involved in the incident issued a public statement published in the *Los Angeles Times*. Korean representatives, he explained, had arranged a meeting with grower Joseph Simpson and the farmers had agreed to compensate the Koreans for their train tickets out of Hemet and the loss of wages for two days of work, which amounted to about $70.[15] Asserting that Koreans were unequivocally not Japanese, the Korean laborer expressed his indignation at the continual attempts by the Japanese to represent the interests of Koreans in America:

> We don't want to see the Japanese Consul, or for that matter have any Japanese interfere with our affairs whether they are personal or even of an international character. We are responsible for ourselves even though we should perish in this or any other country, the victims of fanatical hatred of any other people, we should not look to Japan for redress of our problems. We are Koreans, not Japanese, and Japan has no reason to protest at Washington because of our troubles.[16]

The Hemet incident is a prism into the ways in which Korean immigrants in the United States claimed and asserted a national Korean identity in their daily experiences. This book examines the consequences and implications of such diasporic identifications with the homeland in a U.S. setting. The efforts of Korean immigrants to fight for the independence of their homeland prompted their participation in, and identification with, U.S. political institutions that established them as an American ethnic group. Korean nationalism was ironically central to the Americanization of Korean immigrants.

As seen in the Hemet incident, Korean immigrants zealously sought to affirm a national identity as *Koreans* that was separate and distinct from the

Japanese. These efforts occurred within a triangulated web of geopolitical relations involving the interests of a colonized Korea, imperialist Japan, and exclusionist United States. This international context decisively impacted the processes of community and identity formation for Koreans in America. The experiences of the 10,000 Koreans, most of whom migrated to the continental United States and Hawaiian Islands between 1903 and 1924, were framed by a continual involvement in homeland politics as a result of Japan's colonization of Korea between 1910 and 1945. Korean immigrants, many of whom had been recruited to the United States as contract laborers between 1903 and 1905, had to contend with daily struggles against racial discrimination and class exploitation. As in Hemet, they were subjected to anti-Asian movements in the United States that uniformly racialized Koreans and other Asian immigrants groups. These hostilities were manifested in various legal and extralegal forms, including exclusionary immigration laws, denial of naturalization rights, discriminatory economic sanctions, and physical violence.

The colonization of Korea left Koreans abroad without a state or nation. At the same time, Koreans in America were racially barred from becoming citizens as "aliens ineligible for citizenship." Without the right of naturalization and the franchise, they lacked legitimate recognition in the eyes of the U.S. state. As a result, issues of state power and its uses were central to all Korean immigrant political concerns. To which state did Koreans turn in order to advance and to protect their interests and well-being? And which state would assume such responsibilities?

This book examines these questions of state power by tracing the changes in the internal and external politics of Korean diasporic nationalism. Regarding Japanese rule as alien and illegitimate, Koreans in and out of the Korean peninsula viewed themselves as stateless peoples who wanted to establish a sovereign state of their own. Given the extremely repressive nature of Japanese colonial rule in Korea, independence activities had to be carried out from abroad. By 1944, nearly 12 percent of all Koreans were living outside the Korean peninsula. Koreans had migrated not only to the United States but also to Manchuria, Siberia, China, Europe, Mexico, and Cuba.[17] These circumstances provided the basis for the development of a diasporic nationalism that created a political community extending beyond national borders of the homeland. Given the conditions of statelessness and exile, Korean diasporic nationalism was fundamentally rooted in concerns for state-building, manifested in a quest to establish a sovereign national state outside the territorial boundaries of Korea.

The movement systematically employed a nationalist discourse rooted in the principle of the territorially sovereign state derived from the Westphalian system of states, which has served as the basis for modern political identity and organization in the form of the modern Western nation-state system. It consistently espoused principles of democracy, self-determination, and popular sovereignty in trying to establish legitimacy as a recognized actor within the international system of nation-states.[18]

Situated at the nexus of geopolitical relations involving Korea, Japan, and the United States, Koreans in America emerged as vital actors in the Korean independence movement. With the rise of American global power during the first half of the twentieth century, the U.S. polity emerged as a key arena for the articulation of transnational practices associated with the Korean nationalist movement, enabling U.S.-based Koreans to mobilize international support and influence. Moreover, American political values served as key rhetorical and political strategies and empowered Koreans in America to play an instrumental role in the state-building project of Korean diasporic nationalism.[19]

As a diasporic community, Koreans in the United States remained socially and politically rooted in their connections to their homeland. All diasporic formations begin with the dispersal and displacement of particular groups of people from their ancestral homelands to at least two or more different foreign locations. These groups, in turn, mobilize various forms of collective action around shared themes of displacement and exile that create sustained ties, symbolic or real, to their homelands. The ties created and maintained with other migrants, displaced in other locales and sharing a common sense of marginalization, are also integral to the formation of diaspora. For Korean émigrés, relations among the homeland, host countries, and dispersed settlements of the diaspora itself provided the basis for a diasporic nationalism that linked dispersed Korean settlements in the common struggle to establish a sovereign Korean state.[20] These migrants forged and maintained economic, political, and sociocultural ties that crossed national borders. Korean diasporic nationalism developed from these transnational practices as people, money, values, ideologies, and information spread throughout an array of Korean settlements dispersed around the globe.

The dynamics of both transnationalism and diaspora were certainly evident in the 1913 Hemet incident. As seen in the Korean community response, a transnational orientation toward homeland politics provided the primary lens through which Korean immigrants understood their experiences in the United States. The recognition of Korea's national sovereignty was central to their response to the racial hostilities directed against

Korean and Japanese immigrants alike. Over three decades, Koreans in the United States and throughout the diaspora would continue their quest to establish a sovereign political state of their own.

Systematic efforts to create a national state presented serious challenges for coherent political action, however. By 1920, two major ideological camps had emerged within the diaspora, both of which advocated competing policies and strategies for achieving Korean independence. One contemporary observer aptly referred to them as the "American group" and the "Siberian-Manchurian group."[21] The American group actively pursued international diplomacy as the primary means for gaining independence. Engaged in a variety of propaganda and lobbying activities in the United States, it sought to enlist support for Korean independence from the United States and other Western powers. These activities were imbued with the U.S. government's rhetoric of self-determination, democracy, and freedom, embodied in President Woodrow Wilson's Fourteen Points. In contrast, the Siberian-Manchurian group, inspired by Leninist-based notions of self-determination, believed that direct armed struggle against the Japanese was the only way to achieve unconditional independence for Korea.[22] With Russian and later Chinese financial and military assistance, this socialist-oriented group sought to mobilize the large number of Koreans living in Siberia and Manchuria to conduct guerilla-style military attacks against the Japanese in the northern parts of Korea, believing that it would motivate the Korean populace to overthrow Japanese colonial rule. Beginning in the 1920s, the socialist-oriented component of the independence movement competed vigorously with the U.S.-based strand of the diaspora for ideological dominance and the best means to achieve independence, leading to deeply conflicting visions of an independent Korea. These factional debates and conflicts greatly constrained the ability of the nationalist movement to create a state that could act with sovereign authority to respond to the needs and well-being of its national constituents in the diaspora.

Due to these constraints, U.S.-based Koreans increasingly came to rely on the United States to act as a sovereign state to pursue the national interests of Koreans throughout the diaspora. This strategic reliance on U.S. state power reflected the development and articulation of an ethnic consciousness—a collective sense of peoplehood—among Korean immigrants in the United States. Thus, in unforeseeable ways, zealous transnational commitments to homeland politics among Korean immigrants prompted them to establish a politico-legal presence within U.S. state structures and institutions to attain independence for Korea. Immigrant organizations vigorously lobbied the executive, legislative, judiciary, and military branches. In the process, Korean immigrants emerged as a distinct political interest group, whereby ethnicity served as a basis for making nationalist claims.

Paradoxically, attachments to homeland political issues associated with the transnational practices of Korean nationalism led to the incorporation of Korean immigrants in American political structures. On the one hand, enduring transnational ties challenge conventional notions of immigrant assimilation that expect newcomers to shed their involvement and identifications with their home country as they seek full political and social integration in the United States. For a racialized group like Koreans in America, their transnational attachments ostensibly reified their racial difference, further alienating them from American society and politics. On the other hand, the strong homeland orientation associated with transnational political activities does not automatically inhibit the immigrant propensity to participate in American society and politics and may actually prompt such involvement.[23] This study contends that transnationalism was necessary for Korean immigrants to form an ethnic identity.

Much of the recent scholarship in American immigration and ethnic history has framed discussions of ethnicity in terms of cultural adaptation, emphasizing the persistence of homeland values, traditions, and cultural practices among immigrant communities in the United States.[24] This study, however, highlights the ways in which politics and political participation constitute sites for the construction of ethnicity.[25] Ethnicity was an ongoing process that emerged from daily interactions between the dominant host society and immigrants as they adapted to specific realities at particular historical moments.

In foregrounding the significance of politics in the process of ethnic group formation, this study specifically calls attention to the often overlooked ways in which the modern state promotes the creation and maintenance of ethnic identities through its official recognition of ethnicity as a basis for political access and participation. In this context, the state serves as the primary arena in which competing groups vie for power and resources. The state, with its capacity to resolve conflicts and distribute privilege and resources in response to group claims, is the direct arbiter of an ethnic group's interests, well-being, and status in the polity. Thus, only by constituting themselves as part of American society could Korean immigrants gain the "right" to make claims on the U.S. polity, pressuring the latter to support their aspirations and efforts to recover Korea's independence. In this way, the transnational and local interests of Korean immigrants were not mutually exclusive but inextricably linked. The significant role of ethnicity in American political processes is a defining characteristic of the state-society relationship embedded in twentieth-century American interest group politics.[26]

Of course, this interrelationship between ethnicity and political incorporation is not unique to the experiences of Korean immigrants. Throughout American history, immigrants have entered and participated in the American polity as ethnic groups. The Irish, Jews, Italians, Poles, Germans, Greeks, Yugoslavians, Hungarians, and Czechoslovakians, for instance, all relied on a range of political means to access and influence American public opinion and political decision-making processes for various causes related to their respective homelands. During World War I and World War II, in particular, an array of American immigrant groups from stateless territories inundated U.S. government officials in Washington, D.C., with petitions for some sort of official diplomatic recognition or intervention on behalf of their respective homelands. In this way, the political activities of Koreans in the United States closely adhered to established patterns of ethnic group politics.[27]

While Korean immigrants employed highly conventional political tactics to access the U.S. political arena, they were a highly unconventional group to do so because, unlike most of the other aforementioned American immigrant groups, they were legally denied the right of naturalization and could not vote. For many European immigrant groups, electoral politics provided a key point of entry into the U.S. political arena. In American cities with large immigrant populations, urban political machines actively canvassed ethnic neighborhoods seeking to secure immigrant votes. By recognizing and advancing the status and interests of ethnic groups, political machines helped immigrant groups integrate into the larger American society while simultaneously fostering ethnic group formation. In the process, the urban ethnic voting bloc emerged as a salient presence in the American political landscape.[28]

Ideologies of race and citizenship constrained the nature of political activities among Korean immigrants and their relationship to U.S. state institutions and society. Access to the vote gave immigrant ethnic groups from Europe opportunities for political advancement that was generally unavailable to Korean immigrants until after World War II. Political leverage for Koreans was further constrained by the fact that the largest concentration of Koreans resided on the Hawaiian Islands, which remained a U.S. territorial possession until 1959. As a result, Korean immigrants relied on a clientalist political model, which operated almost entirely by competing for and securing the support of powerful patrons. Though they were able to forge viable political spaces for themselves through these activities, political sponsorship was generally far less solid than that for other groups who could pressure potential political supporters through electoral processes.

This study stresses the distinctions between citizen-based and noncitizen-based ethnic politics. Ethnic group participation in the political system has been a central component in American ethnic pluralism, providing a model of belonging based on the assertion and maintenance of ethnic difference within the public sphere. In the pluralist model, recognition of the right to difference is not incompatible with a unified republic. The multiplicity of identities and multiplicity of interests in society are held together by a collective commitment to a common core of democratic values and ideals that constitute a unified national American identity. Despite this capacious vision of American society, it is almost exclusively based on the experiences of European immigrants, and ethnicity has been understood in terms of cultural differences rather than notions of race.[29] Racial minorities, Koreans and other Asians, have been historically perceived as inherently unfit for full and equal participation in the American nation and thus excluded from its political and social processes.

Meaningful discussion of the historically specific ways in which political, economic, social, and legal barriers for racial minorities have constrained their relationships with the dominant host society has been infrequent. Of course, immigrants from Europe, notably the Irish and then immigrants from southern and eastern Europe, struggled against various forms of discrimination in American society as "in-between people" who were considered neither fully white nor nonwhite.[30] Yet, all the "in-between" immigrant groups from Europe were eventually able to claim "whiteness," which enabled them to improve their social status in the United States and enter mainstream society. In contrast, Asian immigrants, racialized as "perpetual foreigners," were institutionally barred from becoming full members and participants of the American nation.[31] The state in the pluralist model of politics is thus not a neutral, impartial arbiter of group status and interests; rather, the coercive powers of the state have been selectively used against certain groups to limit and deny their access to, and participation in, the U.S. political arena. Lack of serious engagement with questions of race in conventional pluralist models of democratic participation has obscured fundamental issues of power, inequality, and racism.[32]

In tracing the development of Korean immigrant participation in the diasporic politics of the Korean independence movement, this book focuses on the experiences and activities of the U.S. component of the diaspora in four key sites: Honolulu, San Francisco, Los Angeles, and Washington, D.C. These cities were home to political organizations dedicated to mobilizing support and disseminating information and resources for the movement, and were at the heart of the emergent transnational networks. Focusing on these organizations' activities, this book closely examines questions of state power that informed the politics of Korean diasporic nationalism in its quest to achieve sovereign statehood.

Chapter 1 delineates the migration and settlement patterns of Koreans immigrating to Hawaii and the continental United States in the years prior to 1945, with an eye toward the geopolitical factors leading to Korea's loss of national sovereignty to Japan between 1905 and 1910. Geopolitical events created a shared sense of marginality and displacement across the Korean diaspora that provided conditions for the eventual development of a diasporic nationalism in search of statehood.

While most Koreans immigrated to the United States as labor migrants, the political situation in Korea had a profound politicizing effect on their daily lives as they zealously endeavored to claim and assert a national Korean identity that was separate and distinct from the Japanese. Chapter 2 examines the ties forged around homeland issues that were integral to the process of community formation among Koreans in America. It reveals the emergence of a diasporic consciousness among Korean immigrants as they saw themselves inextricably linked to their compatriots in their homeland and other locales between 1905 and 1945.

An array of nationalist organizations emerged in the Korean diaspora. The leadership of the intelligentsia performed the essential ideological work necessary in generating and mobilizing nationalist and ethnic identities within a particular population or group. While representing group interests, the collective claims and actions arising from organizations are often the product of contestation and negotiation.[33] Chapter 3 narrates the systematic efforts of nationalist leaders in the diaspora to establish a national Korean state that could represent the authentic sovereign of the Korean people in the aftermath of Japan's brutal suppression of the 1919 March First uprising. These efforts resulted in the formation of the Korean Provisional Government (KPG) in Shanghai, which developed out of multiple ideological and strategic strands within the diaspora. The globalization of American power following World War I empowered the U.S. component of the Korean diaspora to play a significant role in defining the vision of a new Korean nation-state.

Chapter 4 looks at the challenges and dilemmas in developing coherent political action in the diaspora. The independence movement particularly faced the challenge of centralizing the national authority of the KPG within the diaspora and creating focused policies toward the homeland. Shortly after the formation of the KPG, a highly contentious power struggle arose between the Korean Commission, under the leadership of KPG President Syngman Rhee, and Korean immigrant organizations in America under the direction of the KNA. This conflict exacerbated deep ideological and factional rifts within the national independence movement.

A period of retrenchment followed the breakdown of the KPG in the 1920s. Struggles for power and leadership continued at the local level, however. Chapter 5 focuses on the internecine conflicts among Korean nationalist organizations in Hawaii in the early 1930s. With no central sovereign authority of their own, Koreans in America turned to U.S. state structures to legitimate leadership within the community.

This reliance on U.S. state power was further articulated in the 1930s. Chapter 6 examines the activities of Kilsoo Haan, a Korean nationalist figure from Hawaii who emerged as a leading voice among Koreans in the diaspora during the 1930s. His activities promoted an unconditional acceptance of U.S. sovereignty as fundamental to Koreans achieving their national goals.

Soon after the U.S. entry into World War II, Korean nationalist organizations renewed intensive lobbying for the official recognition of the exiled Korean Provisional Government in China, which is detailed in Chapter 7. Seeing themselves as part of a common international struggle against Japan, Korean nationalist leaders expected the Allied powers, particularly the United States, to play a more active role in the liberation of their homeland. For the U.S. component of the diaspora, recognition from the U.S. state rather than the immediate independence of Korea became a focal point of their political activities. This claims-making on the American state reflected the articulation of an ethnic orientation among Korean immigrants. Their quest for statehood ended as they became ethnic subjects of the U.S. liberal state. Nonetheless, during the previous four decades, the quest embedded the Korean diaspora within the global geopolitics of the twentieth century.

CHAPTER 1

Mapping the Geopolitical Terrain of the Korean Diaspora

Korean migrations to the United States during the first half of the twentieth century occurred within a relatively short window of time. Between 1880 and 1902, just 50 Koreans including merchants, diplomats, and students entered the United States. A much larger wave of immigration commenced in 1903. Between 1903 and 1905, approximately 7,400 Koreans, most of them men, were recruited to work on the Hawaiian sugar plantations. About 1,000 Koreans, who had initially immigrated to Hawaii, made their way to the U.S. mainland in the years between 1905 and 1907. Further migrations from 1906 to 1924 consisted of about 600 political refugees, made up of mostly intellectuals and ex-government officials seeking to escape the tightening control of Japanese colonial rule, and over 1,000 "picture brides," who emigrated to marry earlier male immigrants. Together, this diverse group of laborers, picture brides, and intellectuals formed the foundations of the Korean immigrant community in the United States until large-scale emigration from Korea resumed in the post–World War II period.

This chapter traces the migration of Koreans to the United States in the years prior to 1945 and their adaptive strategies upon arrival. In mapping the migration and settlement patterns of Korean immigration the United States, it discusses the geopolitical circumstances that led to Korea's loss of national sovereignty to Japan in 1910. Beginning in the late nineteenth century, Korea emerged as a central battleground for geopolitical power struggles among its neighbors, thrusting Korea into a global system made up of individual nation-states competing for economic and military power.[1] These international rivalries not only precipitated the mass dispersal of Koreans from their homeland but also profoundly shaped their experiences as migrants abroad. Migration to the United States was thus inextricably intertwined with the machinations of international diplomacy, industrial capitalism, and restrictive immigration policies, all of which unfolded within a triangulated web of geopolitical relations involving a colonized Korea, imperialist Japan, and exclusionist United States.

In the mid- and late-nineteenth century, a series of imperialist rivalries engulfed the East Asian region and precipitated mass migration from the Korean peninsula. By 1944, nearly 12 percent of all Koreans were living outside of their homeland in destinations around the globe that included Manchuria, Siberia, China, Japan, Hawaii, the continental United States, Mexico, and Cuba.[2] The magnitude of this exodus was truly extraordinary considering that Korea had tightly closed its borders to all emigration for the previous two and a half centuries, garnering it the nickname "Hermit Kingdom."

The "opening" of East Asia by Western imperialist nations in the mid-nineteenth century set off a political maelstrom. China was the first to fall to European imperialist encroachments following its defeat by the British in the Opium War of 1839–40. Japan succumbed to Western imperialist pressures initiated by the gunboat diplomacy of American Commodore Matthew Perry in 1853. In both China and Japan, the European imperial powers imposed unequal treaty systems granting them territorial control in the form of extraterritorial legal rights and exclusive trading privileges at selected port cities.

Korea would meet a similar fate. Though the Koreans successfully fought off debilitating invasions by the Japanese and Manchus in the sixteenth century, the foreign intruders and invasions left the Korean nation and its people in near ruin, after which Korea sealed itself off from outside contact for two and a half centuries. Korea's long isolation abruptly ended with the arrival of Western imperial powers in East Asia. Ironically, Japan became the first nation to sign a modern international treaty with Korea. In a series of Meiji reform programs commencing in 1868, Japan instituted a state policy of adopting Western technology and rapid industrialization in an effort to acquire the power and international prestige of the European imperialist nations.[3] Under the threat of military force, Japan pressured Korea into signing the Kangwha Treaty in 1876, which established a Western-style unequal treaty system that gave Japan many of the same political and economic privileges the West had extracted from Japan and China in the decades before 1876. More importantly, the Kangwha Treaty represented the international recognition of Korea's sovereignty, which effectively ended China's age-old suzerainty over Korea. Though strictly adhering to its isolationist policy, the Korean court had maintained for centuries a traditional Confucian-based tributary system that recognized China as its superior "elder brother."[4] By declaring Korea's independence in the Kangwha Treaty, Japan sought to dismantle the East Asian world order, whereby Japan and Korea were perpetually subordinated to China.[5] By replacing this world order with a modern Western nation-state system, Japan had set a path to pursue its imperialist ambitions and begun the long and arduous odyssey in which Korea sought to redefine itself as a nation-state.[6]

Japan's actions set off a power struggle between China and Japan over dominance in Korea, culminating in the Sino-Japanese War in 1894. During the 1860s, China, like Japan, responded to the domestic upheaval caused by Western encroachment, but it sought to remedy its national ills by restoring the traditional Confucian system. The reform efforts included attempts to reassert China's suzerainty over Korea. Under the leadership of Li Hung-chang, China sought to pit imperial powers against each other in Korea. Li calculated that Korea would ultimately turn to its trusted "elder brother" China to help restore peace and stability. He encouraged the Korean court to open relations with Western nations.[7] In 1882, the United States became the first Western nation to enter into a modern treaty agreement with Korea. By 1893, Britain, Germany, Russia, Italy, Austria, and France had all signed similar treaties with Korea. Like previous unequal treaties in China and Japan, these international agreements gave Western nations inordinate commercial and diplomatic benefits in Korea, which ultimately led to increased international rivalries over influence and power in Korea. Within a short period, the Korean peninsula emerged as the central battleground for competing international powers.

This escalation in foreign involvement in Korea affairs created growing unrest among the Korean populace. Adopting the slogan, "Drive out the Japanese dwarfs and the Western Barbarians," a mass peasant movement arose in the 1860s under the name of Eastern Learning or Tonghak, which sought to rid Korea of all foreign intervention.[8] In the spring of 1894, the Tonghak movement led a massive rebellion. Unable to suppress the rebellion on its own, the Korean government requested assistance from China, which dispatched 3,000 troops to Korea and then notified Japan of its military deployment in Korea in accordance to the 1885 Treaty of Tientsin, which had been signed by China and Japan in the aftermath of the abortive

1884 Kapsin Coup in Seoul that brought Chinese and Japanese soldiers into a brief episode of armed conflict. Alarmed by the suddenly large Chinese military presence in Korea in 1894, Japan sent an even larger military force of 8,000 troops to the Korean peninsula. By the time the Japanese troops arrived in Korea, the Tonghak rebellion had lost much of its steam, eliminating the need for further Chinese and Japanese soldiers. Concerned by the large number of Japanese troops, China proposed a joint withdrawal of Chinese and Japanese military forces. Japan, however, saw the situation as an opportunity for a strong military presence in Korea to counterbalance and even displace Chinese influence on the peninsula. It suggested a joint Sino-Japanese reform of Korea's government in order to preserve peace in East Asia. China rejected Japan's proposal as "preposterous" interference in the internal affairs of Korea.[9] The two sides remained deadlocked, prompting a military clash. On July 23, 1894, Japanese troops suddenly seized the royal palace in Seoul and attacked Chinese soldiers, marking the beginning of the Sino-Japanese War and the emergence of Japan as an imperial power.

With its technological superiority, Japan's military handily defeated China. In 1895, the two powers signed the Treaty of Shimonoseki, awarding Japan valuable Chinese territorial possessions as well as predominant influence in Korea.[10] The Japanese victory effectively ended China's supremacy in Korea and marked a new period in Korean history. This victory and the revision of its unequal treaties did not fully translate into Japan being recognized by the international community as an equal world power. Japan's territorial gains in China greatly alarmed Russia, France, and Germany, which harbored their own imperialist ambitions in China. In what was called the Triple Intervention, the three Western nations immediately protested the provisions of the treaty and forced Japan to give up major portions of its newly acquired Chinese territories. Ultimately, the Triple Intervention enabled Russia to emerge as a formidable rival in Northeast Asia and to claim a stake in Korea. To counter this threat, Japan promptly moved its military forces back into Korea, eventually leading to the Russo-Japanese War in 1904.

Japan shocked the world in routing Russia, a powerful Western nation, in 1905. In July, U.S. President Theodore Roosevelt presided over peace treaty negotiations between the two countries. The Treaty of Portsmouth officially ended the Russo-Japanese War and announced Japan's emergence as a world power. Under the treaty, Japan appropriated all of Russia's possessions and interests in Korea and Manchuria. Unbeknownst to most Koreans, Americans, and even Japanese at the time and for many years thereafter, the U.S. Secretary of War, William Howard Taft, and the Japanese Prime Minister, Katsura Taro, entered into a secret accord during the peace negotiations at Portsmouth. In the Taft-Katsura agreement, the United States, under the authorization of President Roosevelt, agreed not to interfere with Japan's interests in Korea in exchange for Japan's noninterference in America's interests in the Philippines. American acquiescence removed all remaining obstacles for Japan to assume full control of the Korean peninsula.[11] Soon thereafter, Japan declared a protectorate over Korea as an open pronouncement of its newly arrived stature on the international stage. Though Japan recognized the sovereignty of the Korean nation and kept the Korean monarchy intact, Japan assumed control over much of Korea's administrative powers. In 1910, Japan formally annexed Korea as a colony, taking full control over every aspect of Korean life and culture.

During this period of disorder and foreign intrusion in Korea, the Hawaiian Sugar Planters' Association (HSPA), the main organization among plantation owners, was seeking new sources of cheap labor. By 1900, Chinese immigration to the United States had come to a nearly complete halt due to exclusionary legislation first enacted in 1882. At the same time, Japanese workers, who comprised about 80 percent of Hawaii's workforce, were becoming a source of concern for plantation owners due to frequent strikes for higher wages and better working conditions. Increasing numbers of Japanese were migrating to the U.S. mainland in search of better jobs. In order to ensure that wage levels would remain low by keeping its labor force divided along ethnic lines, the HSPA turned to Korean laborers. Between 1903 and 1905, Hawaiian sugar plantations recruited approximately 7,400 Korean laborers, who made up 11 percent of the sugar plantation workforce by 1905.[12]

Horace Allen, the United States Minister to Korea, was eager to promote American commercial interests in Korea and actively aided American companies in Korea, including the Hawaiian sugar plantations. In 1902, he persuaded the Korean king to allow Koreans to migrate to Hawaii, arguing that emigration would alleviate some of its domestic economic problems. He also convinced the king that immigration would increase Korea's international prestige since Chinese immigrants had been barred from entry.[13]

In contrast to the Chinese and Japanese who had originated from a single region or province, the majority of Korean immigrants to Hawaii came from town and cities throughout the Korean peninsula and from diverse social and occupational backgrounds. Farmers and rural laborers constituted only one-third of the total pool of migrants; the largest group was laborers from port cities and towns.[14] Many emigrants left due to the economic hardships brought on by the political and social turmoil in Korea. Attracted by reports of high wages in Hawaii, most migrated with the hope of amassing great wealth and returning to Korea after a few years.[15] Labor recruiters advertised opportunities for a Western education in Hawaii that would enable Koreans to improve the economic future for themselves and for their country. Religious freedom offered Korean Christians another reason for emigration. About 40 percent of the immigrants to Hawaii were recent Christian converts. At the turn of the twentieth century, American Protestant missionaries vigorously proselytized in Korea and successfully tapped into the frustration and dissatisfaction of Koreans prevalent in troubled times. Missionaries spoke favorably of the efforts of labor recruiters and encouraged converts to go to Hawaii to seek better lives. Koreans thus began to make a positive association between missionaries and the United States.[16]

Despite their varied backgrounds and motivations, more than 90 percent of Koreans entering the United States listed their occupations as farm laborers.[17] Since the Korean government and Hawaiian plantation owners sponsored Korean immigration, they most likely did so to ensure entry. Moreover, nearly all Koreans initially immigrated to Hawaii as contract laborers in order to fulfill the terms of their contracts with the plantations.[18]

Upon arrival in Hawaii, the Korean newcomers quickly discovered plantation life was incongruous with their high expectations of economic prosperity and increased social status. They were merely cheap labor for the plantation owners, who needed them to supplant insurgent Japanese workers. Koreans who had been farmers in Korea more easily adjusted to life in Hawaii. However, those who originated from urban areas with nonagricultural backgrounds found themselves ill suited for work on the plantations. In her 1937 master's thesis on the Korean community of Hawaii, Bernice Kim recorded stories from immigrants of "how some boys and even men, with fair hands blistered, faces and arms torn and scratched by the cane leaf stickers, would sit between the rows of cane and weep like children."[19]

Unsurprisingly, Koreans left the plantations as quickly as possible, faster than any of the other 33 ethnic groups who worked in the sugar plantations. At the peak year of immigration in 1905, Korean laborers made up 10.9 percent of the workforce on the plantations in Hawaii; within 10 years, they constituted only 3.1 percent. Between 1905 and 1910, 65 percent of Korean laborers migrated to the cities in Hawaii or to the U.S. mainland.[20]

The Koreans in Hawaii saw plantation labor as a temporary condition. Historian Wayne Patterson cites lack of agricultural experience as an important reason for their mediocre performance as field laborers compared with the Chinese and Japanese. The Japanese came primarily from farming backgrounds, and many probably planned to remain on the plantations for a longer time. As a result, they were motivated to improve their living conditions and wages, and engaged in frequent strikes and other labor-organizing efforts. By contrast, Koreans did not see a future on the sugar plantations, which accounted for their relative docility in dealing with low wages and poor living conditions. In 1910, the Korean National Association reported that about 4,000 Koreans, including approximately a hundred Hawaii-born Koreans, remained in Hawaii, primarily in the cities. Some 1,000 returned to Korea, while another thousand migrated to the mainland.[21]

The mass migration of Korean laborers to Hawaii came to an abrupt halt in April 1905. Two main factors are often cited as influencing the Korean government's decision to end further migrations. In 1904, about 1,000 Koreans left Korea to work on Mexico's hemp plantations on the Yucatan peninsula. A year later, news of the severe mistreatment of these laborers made national headlines. The Korean government banned further immigration to Mexico.[22]

Soon afterwards, the Japanese government, which had taken control of Korea's diplomatic affairs as a result of its protectorate treaty, demanded that the Korean government extend the ban to Hawaii. It was concerned about rapidly growing anti-Japanese sentiments on the U.S. mainland as increasing numbers of Japanese migrated from Hawaii to California. The Japanese government feared that the anti-Chinese exclusion legislation would be enacted against Japanese immigrants. As a newly emergent world power, the Japanese government was particularly concerned about the deleterious effect such legislation would have on its international reputation and standing among other powers.[23]

Japanese government officials asserted that Koreans consistently underbid the Japanese for work in Hawaii, which caused many Japanese laborers to leave in search of higher wages in California. As a result, the Japanese government believed that a ban on Korean immigration to Hawaii would substantially reduce the migration of Japanese to California and thus lessen the clamor for anti-Japanese legislation in the United States. Moreover, Japanese labor recruitment companies, which complained their business activity would be hampered if Korean immigration to Hawaii continued, strongly pressured the Japanese government to order the cessation of

Korean emigration.[24] These triangulated entanglements caused the mass migration of Koreans to Hawaii to virtually halt in 1905.

Meanwhile, Koreans already in Hawaii had begun to migrate to the U.S. mainland in search of new opportunities on an average of one or two years after completing the terms of their "informal" contracts with plantation owners. With a high demand for unskilled laborers, the expanding agricultural and railroad industries on the Pacific Coast offered wages well above the average 70 cents per day paid on the sugar plantations. In addition to economic motives, Koreans discovered that educational pursuits on the islands were limited, and word spread of the abundant opportunities for an education on the mainland. From 1905 to 1907, about 1,000 Koreans migrated from Hawaii to the mainland.[25]

These secondary migrations dropped off sharply after 1907. In response to the pressures of a virulent anti-Japanese movement throughout the Pacific Coast states, President Theodore Roosevelt signed Executive Order 589 in March 1907 that prohibited Japanese and Korean laborers, who held passports for Hawaii, Mexico, or Canada, from migrating to the U.S. mainland. In the winter of 1907, the Japanese government consented to the Gentlemen's Agreement and ceased issuing passports to Japanese and Korean laborers bound for the United States.

Despite these restrictions, a relatively small but steady stream of emigrants entered the United States between 1905 and 1924. During those years, over 1,000 "picture brides" arrived in the United States through a legal loophole in the Gentleman's Agreement that allowed wives to unite with their immigrant husbands who were already in America. Most of the picture brides were young women from poor rural families. During the same period, about 600 political refugees fled to the United States to escape Japan's repressive colonial policies. These exiles were primarily former soldiers of the Korean army, intellectuals, and ex-government officials from the upper echelons of Korean society. Korean immigration to the United States halted after the passage of the 1924 Immigration Act that denied entry to virtually all Asians.[26] As a result, the total population of approximately 10,000 Koreans in America remained relatively constant until the 1950s, far fewer in number than their Chinese, Japanese, and Filipino counterparts.

Korean settlements were widely scattered throughout the continental United States. About 800 settled in California, with the rest dispersed around railroad construction sites in Washington, Utah, Nevada, Colorado, and Nebraska. In 1910, a small number of Koreans resided in large cities such as San Francisco and Los Angeles, most of them students employed as "school boys." These young men attended school and earned a living as domestic servants in American households for room and board and a small stipend. During the summer, they worked as laborers in agriculture fields or on railroad construction sites to earn money for their tuition.[27]

From 1910 to 1920, nearly 83 percent of Koreans lived in small California agricultural towns such as Willows, Riverside, Oxnard, Reedley, Lompoc, Stockton, Dinuba, Walnut Grove, and Bakersfield.[28] Because most of their work was in the agricultural sector, their residential distribution was determined by the demand for agricultural labor. While plantation labor was stationary, farm work on the mainland involved constant migration based on crop seasons. California farms specialized in the cultivation of intensive crops, such as sugar beets, grapes, deciduous and citrus fruits, berries, vegetables, and hops, which required large amounts of hand labor during harvest seasons.[29] Given the large variety of crops cultivated throughout the Pacific Coast at different times of the year, there was a demand for harvest labor almost every month of the year. However, each harvest lasted only two to six weeks, requiring laborers to move constantly to find work.[30] One Korean laborer described his frequent moves from town to town:

> About ten days after I arrived in San Francisco (in 1916), I went to Stockton, and through a Korean contractor I went to work on a Caucasian-owned bean farm. There were about 20 other Koreans working there.... We were hoeing the bean fields and when we finished we went to another bean farm for hoeing. It was hard work.... Then we went to Dinuba picking grapes. I was flocking with other Koreans, and I went wherever they went for available farm jobs.[31]

Despite their urban occupational backgrounds, most Korean immigrants discovered that they could not get jobs in the cities due to anti-Asian sentiment. Agriculture offered an opportunity for upward socioeconomic mobility since laborers could save up money to lease land as tenant farmers and eventually buy land as farm owner-operators.[32] Given the demand for a mobile supply of labor, Koreans could gain some measure of independent economic prosperity through agricultural activities. At a time of rapid growth in Western agriculture, a significant number of Asians, including Koreans, were able to make the transition from laborer to farmer. Between 1905 and 1910, many Koreans found work in the Lower Sacramento River picking grapes on farms near Fresno and on the orange groves near

Riverside and Redlands.³³ The rapid growth of the rice industry in the Upper Sacramento Valley from 1914 to 1920 offered a chance for Koreans to create an economic niche for themselves. Some Korean farmers, as well as other Asian immigrants, even amassed small fortunes from their agricultural work.³⁴

Areas of extensive agricultural cultivation, especially during harvest seasons, offered numerous employment opportunities for Asians. As a result, Koreans did not tend to concentrate in any specific city or in a particular district within a city that would constitute a "Koreatown" until after the 1960s. Instead, they usually resided near established Chinese and Japanese settlements in cities and rural towns throughout California.³⁵ As relative newcomers to the mainland and a smaller minority than the Chinese or Japanese, Koreans often benefited by living in areas where Japanese farmers and laborers had already congregated and gained footholds in certain agricultural industries.

Between 1920 and 1930, the occupational patterns among Korean immigrants shifted from agricultural activities to commercial ventures, particularly family-operated small businesses, due to adverse conditions in agricultural work and restrictive land laws that targeted Asian farmers. During World War I, many Korean farmers in California benefited from the high agricultural prices spurred by the worldwide demand for American foodstuffs. After the war, market prices dropped sharply, leaving many Korean farmers devastated. Moreover, the state of California enacted revisions to the 1913 Alien Land Law. During the war, the law, which had prohibited Asian immigrants from buying or leasing land for more than three years, was not strictly enforced due to the high demand for American agricultural goods. As a result, Asian immigrant farming flourished between 1914 and 1920. In response to renewed anti-Asian agitation in the postwar depression, California legislators imposed more stringent restrictions on the Alien Land Law in 1920 and 1923 that made it nearly impossible for Asian immigrants to own or lease land for farming.³⁶ As a result, many Korean farmers found it extremely difficult to maintain their economic self-sufficiency in farming after 1920. Like tenant farming, opening a small business was also a pragmatic economic choice, since little capital was required, and unpaid family members could satisfy labor needs. Typical commercial ventures included fruit and vegetable stands, grocery stores, pressing and laundry shops, and restaurants.

This occupational shift was accompanied by a residential transition from rural to urban life. In 1910, 83 percent of the Korean population in California resided in farming areas and in 1920, 79 percent, but the United

States Census of 1930 recorded 1,860 Koreans residing on the mainland, with 1,250, or 67 percent, living in urban areas.[37] Los Angeles and San Francisco became the main urban centers for the Korean community. The numerous agricultural towns and communities near Los Angeles, such as Oxnard, Pomona, Upland, Riverside, and Redlands, that had earlier attracted Koreans fed the migration to Los Angeles County. By the end of the 1930s, Los Angeles had the largest Korean community on the mainland, with a population of about 650. San Francisco, which had assumed an early importance as the port of entry for Koreans coming from Hawaii and abroad, was home to approximately 150 Koreans in 1930.[38]

Korean occupational and residential patterns indicate the paramount importance of the search for economic autonomy in the development of Korean communities in Hawaii and the U.S. mainland. However, as political conditions worsened in Korea, homeland affairs increasingly played a significant role in the daily concerns of Korean immigrants as they organized their community lives around the struggle for national independence. Like their counterparts elsewhere in the diaspora, Korean immigrants in the United States were at the center of various geopolitical circumstances involving Japan, underscoring their sense of statelessness and powerlessness.[39] Under the conditions of Japanese colonization and exile, Japan consistently attempted to use Koreans throughout the diaspora to advance its own geopolitical interests.[40] Deeply politicized by events both in Korea and in the United States, Koreans in America began to see themselves as a diasporic community inextricably linked to their compatriots displaced in other locales.

CHAPTER 2

Becoming Diasporic

From Labor Migrants to Political Wanderers, 1905–19

My name is M.W. Chun. I am 25 years of age. I came to America as a student, but have no money. I am now farming. I was out in the country and came back five days ago, but I could find no work to do in the city. All the world looks on Corea as a low country and I was very sorry for it. I left my home for studying to help our country as other nations, but since I left the condition of Corea became worse. Japan thinks might is right, and would force our Government to make some treaties. And after that the great trouble has been started in our country. My brothers and relatives have been killed by the Japanese, but I have no power to do anything here, and so I have always had to stand around helpless.
—Chun Myung-won, *1908*

We are not the immigrants sent by the national policy, nor do we want to become the new world citizen. . . . Now our business should be for all Koreans and our activity should be based on the welfare of our mother country. Thus we are not sojourners, but political wanderers, and we are not laborers but righteous army soldiers.
—Sinhan Minbo, *1910*[1]

Although the search for economic self-sufficiency among Korean immigrants remained important, Korea's loss of national sovereignty to Japan between 1905 and 1910 would soon become the single most important issue for Korean immigrants. After annexation, Koreans in the United States no longer perceived themselves to be solely sojourning labor migrants in search of opportunities for economic betterment, but rather stateless "political wanderers" in search of ways to help their homeland.

Individuals such as Chun Myung-won would no longer "stand around helpless" as Japanese imperial encroachment destroyed their homeland and killed their brethren.

This chapter examines a series of dramatic events in San Francisco beginning in the spring of 1908 that heightened the political consciousness of Korean migrants in the United States as they came to view themselves as "political wanderers." The responses elicited by these events of 1908 marked a decisive moment in the development of a diasporic nationalism that would seek to establish a sovereign Korean state and create ties that bound dispersed Korean settlements to each other. On March 20, 1908, American diplomat Durham White Stevens arrived in San Francisco from Korea aboard the S.S. *Nippon Maru*. Stevens was en route to visit his sister in Atlantic City, New Jersey, after four years of service as a foreign affairs advisor for the Korean government. His diplomatic career began in 1873 when President Ulysses Grant appointed him secretary to the U.S. legation in Tokyo, Japan. He quickly mastered the Japanese language and became a highly valued translator.[2] In 1882, he entered the employ of the Japanese Ministry of Foreign Affairs as English secretary to the Japanese legation in Washington, D.C., and then was transferred to Tokyo, where he served as advisor to the Japanese Foreign Ministry. In Japan, Stevens quickly emerged as a prominent figure within Japanese diplomatic circles and was decorated with several prestigious national honors.

During his thirty years of service to the Japanese government, much of Durham Stevens' diplomatic work was shrouded in secrecy. His trip to visit his sister was a cover for a covert mission. Earlier in 1907, the Japanese government had consented to the Gentlemen's Agreement that restricted further Japanese immigration to the United States. However, Japanese officials were still concerned that the strong anti-Japanese movement in America would pressure U.S. federal officials to pass a national exclusion law targeting the Japanese. They decided to dispatch Durham Stevens to the United States to lobby members of the U.S. Congress against the passage of such legislation.[3]

Like his diplomatic work for Japan, Stevens' activities in Korea as advisor on foreign affairs for the Korean government were cloaked in deception. During the Russo-Japanese War, Japan had sought to tighten its political control over Korea to prevent Russia from making further political gains in Korea. A special provision in a diplomatic agreement signed between Korea and Japan in August 1904 empowered the Japanese government to "recommend" a non-Japanese third-party advisor to the Korean Foreign Office, who was responsible for counseling the Korean government on all matters of significance involving foreign affairs in Korea. After careful deliberation, the Japanese government appointed the loyal Durham Stevens to this delicate and challenging position. Although Korean officials initially protested the imposition of a Japanese-appointed official, they were pleased to learn that the new position would be filled by an American. King Kojong's long-term friendship and trust in the American minister to Korea, Horace Allen, the favorable image of American missionaries in Korea, and the "good offices" pledge in the 1882 Treaty of Amity and Commerce with the United States convinced the Koreans that Stevens' presence would help the country safeguard its national independence.[4]

Japanese officials had notified the Koreans that Stevens' employment contract with the Japanese government had been terminated and he would now be an official employee of Korea, to be paid a monthly salary and housing allowance by the Korean government. Soon after Stevens arrived in October 1904, however, Japanese Foreign Minister Komura Jutaro sent Stevens a letter explicitly instructing him on his responsibilities and duties as foreign affairs advisor in Korea.

Komura emphasized, "The administration of the Korean foreign affairs has, as you are no doubt aware, a very close and important connection with the interest of this Empire, and consequently ... it is absolutely indispensable for the Imperial Government to exercise a proper degree of control over the said administration." As such, Komura stressed the need for Stevens to protect and promote Japanese interests in Korea at all times. "The course of our policy vis-à-vis Korea will from time to time be confidentially made known to you through our Representative at Seoul, and you will always be careful not to act in divergence there from." Komura further instructed Stevens that "in all matters of high importance in the Korean foreign intercourses, you will promptly and frankly communicate with the Japanese Representative" and "in case you desire to present any reports or submit your views to the Imperial Government, you will forward them either through the Japanese Representative or directly to this Ministry." In direct contradiction to the official understanding of Stevens' position, Komura notified the Japanese representative in Korea that "Mr. Stevens must be maintained in his status as an employee of the Japanese government regardless of his status having been transferred to that of a councilor of the Korean government. Furthermore this fact should be a secret between Mr. Stevens and yourself."[5]

Throughout his tenure, Stevens faithfully advanced Japan's interests in Korea. In his support for the Protectorate Treaty with Japan in November 1905, Stevens publicly denied reports of former Japanese Prime Minister

Ito Hirobumi's use of coercion to secure the agreement from the Korean government. Though Stevens was not present at the signing, he wrote to Horace Allen in 1906 discounting the charge of Ito's threat to members of the Korean court:

> You know and I know that the Emperor [Kojong, Korea's sovereign hereditary ruler] would not have yielded willingly . . . but the cabinet failed him. Pak Chai Soon would never have signed the treaty if the Emperor had not given him express command to do so. He did sign the treaty and the seal was brought from the Foreign Office by his express orders. The stories about soldiers in the palace, and concessions forced at the point of the bayonet and all the rest of the skull and cross bones are silly rot. The man who made the settlement possible on the Corean side was Yi Wan Yong. He stood for it from the beginning. I talked the whole matter over to him and Pak Chai Soon before Ito came and it was plain from what they told me that they had no intention of yielding to palace influences or being used as catspaws.[6]

With the establishment of the Japanese protectorate, the Korean Ministry of Foreign Affairs was eliminated and with it Stevens' position as advisor of foreign affairs. Consequently, all foreign legations withdrew their offices and representatives from Korea, with the United States the first to do so. On February 1, 1906, the Japanese Residency-General was established and Ito Hirobumi returned to Korea as the first Resident-General. Stevens remained in Korea and was reassigned to the Bureau of Foreign Affairs as Counselor to the Residency-General and was once again a public employee of Japan.[7]

As Resident-General, Ito ruled Korea with a heavy hand. Japan increasingly resorted to force and violence in its dealings with the Korean people. Stevens justified this rise in Japanese political and economic exploitation of Korea's institutions and resources because ironically he found "the Korean way of official handling of business brutal and unjust."[8] Japan's coercive methods increasingly drew the ire of Koreans in and out of the government. The Righteous Armies, led by former officials and soldiers of the disbanded Korean army, in particular intensified their militant anti-Japanese activities after Japan had forced their dissolution in 1907. As growing discontent among the Korean populace fueled open agitation against Japan, Stevens reportedly became the target of assassination plots and he left for Washington, D.C., amidst widespread rumors of threats against his life by Korea.

Given his high profile with the Japanese government, Durham White Stevens' arrival attracted the attention of the San Francisco press. In a press interview, he expressed his opinion that the Korean nation and its people had benefited greatly from Japan's protectorate, stating, "Japan is doing in Korea and for the Koreans what the United States is doing in the Philippines for the Filipinos, modifying its methods only to suit the somewhat different conditions with which it has to deal."[9] He commented that Japan would withdraw from the Korean peninsula once Korea became sufficiently capable of governing itself. In the meantime, he asserted, the Korean government needed Japan's help and the Korean people had welcomed the Japanese presence.[10]

The next day, Stevens' interview appeared in all of San Francisco's major newspapers. His comments about the beneficial impact of the Japanese protectorate in Korea infuriated the city's small but vocal community of Korean émigrés, who already knew of him from Koreans in Korea.[11] The following afternoon, a Sunday, nearly the entire community of approximately 50 Koreans gathered at the Korean Methodist Church, also known as the Korean mission, in San Francisco. Members of local chapters of two rival Korean organizations, the Konglip Association and the Taedong Association, attended the meeting, their factionalism bridged by Stevens' arrival. After hours of deliberation, the attendees decided to select four men, two from each association, to meet with Stevens to personally confirm the validity of his statements about the Korean situation.[12]

That night, Lee Hak-hyun, Chung Chae-kwan, Moon Yang-mok, and Choy Yu-sop went to the Fairmount Hotel to see Stevens. Lee Hak-hyun, who was fluent in English and often went by the name of Earl Lee, approached the front desk to inquire if Durham Stevens would meet with him. Lee stated that he and his fellow Koreans wanted to express their gratitude for Stevens' services to Korea. Stevens came down to the lobby to meet with the young Korean men. Because the lobby was filled with hotel guests engaging in after-dinner conversations, Stevens suggested conversing in an empty room near the lobby. Upon entering the room, Earl Lee handed Stevens a newspaper and asked if he had indeed made those statements to the press. When Stevens replied in the affirmative, the conversation quickly escalated into a heated debate. The Korean men pressed Stevens to elaborate on the impact of Japanese policies in Korea, while Stevens staunchly defended his views on the benefits of the Japanese presence. Enraged by Stevens' refusal to recant, one of the men struck the American diplomat in the face, knocking him to the floor. As Stevens struggled to get up, all four Korean men began to beat him with rattan chairs lying around the room. The brawl threw the crowded lobby into a frenzy.

The hotel staff quickly responded to the commotion and pulled the Korean men away from the injured Stevens, who demanded that the men be expelled from the hotel.[13]

The disturbance at the hotel drew local press coverage. After the cut on his face was treated, Stevens described the incident as something "in the nature of a comedy" and dismissed the assailants as a group of young students misguided by their naive patriotism. Refusing further comment, he returned to his room.[14]

The Koreans, in contrast, had a much more somber assessment of the incident. Earl Lee told the press soon after the incident:

> We went to the Fairmount Hotel to teach Stevens a lesson. . . . We do not regret what we did, and we are willing to be punished. . . . We are willing to suffer and die for Corea. Liberty or death is our motto, and we are all willing to live up to it. . . . We are all sorry we let him off so easy, but what could we do with all the people at the hotel holding us back?

Accusing Stevens of spreading false Japanese propaganda, Lee asserted that the Korean people were unequivocally opposed to the Japanese presence in Korea, and that the Japanese had only brought violence and suffering to the Korean people since the 1905 protectorate.[15]

Later that night, the four Korean men returned to the Korean mission to report on the event to a crowd of compatriots. Incensed by Stevens' disparaging and condescending comments about the Korean people, they began to discuss additional ways to protest. During the late-night meeting, several members learned that Stevens was to take a ferry from San Francisco to Oakland to catch a train headed for Washington, D.C. Seized by the "liberty or death" motto, two young Korean men in attendance at the meeting, one from the Konglip Association and the other from the Taedong Association, took it upon themselves to make sure that Stevens would not again be "let off so easy."[16]

On Monday morning, March 23, Stevens left the Fairmount Hotel accompanied by Japanese Consul-General Koike Chozo. Koike was the first to exit the automobile at the ferry building. As Stevens stepped out of the car, Chun Myung-won, who had been waiting at the dock, quickly ran up to Stevens and pointed a pistol, concealed under a handkerchief, at him. To Chun's surprise, his gun jammed and failed to fire. Unable to shoot him, Chun lunged at Stevens and struck a vicious blow to Stevens' face with the butt of the pistol. Despite suffering a severe cut on his face, Stevens managed to collect himself and chase after his assailant.[17]

As Stevens was running after Chun, the sound of three gunshots reverberated. Another Korean man, Chang In-whan, who had been standing in a crowd gathered near the car, fired the shots from his own gun. The first missed Stevens and hit the fleeing Chun in the chest just as he was looking back at his pursuer. The other two struck Stevens, with one bullet entering near his right shoulder blade and the other his lower back. Before Chang could fire again, a passerby struck Chang in the arm, causing him to drop the gun. Chang quickly fled the scene. Hearing the gunshots and the ensuing pandemonium, two policemen rushed to the scene and managed to chase down Chang and the wounded Chun. As one of the officers apprehended and arrested Chang, a crowd of onlookers surrounded him and shouted, "Lynch the murderer!" Meanwhile, Stevens was rushed to a nearby hospital. Chun Myung-won was taken to the same hospital under police custody.[18]

At the hospital, a group of surgeons treated both men. They found two bullets deeply lodged inside Stevens' body, but a preliminary medical examination indicated that neither had punctured any internal organs. As a result, the surgeons decided not to try to remove the bullets immediately and anticipated a quick and full recovery. Chun's wound appeared to be much more critical. The doctors discovered that the bullet from Chang's gun had pierced his right lung, and they declared that he had little chance of recovery.[19]

Following his surgery, Stevens appeared lucid and high-spirited as he provided his own account of the shooting to a throng of reporters surrounding his hospital bed. He denied reports that the assassination attempt was part of a conspiracy led by a Korean revolutionary organization in Korea with links to the San Francisco Korean community. He asserted, "I do not regard the attack upon me as having any political significance. I consider it merely the work of fanatical students, who may be classed as anarchists. It has no bearing on the Japanese-Corean situation."[20] He jokingly remarked, "This is a nice way to begin the vacation I had looked forward to with so much pleasure."[21]

Public statements from Chun Myung-won and Chang In-whan about the shooting were much more ruminative. Hours after the shooting, the police brought Chang to the hospital to determine if Chun had acted as his accomplice. They claimed not to be acquainted with each other, and each stated that he had acted on his own, even though both had been present at the mass meeting at the Korean mission.[22] In individual statements, both men provided very similar explanations for shooting Stevens. They showed neither remorse nor concern for their own personal welfare.

Imbued with an overriding sense of patriotism, Chang and Chun both declared that they were willing to sacrifice their lives for the sake of their homeland brethren, belying Stevens' assertion that the assassination attempt had no political connection to the Japanese protectorate in Korea. Like many of their compatriots in the United States, Chang In-whan and Chun Myung-won migrated to Hawaii in 1905 as plantation laborers with the goal of obtaining a Western education. In 1906, each made his way to California and found work as an itinerant laborer along the Pacific Coast before coming to San Francisco.[23]

From his hospital bed, Chun gave a deposition to the police through interpreter Yang Doo-sam, who headed the Korean mission. Chun explained that he felt powerless in the United States to help his brethren in Korea:

> This day I shot Stevens. I shot him because he was the main factor in the Japanese reign of bloodshed and oppression in Korea, and because he, as the head and adviser of the regime, was responsible for the deaths of our fathers, mothers and brothers in Korea. . . . I shot the man as an expression of the sentiment of the Korean race and its hatred of Japanese government. I knew I would die when I shot him, but so angered was I at his falsehoods and the misuse of his power that, with the knowledge of my own death, I shot him. What is life without liberty? How can I be calm, knowing that our fathers, mothers and brothers are being murdered by agents of the Japanese government? A man in whose breast there is not a love for his country greater than all else and who can remain passive, knowing that the fathers, mothers and brothers of this country are being murdered, has no right to live. If I kill him and I die it will be a warning to others who take his place to rule justly and to deal with the people in his care with kindness and humanity. I will make no complaint to the punishment that will be meted out to me and should my act aid my country in struggles for freedom, I will die nobly and well. . . .[24]

Chang expressed very similar motives in a letter written from his jail cell and translated into English:

> My country is completely wrecked by the Japanese since the Japanese protection. Mr. Stevens helps Japan to make out the plan to destroy Corea, for he was appointed advisor in the interest of Japan, and as he said here, he is a great friend of Japan. He did many things cruel to Coreans through Japanese for Japan's sake while he was paid by the Corean government to do service

for Corea. . . . Why would I not kill him? Thousand of thousands of people have been killed through his plan, and as much will be killed if he returns to Corea from the United States America. So I shot him for the sake of my country and to sympathize with the people who have already been killed, and to save the people from another killing by Stevens. What is life? Everybody ought to know how to die. If I kill him and die, it will be glory to my country and happy to the people.[25]

Two days after the shooting, Stevens' health took a sudden turn for the worse. Doctors had planned to x-ray him to determine the exact location of the bullets in preparation for their surgical extraction. That same

Figure 2.1.
Photo of Chang In-whan taken in the late 1920s.
Source: K. W. Lee.

morning, Stevens complained of extreme abdominal pain, displaying symptoms of peritonitis. As his condition rapidly deteriorated, doctors rushed Stevens into emergency surgery. To their chagrin, the surgeons found that Stevens' intestines had been severely punctured and determined that he had no chance of survival. Stevens died in his hospital bed later that night. The autopsy reported that Stevens had died of shock and hemorrhaging from the gunshot wound to his abdomen. Chun, whose wound was initially thought to be fatal, made a surprising recovery.[26]

Following Stevens' death, Chang In-whan was charged with murder and Chun Myung-won as an accessory to murder.[27] Chang was formally arraigned for murder on April 10 with the trial to begin on July 27.[28] Still recovering from his gunshot wound in the hospital, Chun was unable to attend court for his preliminary hearings until June 10.[29]

The San Francisco Korean community quickly came to the aid of both men. On the night after the shooting, about 40 local Koreans gathered at the Korean mission to discuss ways to help their two compatriots. They agreed that the local chapters of the Taedong Association and the Kongnip Association needed to combine their efforts in organizing a campaign for a legal defense. The two organizations, each with seven to eight local chapters dispersed throughout the U.S. mainland, merged into a single body under the name of the Kongnip Association, agreeing to put their provincial differences aside. The meeting concluded with participants donating $700 to the defense campaign.[30]

As news spread about the shooting of Durham White Stevens, Chang and Chun also received support from Koreans outside of the San Francisco area. On the day after the shooting, the Korean community in Los Angeles publicly announced their support for both men and their intention to raise funds for their legal defense. They also sent an articulate bilingual Korean student, Hugh C. Cynn, who was attending the University of Southern California, to assist the defense team.[31] Cynn often acted as a public spokesperson for the Koreans and later served as an official court interpreter at Chang's trial.[32]

Koreans in Hawaii, represented by the Hanin Hapsonghoe (Korean Consolidated Association), also approached the newly consolidated Konglip Hyophoe (Mutual Cooperation Federation of North America) to offer their assistance and support for the defense of Chang and Chun. Like the Kongnip Hyophoe, the Hanin Hapsonghoe was the result of a recent merger of twenty-four different associations dispersed throughout the Hawaiian Islands. In October 1908, amidst Chang In-whan's ongoing trial, representatives from both umbrella organizations met in San Francisco and agreed to unite to help their compatriot, as well as to achieve their shared political objectives of aiding their homeland in the face of Japanese oppression. On November 20, 1908, leaders announced the merger of their two associations under the name of Kungminhoe or Korean National (People's) Association under the following terms:

1. All the organizations of Korean residents in America shall be merged into one association for greater unification and effective resistance against the Japanese atrocities in Korea.
2. The name of the consolidated association shall be the "Korean National Association in America."
3. The Korean National Association in America shall include all the Korean political organizations in the United States, Hawaii, and Mexico, and it shall establish Far Eastern branches wherever contacts are available.[33]

Prior coordinated political activities between Korean immigrant groups in Hawaii and the mainland had been minimal at best. The Stevens case provided a catalyst for these groups to work together, as they began to see themselves part of a common transnational movement for justice and freedom for their persecuted brethren in California as well as back home in Korea.

Monetary contributions poured in from Koreans living in and out of California. Compatriots from Korea, Japan, Siberia, Manchuria, Mexico, Hawaii, and throughout the continental United States contributed over $8,500 to the defense of Chang and Chun.[34] According to one report, 506 individual Koreans in the continental United States had donated nearly $5,000. Such monetary commitments were extraordinary given that the small population of Koreans on the mainland numbered no more than 1,000 in 1908. Since most earned meager wages, many likely donated at least a week's worth of wages.[35]

Chang and Chun received legal counsel from three prominent American lawyers, led by well-known San Francisco attorney Nathan C. Coughlan. Coughlan, of Irish descent, reportedly took the case for free, citing his empathy for Korea's plight under the Japanese given his own Irish background.[36] Attorney John Barrett and a former judge, Robert Ferral, joined Coughlan to form a distinguished and formidable defense team. Under Coughlan's direction, Chang pleaded innocent on the grounds of "patriotic insanity." Coughlan argued that the atrocities and oppression committed by the Japanese in Korea had driven Chang to insanity, which led him to shoot and kill Stevens. He intended to highlight Japan's oppressive policies in Korea as key evidence in the defense of his client.[37] As such, the case appeared to take the form of an international tribunal revolving around Japan's relations with Korea, rather than a criminal murder trial.

Koreans in the United States were quick to recognize the larger political implications of the Stevens case. The day after the shooting, the *Konglip Sinbo*, a Korean-language immigrant newspaper, declared that the "trial will be the judgment of our sorrow in the open public court."[38] The publicity provided Koreans with a national stage to voice their opposition to the Japanese presence in Korea. In an editorial in the *Konglip Sinbo*, Hugh Cynn exhorted that Koreans in the United States had a patriotic responsibility not only to support Chang and Chun in their legal trials but also to publicize to the world the oppressive and hostile nature of Japan's policies in Korea.[39] An acquittal or minimum sentence for Chang and Chun would validate their claims of Japanese oppression in Korea.

Members of the Korean community also saw the Stevens case as a rallying call for the mobilization of Koreans abroad under a common cause. The *Konglip Sinbo* published an editorial entitled, "One sound of pistol will be heard in all the world. The sound of two bullets cry for the spirit of freedom," which declared that the assassination of Stevens should be perceived not as a random act of individual violence but rather as part of a larger collective movement for national independence, not unlike the patriotism that inspired similar movements in America and Europe.

> The Coreans, who are so hungry for liberty and independence, how could they see [Stevens] without anger? The assassination was hatched by the spirit of patriotism. . . . When the thirteen colonies of America rebelled against Great Britain; when Switzerland rebelled against Germany, and when Italy rebelled against Austria, let us remember that there were many instances of such a thing as happened yesterday. The Corean people must get the eighteenth century idea of European and American patriotism. Come patriots! Come patriots! Let us awake by the sound of the pistol.[40]

The editorial justified the killing of Stevens as a patriotic act that had important historical precedents and urged all Koreans to seize the moment.[41] Korean immigrants would indeed heed these calls for unified action in subsequent months.

Despite the inflammatory rhetoric of the editorial, Korean spokespersons such as Hugh Cynn made it very clear that the members of the Korean community did not intend to harm any other Japanese officials in San Francisco.[42] In the days following the shooting, a number of newspapers reported that the Japanese Consulate General in San Francisco, Chozo Koike, was in grave danger. Though recognizing that Chun and Chang had violated American laws, Cynn and others emphasized that Koreans were a law-abiding people who greatly respected the laws of America. Nevertheless, they offered no apologies for Stevens' death and adamantly affirmed support for their compatriots under police custody, maintaining that Stevens' actions in Korea had brought so much pain and suffering to the Korean people and that he deliberately provoked the Korean community with his blatant lies about Japan's policies in Korea. For Koreans everywhere, Chang was not a murderer, but a heroic patriot who was willing to sacrifice his life for his people.[43]

The Japanese government was also cognizant of the larger political implications of the Stevens case. Immediately after the shooting, Japanese government officials downplayed the severity of the incident and its bearing on the Japanese-Korean situation.[44] Japanese Consulate General Koike initially explained that the assassination attempt on Stevens was an act of violence committed by a few discontented individuals whose "private interests were injured by Stevens' opposition."[45] However, the extensive local and national press attention made Japanese officials increasingly concerned about the potential damage to Japan's international reputation. Most of the newspaper coverage devoted substantial space to Korean grievances against Japan, with numerous articles providing in-depth information about the political situation in Korea under Japan.[46] A court ruling sympathetic to the Koreans in the Stevens murder trial would likely bring even greater international attention to the situation in Korea.

Given these concerns, the Japanese government took great measures to ensure that Chang In-whan and Chun Myung-won received maximum sentences for the shooting and death of Durham Stevens.[47] The Japanese Consulate hired a high-priced American lawyer, Samuel Knight, to assist the prosecution led by Assistant District Attorney James M. Hanley.[48] The Japanese government also sent numerous official publications from Tokyo that outlined and explained its policies in Korea and their beneficial impact on Korean society, with titles such as *Administrative Reforms in Korea*, *Summary of the Financial Affairs of Korea*, and *Report of the Progress of the Reorganization of the Finances of Korea*. While they intended these publications to serve as evidence in the trial, they were also part of a concerted effort to garner American public support.[49]

Although Chang's trial date had been set for July 27, the trial did not begin until December. The delays primarily involved the prosecution's case against Chun Myung-won. Due to his gunshot wound, Chun was physically unable to attend his hearings for months. When his preliminary hearings finally began on June 13, the prosecution could not indict him as part of the murder plot. Because his gun had failed to fire, no witnesses had seen

Chun attempt to shoot Stevens. Though his gun had been found at the scene, there was no reliable evidence directly linking him to it. Moreover, defense attorney Nathan Coughlan contested Chun's confession to the shooting, which had been translated by Korean mission pastor Yang Doo-sam at his hospital bedside. Coughlan argued that Yang was not a court-approved translator and so his translation could not be entered as trial evidence. The judge requested that Yang appear before the court to corroborate the veracity of his translation before the court. The prosecution, however, was unable to locate Yang, who was reportedly out of town indefinitely to conduct church work. On June 27, the judge ruled that the prosecution failed to provide sufficient evidence to indict Chun on murder charges. He also ruled that evidence did not conclusively prove that Chun had any connection to Chang in relation to the shooting and thus could not be tried as an accessory to murder. With Chun no longer legally linked to the murder case, Coughlan requested that he be released on a bail of $500. In a surprising move given strong anti-Asian sentiment, the court released Chun without bail, citing Coughlan's reputation.[50] Chun fled to Siberia in September, and the charges against him were subsequently dropped due to the lack of sufficient evidence.[51]

Chang In-whan's trial finally commenced on December 14, 1908. The prosecution, led by Assistant District Attorney James H. Hanley and Special Prosecutor Samuel Knight, sought a first-degree murder conviction against Chang, arguing that he had conspired to murder Durham Stevens. The prosecution presented an array of testimony from witnesses at the scene of the shooting. The witnesses identified Chang as the gunman who shot Stevens. Other witnesses, including the arresting police officers, testified that Chang had admitted to firing the three gunshots. The prosecution also presented to the court the murder weapon that Chang used. Additional witnesses claimed that Stevens had identified Chang as his assailant when the two men encountered each other at the hospital after the shooting. The police had escorted Chang to the hospital in order to identify Chun as his accomplice. Noticing that Stevens was also in the room, Chang confronted him, calling him a "bad man" for taking money from Korea and giving it to Japan. The prosecution concluded its case asserting that Chang was indisputably the man who shot and killed Stevens and that his actions were premeditated with malicious intent.[52]

Chang's defense team sought his acquittal on grounds of temporary insanity and justifiable homicide. Regarding the latter plea, attorney Nathan Coughlan argued that Chang fired at Stevens to protect Chun. When Chang saw Stevens chasing after Chun at the depot, Chang believed that

Stevens was holding a gun and intended to shoot Chun. As for the plea of temporary insanity, Coughlan maintained that Chang suffered from a form of insanity caused by the brutal atrocities committed by Japanese troops in Korea. Several Korean witnesses took the stand for the defense, testifying that Chang had displayed erratic behavior in the months prior to the shooting and incessantly talked about Korea's situation under the Japanese.[53]

According to press reports, the defense team's dramatic summations about Korea's subordination under Japan were so moving that several members of the all-white jury were moved to tears during the trial. The prosecution vehemently discounted such legal arguments as tactics intended to divert attention from the charges at hand. The prosecution forcefully reminded the jury that Chang In-whan, not Japan, was on trial.[54] Challenging the defense claim of patriotic insanity, the prosecution summoned four experts in psychiatric disorders who testified that they believed Chang was not and could not have been insane when he shot Stevens and was feigning signs of insanity during the court proceedings. In an intense cross-examination of the expert witnesses, the defense vainly attempted to secure an admission that Japanese atrocities in Korea could have driven Chang to insanity by posing multiple hypothetical scenarios to the witnesses. The prosecution eventually objected strongly to the high improbability of such scenarios, at which time the judge ordered an end to the cross-examination.[55]

Heated harangues over legal arguments and tactics often boiled over into acrimonious personal exchanges between the attorneys for the prosecution and defense. Defense attorney Robert Ferral, for instance, strongly objected to Special Prosecutor Samuel Knight's request that defense witnesses provide the names of their relatives and friends in Korea. Denouncing Knight as a tool of the Japanese government, Ferral accused him of attempting to intimidate witnesses with the threat of handing those names over to the Japanese government, which had the power to take punitive measures against such individuals. Knight in response called Ferral a "Korean highbinder" and at another point in the trial pointedly asked defense attorney Barrett where he was getting his "blood money" to defend Chang. On the last day of the trial, Coughlan and Knight came close to blows, with the judge threatening to cite both men with contempt of court. Closing statements from both sides were completed on December 23, and the case went to the jury.[56]

Evidently, the jury was divided on the degree of Chang's guilt, going through eight rounds of voting to reach a unanimous verdict. The first vote was split three for first-degree murder, five for second-degree murder, and four for manslaughter. By the seventh vote, the jury stood at three for manslaughter and nine for second-degree murder. Finally on the eighth vote, the jury reached a unanimous decision for second-degree murder, which carried a sentence of ten years to life and no possibility of capital punishment.[57] During his sentencing hearing, Chang, through his interpreter, pleaded with the judge to change his sentence to the death penalty, stating: "I do not want to live if I am to be sent to prison for a long time. . . . If sent to prison I will do nothing but weep for my country's wrong. . . . I do not want to live. I wanted to give up my life for my country."[58] On January 2, 1909, Judge Carroll Cook sentenced Chang In-whan to 25 years at San Quentin prison.[59] Stoically accepting the sentence, Chang told the judge, "I did my duty to the country and I don't care what the law does to me."[60]

Given the strong anti-Asian current, the defense campaign must have understood that the possibility of an acquittal for Chang In-whan's killing of a white man, particularly one of Stevens' prominence, would be nearly impossible and instead hoped for a commuted sentence. The mobilized efforts for his defense had, indeed, saved him from an almost certain life sentence and possible capital punishment. As such, his supporters viewed their campaign as a success. The impact of the verdict and sentence resonated beyond the actual legal case. Korean immigrants succeeded in disseminating and exposing information about the political situation in Korea under the Japanese. Moreover, the campaign to aid Chang and Chun marked a fundamental turning point in the diasporic political mobilization of Koreans abroad, which directly led to the formation of the Korean National Association (KNA).[61]

Officially inaugurated on February 1, 1909, the KNA had two regional headquarters—the Korean National Association of Hawaii in Honolulu and the Korean National Association of North America in San Francisco—with each headquarters having a legislative representative assembly and an executive committee. The regional headquarters were responsible for administering local chapters within their respective districts.[62] At its peak in 1914, the North American headquarters administered over 38 local chapters with some 850 members, while the Hawaii division oversaw 73 local chapters with 2,351 members.[63]

At its inauguration, the KNA announced its objectives to be "advancing the education and industry of Koreans abroad, promoting freedom and equality, and regaining the independence of Korea."[64] It emphasized the need for Koreans on the U.S. mainland and Hawaii to overcome the divisions and differences that had separated them into multiple competing groups in order to strengthen their ability to contribute to the struggle against Japan. In this way, the KNA self-consciously viewed itself as a new beginning, a "new era of unification."[65]

The San Francisco headquarters also published a weekly Korean-language newspaper, the *Sinhan Minbo* (New Korea), whose first issue was dated days after the inauguration of the KNA. Financially supported by KNA membership, the *Sinhan Minbo* served as the KNA's main organ, disseminating news and editorials that focused on the issue of national independence for Korea, as well as information about the political and social activities of Koreans living abroad. In its lead article, the inaugural issue explained its name change to a newspaper for all Koreans in the same way that the KNA was a new organization representing all Koreans. Its former name, the *Konglip Sinbo* (The United Korea), had been limited in scope and partial in its affiliation with the Kongliphoe (United Korean Association). The *Sinhan Minbo*, the KNA promised, would be much broader in scope and impartial in its views in order to reach out to a wider body of readers. Thus, the "new" in the name *New Korea* carried multiple meanings: as a renewal, cleansing, revitalization, resurrection, and reconstruction after a period of indolence, stagnation, disablement, and dependence. In these ways, the paper set out to revitalize the spirit and commitment of the Korean people in concert with the objectives of the KNA.[66] The *Sinhan Minbo*'s circulation numbered approximately 3,000, with 700 to 800 distributed throughout the U.S. mainland, 500 to 600 sent to Hawaii, 300 to 400 going to Mexico, and the rest to Korean settlements in Manchuria and Siberia. The Hawaii regional headquarters also published its own newspaper, the *Sinhan Kukbo* (United Korean News), which changed its name to the *Kungminbo* (Korean National Herald) in 1913.[67]

The KNA and *Sinhan Minbo* consciously aimed to link the welfare and well-being of Koreans abroad with the struggle for the independence of their homeland. A *Sinhan Minbo* editorial addressed to "my fellow people in America and Hawaii," for instance, proclaimed that the future of Korea depended on Koreans in America, who had an almost providential mission to aid their homeland. The editorial praised the pioneering spirit of Koreans in America, displayed in their successful ventures in organizing themselves politically, economically, and socially in a foreign land. Explaining that an independent Korea would reap the benefits of the knowledge and money gained from these experiences abroad, it called on Koreans to unite and prosper in preparation for returning to a free Korea, but not to return to Korea in the near future for "selfish motives."[68] In a similar editorial written to "my fellow people in the Far East," the *Sinhan Minbo* encouraged

Figure 2.2.
Sinhan Minbo office in San Francisco.
Source: Korean American Digital Archive, University of Southern California.

Korean patriots in Manchuria and the Russian Far East to naturalize as Chinese and Russian citizens in order to maintain the struggle for Korea's freedom. If they did so, the editorial explained, Japan could no longer claim jurisdiction over Koreans as Japanese subjects and Korean patriots could maintain their anti-Japanese activities without fear of persecution or reprisal from Japan consuls. The editorial declared that becoming a citizen of China or Russia did not mean one was rejecting Korea, but committing an act of great patriotism. The KNA thus envisioned Koreans in America as well as elsewhere in the diaspora as vital participants in a common transnational political movement for Korean independence.[69]

Guided by this vision, the KNA had begun to expand its activities to other parts of the diaspora soon after establishing its regional headquarters in Hawaii and the continental United States. In April 1909, the KNA of North America sent two representatives to Mexico to create KNA chapters. Later that month, the first local chapter in Mexico was established in Merida, Yucatan, where some 300 Korean laborers had been living since their initial arrival from Korea in 1905.[70] Later local chapters in Mexico City and Oxaca were created. In May 1909, the KNA also sent representatives to Manchuria and Siberia to establish local chapters in those regions. By 1911, a Siberian regional headquarters had been established with 16 local chapters under its supervision and a Manchurian regional headquarters with eight local chapters throughout the region.[71] In order to reflect this geographic expansion in its scope, the KNA changed its name from Kukminhoe (Korean National Association) to Daehanin Kukminhoe (All Korea Korean National Association) in May 1910.[72]

To coordinate activities across the 116 chapters, the KNA convened an All-Korean Leaders Conference in San Francisco on November 8, 1912. Represented by delegates from all four regional headquarters, leaders at the conference established the KNA Central Headquarters, which would serve as a central administrative office to ensure uniformity in rules among all local chapters and to direct the activities of the Korean independence movement across the diaspora.[73] The conference resolved that all Koreans living abroad, regardless of their location, were obligated to recognize the authority of the Central Headquarters.[74]

Following Japan's annexation of Korea and their rejection of its legitimacy, Koreans abroad were keenly aware that they were political exiles without a state or government to protect their interests and well-being. The declaration statement of the Central Headquarters highlighted this condition of statelessness. The KNA Central Headquarters claimed itself to be this central governing body. As long as Korea remained under Japanese rule, the KNA declared it would serve as the legitimate democratic government of the Korean people. As a self-governing body, the KNA saw itself as training Koreans abroad for self-governance in preparation for an independent Korea, thus underscoring the significant role of Koreans in the diaspora in the process of nation-building.[75]

The state functions of the KNA would soon be put to test in the aftermath of the Hemet incident in the summer of 1913, which ended with U.S. Secretary of State William Jennings Bryan's unofficially recognizing the state authority of the KNA over Koreans in California. As a consequence of the KNA's efforts, approximately 300 political exiles from Korea, mostly university students, were legally admitted to the United States as stateless persons during the next several years.[76] The KNA would continue to serve as a supranational political entity for the Korean diaspora until the momentous 1919 March First uprising in Korea. Following these mass demonstrations, the Korean diaspora's search for statehood would take another concrete step toward the creation of a new sovereign Korean nation-state that could be recognized as a legitimate actor within the international community of nation-states. U.S.-based Koreans would once again play a dominant role in these state-making efforts.

CHAPTER 3

Inaugurating a "New Korea"

The March First Movement and the Korean Provisional Government

The year 1919 marked a watershed in the development of Korean nationalism. On March 1, 1919, Korean political and religious leaders in Seoul formally proclaimed independence from Japanese colonial rule. Peaceful demonstrations throughout the Korean peninsula immediately followed the proclamation of independence in what has come to be known as the March First movement. Caught by surprise by the massive scale of the anticolonial uprising, the Japanese violently squashed the nationwide demonstrations, killing thousands of Koreans and arresting even more. As news of the demonstrations spread across the diaspora, political activity among Koreans intensified throughout émigré communities in Manchuria, Siberia, China, Hawaii, and the continental United States. Japan's brutal suppression of the March First movement made it necessary for national liberation activities to be carried out from abroad. Japanese repression, in particular, prevented the establishment of a base in Korea that could act with national authority. As a result, the immediate concerns of the diaspora focused on creating a government in exile that could serve as a central headquarters for the national liberation movement. With these goals in mind, nationalist leaders gathered in Shanghai and organized the Korean Provisional Government (KPG) on April 9, 1919.

This upsurge in organizational activity ushered in a new phase in the Korean nationalist movement, in which the locus of activity occurred largely outside the Korean peninsula. Japan's 1905 protectorate over Korea and subsequent annexation as a colony in 1910 had spawned an array of organized opposition groups among Koreans abroad. For the most part, however, these groups operated largely independent of each other. The KPG, created as a unified government in exile, sought to unify the many disparate elements of the nationalist movement.[1]

The founding of the KPG coincided with the growing economic and military power of the United States globally.[2] Three years of neutrality from the war in Europe and a government-sponsored program of war preparedness had enabled the United States to amass enormous economic wealth and to bolster its military strength. Thus, at the eve of America's entry into World War I in 1917, the United States was in a prime position to supplant Europe as the world's premier leader.

Strategically situated at the nexus of the complex web of geopolitical relations involving Korea, Japan, and the United States, Koreans in America came to hold privileged positions, ideologically and organizationally, within the Korean independence movement. U.S.-based Korean leaders, for instance, were appointed to a disproportionate share of high-ranking leadership positions, including the presidency, within the KPG in Shanghai and its ancillaries in the United States. In the process, the U.S. component of the Korean diaspora, though significantly smaller and geographically far removed from the large number of Koreans living in regions of Manchuria and Siberia close to the Korean border, emerged as key actors in charting the course of a new Korean nation-state. For the next several years, the activities of the KPG would remain at the center of the national liberation movement.[3]

As a government in exile, the KPG struggled for power from outside the territorial boundaries of its claimed national territory.[4] In order to establish its legitimacy, organizers of the KPG elected prominent leaders of nationalist groups in Manchuria, Siberia, China, and the United States to high-level cabinet positions, most of whom were not even present at the government's inception. Given these circumstances, the KPG in one of its first directives ordered the creation of a centralized communication network that directly linked dispersed Korean settlements to the KPG in Shanghai.[5]

Formed as a democratic republic, the KPG was a direct outgrowth of the republican impulses of the March First movement. Republican notions of equality and democracy permeated the Declaration of Independence that was promulgated in Seoul on March 1. They deeply influenced the political outlook of many of the 33 signatories of the Declaration of Independence who had been involved in nationalist activities associated with the republican-influenced Patriotic Enlightenment movement prior to annexation and in the early 1910s. The Provisional Government in Shanghai represented the first republican government in Korean history and a major component of the national liberation movement that would become an "all-out republican movement."[6]

Competing political ideologies also came to the fore after March 1919. Most notably, socialism, as represented by Yi Tong-hwi and the Korean Socialist Party, emerged as a significant force in the national liberation movement. From the early 1910s, Yi, a famous major in the Korean Army before its dissolution by the Japanese, had gained prominence in organizing anti-Japanese activities in exile: first in the mountains of northern Korea, then in Manchuria, and finally in the Russian Far East. In June 1918, he founded the first Korean socialist-oriented organization, the Korean Socialist Party (Hanin Sahoedang), in Khaborovsk (see Fig. 4.3., p. 91).[7]

Following the March demonstrations in Korea, Yi organized a conference in Vladivostok attended by representatives from Korean nationalist groups in Siberia and Manchuria sympathetic to the Bolshevik cause. Leaders at the conference agreed to consolidate their resources under the name of the Korean Socialist Party, with Vladivostok serving as its headquarters. Convinced that armed struggle against Japan was the only way of achieving independence, this coalition stepped up preparations for a direct military assault against the Japanese in Korea, drawing on military training centers that proliferated throughout Korean communities in the Russian Far East and Manchuria. In addition to Yi Tong-hwi and his contingent of Korean Communists, Koreans in the Maritime Province, as well as other parts of Siberia and Manchuria, formed a host of other Communist groups. Some joined the KPG, while others opposed the KPG in their rivalry with Yi and the Korean Socialist Party.[8] Yi Tong-hwi and the Korean Communists in Manchuria and Siberia emerged as significant political actors competing for leadership within the Korean diaspora.

Armed struggle groups in Manchuria also expanded their activities following the March First movement. Prior to annexation in 1910, Korean émigré communities in Manchuria near the Korean border served as operational bases for the activities of the Righteous Armies (*uibyong*). Led by former officials and soldiers of the disbanded Korean Army, the Righteous Armies launched numerous guerrilla raids on Japanese military forces along the Korean border. By 1912, however, the Japanese had managed to suppress the activities of the Righteous Armies. The March First uprising in Korea produced a resurgence in armed resistance activities in Manchuria, with over 70 new nationalist organizations established in Korean settlements in the region. In the tradition of the Righteous Armies, these organizations mobilized and trained independence armies in preparation for an all-out war of liberation against Japan.[9]

Dramatic growth in migration from Korea to Manchuria and the Maritime Province after the March First uprising further invigorated the armed resistance movement. After witnessing Japan's brutal suppression of the nonviolent demonstrations, many young Koreans came to view nonviolent tactics as futile and believed that independence could be achieved only through war. Many of these individuals went into exile and joined armed struggle groups.[10]

The expansion of these military-based operations coincided with the establishment of the KPG in Shanghai. The KPG managed to bring some of these armed resistance organizations under its direct authority, particularly those that had joined Yi Tong-hwi's Korean Socialist Party. However, the majority were only loosely affiliated with the military branch of the Provisional Government. Ironically, most of these armed resistance groups were organized around republican principles, much like the KPG, but had already consolidated themselves into larger self-ruling political bodies that functioned as nearly autonomous governments. They saw little benefit in uniting with the KPG for it would have required them to sacrifice their political and financial autonomy.[11] In addition to republican-based armed resistance organizations in Manchuria, other camps included socialist-oriented groups and those that advocated terrorism through numerous bombings and assassination plots against high-ranking Japanese officials in and out of Korea.[12] Though ideological differences divided the various armed resistance groups in the diaspora, they all agreed on the necessity of direct armed struggle for the liberation of Korea (see Fig. 4.3., p. 91).

The upsurge in nationalist activity throughout the diaspora actually gave birth to three different provisional governments in three separate places—the first in Vladivostok, a second in Shanghai, and the third in Seoul—with each claiming to be the authentic national sovereign of the Korean people. The proliferating provisional governments prompted leaders of the Shanghai Provisional Government to try and create a single unified government under its authority.[13]

While the KPG in Shanghai was organized along republican principles, its leaders could not dismiss the more radical military and Communist groups in Manchuria and Siberia. By 1919, nearly 100,000 Koreans lived in Siberia, particularly in the Maritime Province, and over 450,000 Koreans resided in Manchuria, most of them concentrated in the Chientao region.[14]

The large number of Koreans living in regions in close proximity to Korea offered important strategic resources for staging anti-Japanese activities.

As Yi Tong-hwi increasingly solidified his position among Koreans in Manchuria and the Maritime Province, leaders in Shanghai vigorously petitioned Yi to join the Shanghai government. Initially reluctant because of ideological differences, Yi decided to join the Shanghai Provisional Government after its organizers agreed to unify the three provisional governments into a single one in Shanghai based on the cabinet posts and cabinet member lists of the Seoul-based provisional government, which had elected Yi premier and Syngman Rhee president.[15] As premier, Yi believed he could wield substantial influence and authority in determining the policies of the KPG. He hoped to obtain financial and military support from the Soviet government and thus advance his own policies for armed struggle against the Japanese. With these goals in mind, Yi made the decision to move the headquarters of the Korean Socialist Party from Vladivostok to Shanghai and assume the position of premier.[16] In September 1919, the newly unified government headquartered in Shanghai was inaugurated and was officially named the Provisional Government of the Republic of Korea, which would become widely known as the KPG.

The addition of the Korean Socialist Party to the KPG greatly bolstered the status of the Shanghai Provisional Government throughout the diaspora. By the end of 1919, the KPG had successfully consolidated the multiple bases of nationalist activity within the diaspora. Bringing together the various strands of left- and right-wing factions of the liberation movement, it had established itself as a united-front government that sought to serve as the central headquarters of the national liberation movement.

Sustaining a united front presented a formidable challenge for KPG leaders, however. The diverse nationalist activities produced multiple strategies, from which two major tactics for the liberation of Korea emerged that would shape activities for the next several decades. The first approach attempted to gain support for Korean independence from the leading world powers through diplomatic channels. This republican-based approach, exemplified in the activities of Syngman Rhee, emphasized lobbying, propaganda, and representation at international conferences to draw attention to the situation in Korea in order to elicit diplomatic intervention against Japan from the world powers. The second approach advocated direct armed struggle against Japan as the only way to achieve unconditional independence. More specifically, this approach, promoted by Yi Tong-hwi among others, called for mobilizing the large number of

Figure 3.1.
Cabinet and National Assembly of Korean Provisional Government in Shanghai, January 1, 1919. Second row (*left to right*): *tenth* Yi Tong-hwi and *twelfth* Ahn Chang-ho. Notably absent is Syngman Rhee, who was in Washington, D.C.
Source: K. W. Lee.

Koreans living in Manchuria and the Maritime Province to prepare for an all-out war of independence against Japanese forces in Korea.

These two main strands of the nationalist movement reflected not only differences in policies and strategies for the liberation of Korea but also ideological differences over the process of establishing a new modern nation-state in the aftermath of an anticolonial uprising. In collectively declaring Japanese rule alien and illegitimate, Koreans in and out of the peninsula asserted a separate and distinct Korean national identity and claimed the right to a sovereign national state of their own. Thus, for many Koreans at home and abroad, the formation of the KPG signified the creation of a "new Korea," a new sovereign nation-state that legitimately represented the national will of all Koreans. In this light, the concerted campaign to create a united front among national liberation

INAUGURATING A "NEW KOREA" [51]

forces simultaneously represented the systematic efforts to establish a unified nation-state amidst the varying ideological visions of what the new Korea should look like upon liberation from Japan.[17]

One contemporary observer aptly referred to these two ideological camps as the "American group" and the "Siberian-Manchurian group."[18] Primarily linked to U.S.-based Koreans, the American group was guided by political values and ideals embodied in Woodrow Wilson's doctrine of national self-determination set forth in his Fourteen Points.[19] In this famous speech, presented before the U.S. Congress in January 1918, Wilson outlined the basic principles of his peace settlement plan for the end of World War I, including the right of national self-determination for colonized peoples. However, the actual applicability of his anticolonial proclamation was quite ambiguous due to the generality with which he announced his support for the rights of colonized peoples. Engrossed with the wartime issues in Europe, Wilson was very likely referring only to the colonies directly affected by the war in Europe and not to overseas colonies in Asia and other non-European regions of the world. Nevertheless, his speech sparked the hopes and aspirations of colonized peoples around the world.[20]

In the wake of Wilson's wartime proclamations about national self-determination, Koreans in the diaspora, along with a multitude of other groups who suffered under colonial subjugation, sought to gain U.S. support for the liberation of their respective homelands. The anti-imperialist implications embedded in Wilson's speech were accompanied by changing geopolitical circumstances, which further heightened the stature of the United States in the eyes of many colonized peoples around the world. Within this context, Korean nationalists actively engaged in a variety of propaganda and lobbying activities in seeking to enlist support from the United States for Korean independence.

While the American group adhered to a Wilsonian liberal-capitalist vision of an independent Korea, the Siberian-Manchurian group envisioned a revolutionary socialist path that stressed a classless society for an independent Korea derived from Leninist notions of self-determination. This socialist-oriented vision was linked to armed struggle groups in Siberia and Manchuria, which sought to mobilize Koreans for military attacks against Japan.[21] Emphasizing the Bolshevik commitment to the liberation of the weak and oppressed, the Siberian-Manchurian group advocated policies that sought to secure financial and military support from the Soviet government.

In consolidating the diverse array of nationalist groups under its leadership, the KPG expanded the scope and nature of its operational resources. Koreans in the United States and Hawaii, for instance, provided critical financial support and the ability to influence American politicians and public opinion, while those in Manchuria and Siberia offered valuable resources in the form of manpower, arms, and geographical contiguity for military training and fortification. The diverse geopolitical bases of these varied resources called for multiple strategies, but the KPG focused almost exclusively on seeking official diplomatic recognition from the international community, particularly the United States.

News of the March First movement and the establishment of the KPG quickly spread to Koreans living in the United States. The mass movement for self-determination in Korea galvanized the Korean immigrant community. Prominent nationalist leader Philip Jaisohn (So Chae-pil) convened the "Korean Congress" in Philadelphia from April 14–16, 1919, to mobilize support for the Korean independence movement and the new Provisional Government. Attended by nearly 200 delegates from Korean communities throughout North America and as far away as England and Ireland, the Korean Congress provided a forum for Korean immigrants to clarify and affirm their relationship to the recent events in the national independence movement. Appointed chairman of the Congress, Jaisohn declared that neither the distant and remote location of the Provisional Government nor its absentee president Syngman Rhee, who was not in Shanghai but rather in Philadelphia for the Congress, should deter Koreans in the United States from supporting the new government. Jaisohn eloquently stated:

> It does not make any difference whether the President of the Provisional Government is in prison or whether he is in France; he may be in America; that does not make any difference. . . . It does not make the government non-existent, because it is not generally known where it is located. It is the will of the people that makes the government. . . . If you read the history of this country [United States] when the Revolutionary War broke out, you will recall that the Government was not established in any one place, they were forced to move around. When the British chased them from one place, they moved their capital to another. They had a capital in Yorktown, and then they came to Philadelphia. That does not make the government illegal. As somebody has well expressed it in Korean, "The new Provisional Government of Korea is a personification of the will of the people of Korea." It does not make any difference whether the Government is located in Manchuria, Philadelphia or Paris.[22]

At the time of the Congress, the KPG had not yet been restructured into the single unified government headquartered in Shanghai. As a result, participants voiced some concern about its uncertain status and location. Jaisohn argued that physical location did not matter because the KPG was an embodiment of the will and spirit of the Korean people that transcended place.

Another delegate, Henry Chung, voiced similar views, asserting that the Provisional Government was part of a larger universal movement that represented all Koreans regardless of class, gender, or religious beliefs. He also declared that the nationalist movement was an international one in that "every Korean both in and outside of Korea is heart and soul back [sic] of this movement."[23] In conceptualizing the Korean nation-state beyond territorial boundaries, leaders at the Congress sought to position Koreans in the United States as an integral part of the nation-building process.

Explicitly linking the KPG and the American Revolutionaries and the symbolism of the meeting at the "cradle of liberty," Jaisohn took advantage of the auspicious site for the christening of the Republic of Korea.[24] From the outset, the Korean Congress affirmed its zealous commitment to American political ideals and values. After the delegates unanimously elected him chairman of the Congress, Philip Jaisohn expressed some concern that his status as a naturalized American citizen possibly could conflict with the interests and goals of the Congress. Jaisohn had gained prominence for his reform activities in Korea during the last two decades of the nineteenth century. His political activities, promoting the Westernization and modernization of Korea, drew hostility from prevailing conservative forces in the Korean government, compelling him to seek refuge in the United States. He became a naturalized U.S. citizen in 1888, Anglicized his name from So Chae-pil, married a white American woman, and obtained a degree in medicine from George Washington University.[25] Syngman Rhee responded to Jaisohn's concern that the delegates at the Congress "[did not] want any man to preside over this Congress unless he is, above all, 100 per cent loyal American." Rhee explained that the "aims and aspirations" of the Korean people were, in fact, identical to those of the American nation.[26] With this authoritative pronouncement from the new KPG president, the Korean Congress for the next three days proceeded to showcase the importance of an independent, democratic, and Christianized Korea in relation to U.S. ideological, economic, and political interests in East Asia.

Given these strong Americanizing tendencies, the Congress ceremoniously concluded with all of its participants joining together in parade formation, headed by a platoon of mounted reserves and a band. Carrying both Korean and American flags, the paraders marched from the site of the

Congress to Independence Hall, where they gathered in the room in which both the Declaration of Independence and Constitution were signed. President Syngman Rhee read aloud the Korean Declaration of Independence and announced the establishment of the Provisional Government of the Republic of Korea. The body of delegates enthusiastically endorsed them with three loud cheers for the Republic of Korea, followed by another boisterous three cheers for the United States.[27]

While the Congress successfully mobilized loyalty and support among Koreans in the diaspora, its primary objective was to draw American attention to Korean struggles for independence from Japanese colonial rule. Activities throughout the Korean Congress unabashedly championed American democracy and Christianity, and the Korean people's ardent commitment to those ideals and values. However, the Philadelphia Korean Congress was more than uncritical, celebratory exaltations of American political values and ideals. Rather, the proceedings indicated a high degree of political sophistication among the Korean participants as they demonstrated a critical and incisive engagement with the meanings and uses of American power in the new postwar world.

Figure 3.2.
Korean Congress in Philadelphia, 1919. In the second row directly behind the standing woman on the left (*left to right*): *second* Henry Chung (DeYoung), *third* Philip Jaisohn, *fourth* Syngman Rhee.
Source: Korean American Digital Archive, University of Southern California.

Korean leaders at the Korean Congress understood very well that international support was crucial to their quest for independence. They consciously directed their energies toward influencing American public opinion on Japanese imperialism and Korean independence. A significant portion of the proceedings at the Congress were devoted to presenting the "true facts" of the oppressive nature of Japan's actions in Korea. In a press statement beforehand, Philip Jaisohn explained the purpose of the Congress to an American audience:

> We called the Korean Congress because we want America to realize that Korea is a victim of Japan. Korea's wrongs have been insidiously covered up by Japan, and we believe that America will champion the cause of Korea as she has that of other oppressed peoples, once she knows the facts.[28]

Most Korean delegates conducted their speeches and discussions in English. Written transcripts of the Congress proceedings were published and distributed to the American public. Prominent American religious and academic figures from the Philadelphia area were invited to speak, and all expressed their sympathy and support for the Korean people's desire for freedom, while denouncing Japan's motives and actions as tyrannical. The guest speakers also glorified American values of democracy, freedom, and Christianity. As champions of justice and liberty, they asserted that the United States had a moral obligation to aid Korea in its emergent role as a global leader.

One of the first actions of the Korean Congress was to draft "An Appeal to America," in which Korean delegates at the Congress, claiming to represent the 18 million Koreans living in Korea, requested American "support and sympathy because we know you love justice; you also fought for liberty and democracy, and you stand for Christianity and humanity. Our cause is a just one before the laws of God and man. Our aim is freedom from militaristic autocracy; our object is democracy for Asia; our hope is universal Christianity."[29] With their religious appeals, they attempted to connect to the American Protestant missionaries who had been instrumental in promoting Korean immigration to Hawaii at the turn of the twentieth century.[30] Moreover, the majority of Koreans residing in the United States were recent Christian converts, and many had developed strong personal ties to Americans associated with Protestant missionaries in and out of Korea.

Korean nationalists framed Korean subjugation under Japan as a moral, humanitarian issue that required immediate attention from the international community.[31] A strong religious presence permeated the proceedings of the Korean Congress. On each day, the opening sessions began with a speech and prayer by a religious dignitary from the Philadelphia area. Nearly all of the guest speakers were either laypersons with strong religious affiliations or clergymen from a variety of faiths including various denominations of Protestantism, Catholicism, and Judaism. Christian ideology especially resonated with the universalistic moral imperatives associated with the prevailing Wilsonian discourse of the day. In seeking U.S. sympathy for Korean independence, the Congress proceedings extensively chronicled Japan's brutal repression of the March First movement in which the Korean people had peacefully declared en masse their right to national self-determination. The active involvement of Korean Protestants in the nationwide demonstrations was undeniable. Sixteen of the 33 signers of the Korean Declaration of Independence were Christians, many of them Protestant pastors. Christian churches throughout Korea also provided essential networks for planning and coordinating the uprising on a massive scale. Moreover, a disproportionately large number of Korean Christians were arrested in the Japanese suppression of the protests. According to a Japanese military police report published at the end of 1919, more than 17 percent of the 19,525 persons arrested were Korean Protestants, though they comprised only 1 percent of the total Korean population in 1919.[32] By appealing to Christian sensibilities, the Congress sought to make the struggle for Korean independence relevant and meaningful to the American people. As a result, the quest for Korean independence would not be perceived as just a "Korean" issue, but a Christian one too.

In addition to moral appeals, the Congress also underscored the legal claims to Korean independence. In particular, "An Appeal to America" directed attention to the 1882 Treaty of Amity and Commerce between the United States and Korean governments. Korean leaders maintained that they were justified in seeking assistance from the United States based on Article I of the Treaty, which read:

> If other powers deal unjustly or oppressively with either government, the other will exert their good offices, on being informed of the case, to bring about an amicable arrangement, thus showing their friendly feelings.[33]

Jaisohn and other leaders at the Congress believed the American government had already established official recognition of Korean sovereignty and its territorial integrity in 1882, and accordingly, the KPG's first order of action was to obtain official diplomatic recognition from the United States.[34]

For nationalist leaders, the creation of the KPG was a major step in institutionalizing a sovereign political entity that could be considered a legitimate actor within the global community of nation-states. Diplomatic recognition from a powerful sovereign government would provide bona fide acknowledgment and validation of its claims to authority and legitimacy. This understanding of the workings of an international system based on nation-states profoundly shaped the strategies and tactics of the Korean Congress and the overall independence movement.

For Koreans throughout the diaspora, the establishment of the KPG represented the beginnings of a new Korean nation.[35] The Korean Declaration of Independence, which had been promulgated during the March First movement, announced the birth of a new Korea in which "the old world of force has gone and out of the travail of the past a new world of righteousness and truth has been born."[36] Indeed, the establishment of the KPG marked a sharp departure in the political history of Korea. Rather than seeking to restore the 4,000-year old monarchy, Korean nationalist leaders endeavored to create a new democratic republic.[37]

To showcase their new political consciousness, the delegates at the Congress drafted a ten-point resolution entitled "Aims and Aspirations of the Koreans" that set forth the guiding principles of the Korean independence movement. Though the Congress did not make any claims to state power, leaders at the Congress declared that "the very life of the whole nation has to depend on the questions embodied in this resolution."[38] In highlighting the significance of this newly drafted document, Philip Jaisohn predicted that a great number of the participants at the Congress would one day play a leading part in the reconstruction of Korea and that the ideas contained in the resolution would likely be included in the national constitution of a free and independent Korea.[39] Indeed, many of the provisions in "Aims and Aspirations" were incorporated directly into the constitution of the Republic of Korea in July 1948.[40]

As part of the Congress' strategy to attract international attention, "Aims and Aspirations of Koreans" sought to demonstrate the Korean people's desire for freedom and a democratic form of government. The Congress, in particular, sought to counter prevalent Japanese propaganda that portrayed Koreans as incapable of self-rule. Concerned that the American public lacked knowledge about Korea and would question the Korean people's abilities, Jaisohn extolled Korean immigrants in Hawaii as exemplars of Korea's ability to self-govern. He explained that the immigrants to Hawaii were not among the "elite class of Koreans," but rather laborers from rural areas of Korea "without any appreciable education." Despite their humble backgrounds, they successfully created and maintained numerous schools, churches, and benevolent organizations. They managed to raise large sums of money to support these institutions and their activities despite the immigrants' meager earnings. Jaisohn also pointed out that they had already contributed a large amount of money, over $80,000 in bonds, to the cause of independence. He concluded that Koreans in Hawaii were "thoroughly democratic, religious and sincere in their mode of life and strictly obedient to the laws of the land."[41] Through their example, the Korean Congress endeavored to highlight the prominence of Koreans in the United States as the bearers of an American model of democracy that could be propagated abroad.

The Congress was in itself a public exhibit of democratic decision-making processes. Before the first session, the delegates formally elected Jaisohn to preside over the Congress proceedings. In his capacity as president, he ceremoniously appointed delegates to serve on various committees, each of which was responsible for drafting a set of resolutions such as "An Appeal to America" and "Aims and Aspirations of the Koreans." The drafts were then presented to the entire body of delegates, after which the floor opened to every member of the Congress for discussion, suggestions, and debate. Following the initial round of discussions, Jaisohn presented a motion to adopt a particular resolution. In his role as a committee chair, KPG President Syngman Rhee offered a motion to adopt a resolution without the need for any amendments. Jaisohn immediately rejected the idea, stating that the Congress must abide by democratic principles. He exclaimed to Rhee, "You do not want to take any important action unless you get the views of the people. We would like to get the views of this Congress, who represent their people. This is not old Korea; this is new Korea. We want to go by the will of the people, by the majority present." The delegates enthusiastically agreed with Jaisohn. Soon thereafter, a discussion of the resolution commenced, after which it was adopted with the unanimous approval of all in attendance.[42]

This incident revealed the Congress's self-conscious efforts to represent a "new Korea." Jaisohn criticized Rhee's action as one associated with traditional, Confucian-based conceptions of leadership that typically had a strong authoritarian character and an elitist attitude toward the masses. Aware that international patronage was integral to the authority of the Korean nation-state, leaders at the Philadelphia Korean Congress invested much energy into such symbolic activities in order to project a strong image of the diaspora's ability to represent and lead the new Korean nation.

Though nationalist leaders emphasized the birth of a new democratic Korea, continuities with traditional approaches to leadership persisted in the nationalist movement. Syngman Rhee's unrivaled prestige as a nationalist leader was largely derived from the political culture of Confucianism that prized the elite educational backgrounds of the ruling scholar-official class. Indeed, Rhee's successful academic achievements in the United States, graduate degrees from Harvard University and Princeton University, created an almost sacred reverence for him among many Koreans. Such inordinate veneration, however, enabled autocratic tendencies in Rhee's leadership that would be a continual source of friction and conflict within the nationalist movement.

The 1919 Philadelphia Korean Congress ushered in a period of extensive lobbying activities in the United States for Korean independence. Before the concluding ceremonies at the Congress, Philip Jaisohn announced plans for opening a Korean Information Bureau in Philadelphia that would carry on the work of publicizing and disseminating information about the Korean cause of independence.[43] The diplomatic recognition of the KPG also continued to be a focal point for diasporic political activities. In August 1919, shortly after the Congress, KPG President Syngman Rhee established the Korean Commission in Washington, D.C., which he designated the sole diplomatic arm of the KPG and whose daily activities he oversaw.[44]

The Korean Congress also galvanized influential segments of the American public to assist the Korean independence movement. Prominent members of Philadelphia's religious, academic, and social circles created the League of the Friends of Korea in Philadelphia on June 16, 1919. Through the League, they sought to increase public awareness of Korea's situation under Japanese rule and to generate American support for democracy and Christianity in East Asia. With strong links to American Protestant missionaries in Korea, the League declared in its founding statement that the United States had a moral obligation to uphold its principles of justice, equality, and freedom throughout the world. Its goals included the following:

1. To inform the American public of the true conditions in the Far East.
2. To extend sympathy and encouragement to the oppressed people of Korea.
3. To use its moral influence to prevent the recurrence of cruel treatment to which Koreans had been subjected.
4. To secure religious liberty for Korean Christians.[45]

The founding statement stressed that the League did not seek to interfere politically in the affairs of Korea, Japan, or China, but rather to publicize the persecution of Korean Christians and other Japanese atrocities in Korea.[46]

The League coordinated its work with the Korean Information Bureau. Together, the two organizations published a monthly publication entitled the *Korea Review*, edited by Philip Jaisohn, which claimed to be the only English-language publication dedicated to covering political affairs in Korea, China, and Japan. As the official organ of the League of Friends, it published numerous articles and reports written by American missionaries documenting Japan's harsh treatment of Koreans. The *Review* also informed its readers of the activities of the League and the creation of new chapters around the country. By June 1920, it reported that 18 branches of the League of the Friends of Korea had been established from Boston to San Francisco with a total membership of 10,000.[47]

Besides documenting missionary activities in Korea and throughout East Asia, the *Korea Review* also reported on developments within the Korean independence movement in Korea and abroad. Typical articles included updates on the status and activities of the KPG in China and columns such as the "Washington News" and the "Students' Corner," which covered nationalist activities among Koreans in the United States. Nationalist leaders such as Philip Jaisohn, Syngman Rhee, and Henry Chung used its pages to reach a broader English-speaking audience. All three men traveled around America lecturing at schools and churches about Korea's plight under Japanese colonial rule and the need for U.S. assistance. Often providing erudite analyses of the political situation in East Asia, contributors to the *Korea Review* asserted that U.S. political, religious, and commercial interests in Asia all hinged on the "Korean Question." They argued that peace and stability throughout East Asia depended on a free Korea. An occupied Korea was a wedge for Japanese imperialism to expand into the Asian mainland and threatened another global conflict.[48]

The creation of both the League of Friends and the *Korea Review* revealed the prominence of American missionaries in the Korean cause following the March First uprising. Since Japan's annexation of Korea in 1910, American missionary groups had maintained a strict policy of political neutrality in Korea to prevent political partisanship from affecting their evangelical endeavors. Consistent with their disavowal of political involvement in Korea, American Protestant missionaries had little or no involvement in the planning or implementation of the March First uprising. Nonetheless, many missionaries witnessed firsthand the savage beating, torture, and killing of countless Korean civilians by the Japanese during the demonstrations. Korean Christians suffered especially harsh treatment at the hands of the Japanese, who were convinced that American missionaries had instigated the demonstrations. Failing to persuade Japanese officials to refrain from continued violence against the Korean people, American missionaries refused to remain passive onlookers to Japan's policies. Missionary groups asserted what they called "no neutrality for brutality" and began an extensive campaign to document and disclose Japanese acts of violence and cruelty in Korea.[49] Aware that the Japanese government was extremely sensitive to international publicity, missionaries believed that the only recourse available to them was to use the court of world opinion to bring pressure on Japan to alter its policies.

In response to the deluge of missionary reports of Japanese atrocities in Korea from an array of religious, government, and media agencies in the United States, the Federal Council of Churches of Christ in America, the most influential voice of the American Protestant establishment at large, formed the Commission on Relations with the Orient in July 1919. After meticulously reviewing some 1,000 pages of documents from Korea, the Commission carefully compiled reports, personal letters, and eyewitness affidavits from Korea, all of which described or confirmed incidents of unwarranted brutality and extreme violence inflicted on the Korean people by the Japanese, and published them as a 125-page report entitled *The Korean Situation: Authentic Accounts of Recent Events by Eye Witnesses*. Espousing political neutrality on the question of Korean independence, the report asserted that it only intended to mobilize public interest in the hope that "every possible influence may be brought to bear" in ceasing the "brutality, torture, inhuman treatment, religious persecutions, and massacres" in Korea. The missionary report further stated the "need for a sound and enlightened public opinion here in America . . . to secure justice and fair dealing in Korea."[50]

Viewed as objective experts on East Asian matters, American Protestant missionary organizations, such as the Federal Council of Churches and the League of Friends, were uniquely situated to influence foreign policy and public opinion makers in America. During Woodrow Wilson's presidency, American missionaries played prominent roles in American foreign policy toward East Asia. Preoccupied with events in Europe, Americans were generally indifferent toward East Asian affairs during much of the second decade of the twentieth century. Given the high degree of collective ignorance on East Asian matters within American foreign policy circles, missionaries came to play a vital and decisive role in shaping U.S. opinions about East Asia.[51] In contrast to the foreign policy elite, Protestant missionaries had much firsthand knowledge of, and experience in, East Asian affairs and became the principal source of information about the region for government officials as well as the general American public.[52]

American missionary activities on behalf of Korea did have a discernible effect on American public opinion about Korea's plight under the Japanese. Soon after publication of *The Korean Situation*, articles sympathetic to Korea began to fill the pages of mainstream publications. On July 13, 1919, the day after *The Korean Situation*'s publication, the *New York Times* printed an article including excerpts from the missionary report. Similarly, the *Literary Digest* published portions of *The Korean Situation* in its July 26 issue, with additional pieces about Japanese rule in Korea appearing in subsequent issues. In the months that followed, articles in support of Korea and critical of Japan were published in *Current Opinion, Public, World Outlook*, the *Nation, Missionary Review*, the *North American Review*, and *Current History*.[53] Additionally, newspapers throughout the United States printed numerous articles and editorials about Japanese actions in Korea and the Korean struggle for independence. According to the *Korean National Herald* in Honolulu, approximately 9,700 editorials sympathetic to the Korean cause appeared in American newspapers and periodicals between 1919 and 1921, while only 50 pro-Japanese articles were published during the same period.[54]

In deliberating on the "Korean Question" as part of heated debates surrounding U.S. involvement in the League of Nations, the U.S. Congress invariably turned to the American "missionary mind." On July 15, Senator George Norris of Nebraska discussed at length the case of Korea before the U.S. Senate. Quoting extensively from the accounts of Japanese brutality reprinted in a *New York Times* article about *The Korean Situation*, Norris forcefully argued that Japan, if unchecked, would inevitably extend its expansionist policies and violent tactics onto the Asian continent. Though he avoided directly addressing the issue of Korean independence, Norris insisted that the situation in Korea was vital to collective efforts for international peace and stability. The senator from Nebraska concluded with a request that the *New York Times* article be included in the *Congressional Record*, which drew no objections. Two days later, Senator William McCormick of Maryland received the unanimous consent of Senate to have the entire volume of *The Korean Situation* entered into the *Congressional Record* for future reference.[55]

On August 8, 1919, Senator Selden Spencer of Missouri, an ardent supporter of Korean independence, addressed the Senate, offering additional evidence for the need for U.S. assistance to Korea. Spencer presented a series of letters from the distinguished American missionary Homer Hulbert, who had served as special envoy to Korea's King Kojong in 1905. Hulbert reviewed Japan's policies toward Korea that had culminated in a protectorate agreement in 1905, which effectively transferred Korean sovereignty to Japan. Hulbert asserted that the Japanese protectorate over Korea in 1905 was illegitimate. He detailed his attempts to personally deliver letters from the Korean king to U.S. President Theodore Roosevelt at the 1905 Treaty of Portsmouth negotiations, which officially ended the Russo-Japanese War on terms favorable to the victorious Japanese. Explaining how Japan had seized control of Korea with the threat of direct military force, the Korean monarch appealed to President Roosevelt for U.S. intervention based on its 1882 treaty agreement with Korea.[56] According to Hulbert, these letters provided incontrovertible evidence against Japan's claims that the Korean government had voluntarily surrendered its national sovereignty to Japan. Hulbert believed that the Japanese government, aware of his intentions, had deliberately prevented him from meeting with President Roosevelt. Arguing that the Japanese government had carefully concealed the true nature of its belligerent actions, he concluded that the Japanese occupation of Korea had violated fundamental tenets of international law and should not be recognized by the United States, irrespective of Japan's claims.[57]

Between June and December 1919, the U.S. Congress was presented with a sizable body of information and testimony regarding Korea's plight under Japanese colonialism, filling some 64 pages of the *Congressional Record*. Nevertheless, it responded cautiously to the calls to aid the Korean cause. On October 1, 1919, Senator James Phelan of California introduced Senate Resolution 200, which was referred to the Committee on Foreign Relations, stating that the "Senate of the U.S. expresses its sympathies with the aspirations of the Korean people for a government of their own choice."[58] On October 24, 1919, Representative William Mason of Illinois introduced an identical resolution, House Resolution 359.[59] The carefully worded resolutions represented formal expressions of friendship toward the KPG, but fell far short of official recognition of the newly formed Korean government or any promise for future governmental action on behalf of Korean independence. As primarily symbolic gestures, neither resolution moved beyond the Committees on Foreign Relations and Foreign Affairs. The actions of the U.S. Congress made it clear that government officials would not call for any dramatic changes to U.S. foreign policies toward Korea and Japan. However, the lobbying efforts of American missionary groups did generate sufficient publicity to cause policy makers in Washington to devote considerable time to the "Korean Question."

American missionary involvement in Korean affairs reinforced the independence movement's emphasis on democratic processes and Christianity, which helped attract widespread attention from the American public and government officials. The bureaucratic authority of American missionaries also provided Korean immigrants in the United States with some leverage to influence foreign policy issues through official and nonofficial channels of the U.S. polity. These political activities of the U.S. component of the Korean diaspora greatly increased their visibility and prominence in the political affairs of both the United States and Korea and affirmed their authority to define the independence movement's ideological frameworks and its vision of a new Korean nation-state.

CHAPTER 4

Contesting Issues of State Power in the Diaspora

As they sought to sustain their participation in the democratic political processes of the Korean Provisional Government (KPG), Korean immigrants in the United States soon became embroiled in a highly charged conflict over issues of state power that emerged from a contentious feud surrounding fundraising activities between the Korean Commission in Washington, D.C., and the Korean National Association (KNA) of North America headquartered in San Francisco. As a direct branch of the KPG, the Korean Commission was empowered by Syngman Rhee to act as the official national representative of Koreans in the United States. Rhee sought to gain full control over the collection of monetary contributions among Koreans in the United States. In order to do so, he attempted to supplant the local autonomy of the KNA with the state apparatus of the Korean Commission. The KNA, however, refused to relinquish its local authority over Koreans residing on the U.S. mainland.

Operating mostly in a U.S. setting, the KNA and the Korean Commission functioned within two distinctly different institutional contexts. The KNA conducted its activities in the realm of civil society as a self-regulating voluntary association that provided members with a means of collective action in the public sphere.[1] Meanwhile, the Korean Commission exerted its power and authority as the official, bureaucratic, and coercive political apparatus of the state. The fundraising conflict underscored civil society's separate, yet interdependent and complementary, relationship with the state.

Though the fundraising dispute would be resolved by the end of 1919, the conflict exacerbated factional disputes within the KPG in Shanghai. This time issues of state power shifted from the U.S. mainland to the Asian mainland. In organizing the KPG, nationalist leaders attempted to unify scattered Korean communities in exile into a single central administrative body and proclaimed the KPG as the sole and authentic national sovereign of the Korean people. The efforts to create a national state within the diaspora, however, presented serious dilemmas for coherent political action as a multitude of groups competed over determining who had the legitimate right to govern and lead the nation.

Koreans in the United States played an integral role in mobilizing financial resources to support the operational expenses of KPG activities. From the beginning, the government was almost entirely dependent on financial contributions from Koreans in the United States and Hawaii. In May 1919, Ahn Chang-ho, who had been elected to the post of Minister of Home Affairs in the KPG, arrived in Shanghai from San Francisco with $25,000 contributed by members of the KNA. The only KPG cabinet member then present in Shanghai, Ahn used the money to establish a permanent office space for the KPG in a rented building in the French Concession of the Shanghai International Settlement, which was under international control by a consortium of foreign powers. From this location, the Koreans could operate relatively free from the threat of direct Japanese control and persecution that afflicted local Korean diasporic communities throughout the East Asian region.[2]

From Shanghai, Ahn launched a campaign to unite the array of Korean nationalist groups in the diaspora under the single leadership of the Shanghai Provisional Government. In September, the KPG was formally inaugurated as a united front government with Syngman Rhee as president and Yi Tong-hwi as premier.[3] Ahn's centralizing efforts, however, had entailed extensive expenditures for communication and travel. By the end of September 1919, the financial coffers of the KPG were nearly depleted. Reliant on continued financial support from Koreans in the United States, the KPG was soon caught in a bitter conflict between the two main nationalist organizations in the United States: the Korean Commission in Washington, D.C., and the central headquarters of the KNA in San Francisco.[4]

Both the Korean Commission and KNA coordinated their activities with each other and with the KPG through frequent transnational flows of information and money via cablegrams. However, power struggles soon developed over who controlled this flow of information and resources. The transnational links across the diaspora were threatened, jeopardizing the nationalist movement as a whole.

Differences in fundraising policies provided the pretext for the conflict between the two American-based political organizations. Authorized by the KPG in April 1919, the Central Congress of the KNA in San Francisco initiated a Patriotic Fund drive (*Aigukgum*) among Koreans in America, which solicited pledges from individuals that consisted of a poll tax of 5 percent of one's total income. Due to the KNA's highly organized centralized structure that effectively administrated numerous local branches throughout North America, the Provisional Government had designated the KNA to collect Patriotic Funds from its constituents in the United States and remit them to the KPG in Shanghai.[5]

Though their numbers were far smaller than those for Korean émigré communities in Manchuria and Siberia, Koreans living in the United States had emerged as the primary financial supporters of the KPG. According to its financial records, the KNA collected over $88,000 from Koreans in America in 1919, most of which was used to finance the operations of the KPG and the Korean Commission.[6] A significant portion of these funds had been collected from Koreans in California. In fact, nearly half of the total amount collected in 1919 came from Korean immigrant farmers in the Sacramento Valley region, many of whom had prospered from the heavy demand for American foodstuffs during World War I.[7] In contrast, the more populous Korean community in Hawaii contributed about one-fifth of the amount donated by their compatriots on the mainland.[8] Regardless, these were significant sums from such a small population with generally low-earning capacities.

Like the KPG, the Korean Commission depended on Koreans in the continental United States and Hawaii to provide funds for its operations. As KPG president, Rhee presumed the Commission to be a state entity, fully invested with the powers of the state. As part of his mandate to pursue the national interests of the Korean state, he empowered the Commission to collect state revenues from Korean nationals in the United States by replacing the KNA Patriotic Fund program with its own fundraising campaign. On September 1, 1919, the Commission issued $250,000 worth of "Liberty Bonds" (*Kongchaipyo*) in incremental denominations ranging from $5 to $100. Imprinted with the official seal of the Republic of Korea, the bonds were issued as certificates of indebtedness with the pledge that the Republic of Korea would pay the face value of the certificate plus interest within one year after the official recognition of the Republic of Korea by the U.S. government. In the interim, the Liberty Bond would

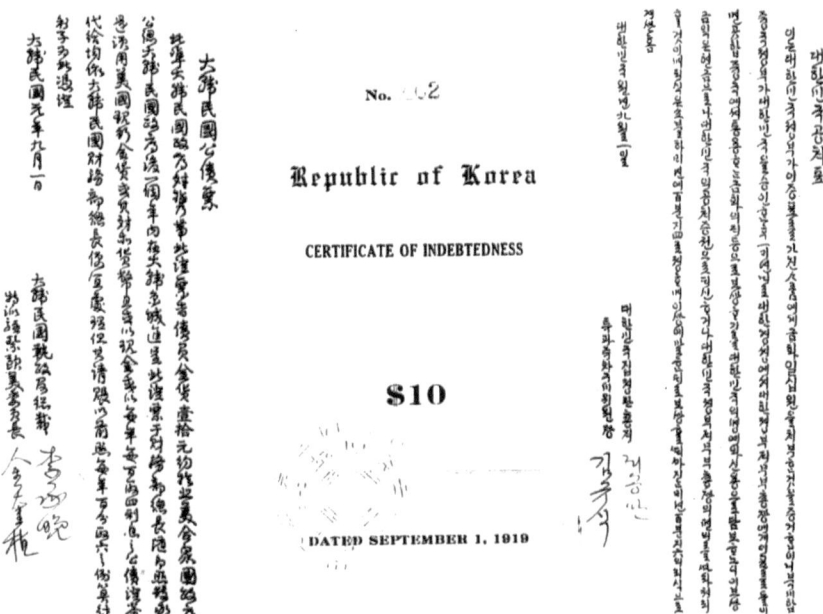

Figure 4.1.
Front and back sides of Korean Commission Liberty Bond or Republic of Korea Certificate of Indebtedness for $10, signed by Kiusic Kimm and Syngman Rhee.
Source: Korean American Digital Archive, University of Southern California.

draw interest at an annual rate of 6 percent.[9] The Korean Commission appointed Rev. David Lee, former president of the Korean National Association of North America, to represent the Commission in its dealings with the KNA office in San Francisco and to oversee the replacement of the Patriotic Fund with Liberty Bonds. Lee explained the Commission's plans to KNA President Earl K. Paik in San Francisco, but he quickly encountered confusion and suspicion from Paik and other KNA officials and went to the West Coast to meet them in person.[10]

The Korean Commission, under its acronym KORIC, cabled KOPOGO, the Korean Provisional Government, in Shanghai, on September 12, requesting that it instruct the KNA headquarters in San Francisco to cease its Patriotic Fund program and to substitute the Liberty Bonds in its place. Rhee criticized the Provisional Government's authorization of the Patriotic Funds, explaining that "all orders of any department must have President's approval and President will issue orders through respective departments." Insisting that "Shanghai and Washington must cooperate absolutely," Rhee asserted that "all communications to our people and Foreign Powers in America and Europe must be handled only through this Commission."[11]

Desperately in need of funds to cover his operating expenses in Washington, Rhee ordered the KNA office in San Francisco to send immediately "all monies on hand raised for governmental purposes" to the Commission to forward to Shanghai.[12] KNA headquarters refused, explaining that it did not have the authority to redirect its funds to Washington. The following day, September 18, Rhee received word from Shanghai that the National Congress had ratified the constitution for the Republic of Korea and had elected him president of the Provisional Government. He immediately wired the information to the KNA in San Francisco, offering it as incontrovertible evidence of his legitimacy as head of state and expected full compliance.[13] Emboldened by his newly found status, he issued a presidential directive that same day, communicated through mass telegrams to Korean communities throughout the Pacific Coast and the Rocky Mountain states.[14] He appointed two to three individuals in each locality to establish KORIC-sponsored local commissions, which were authorized to sell Liberty Bonds in their respective jurisdictions, and to send the collected funds immediately to KORIC Treasurer Hyungju Song in Washington, D.C., instead of following the current route to the KPG in Shanghai.[15] The Commission explained that these local commissioners would only be temporary appointments for the immediate purpose of raising funds. Eventually, permanent local commissioners were to be determined based on elections by Koreans residing in each locality. The Korean Commission emphasized that each local commission would be directly accountable to the Korean Commission in Washington, D.C.[16] In effect, it sought to supersede the local autonomy of the KNA by extending its jurisdiction over Koreans on the mainland through its own centralized state apparatus.[17] KORIC's attempts to control the flow of funds in the United States were thus inextricably linked to its campaign to gain administrative authority over Koreans in America.

Rhee also cabled his representative David Lee in San Francisco, informing him of his directive. He ordered Lee to travel throughout the various KNA localities to help organize elections for the permanent commissions and to ensure that all monetary contributions were channeled directly to the local KORIC commissioners.[18] Lee reported to Rhee a few days later that the KNA's Patriotic Fund drive had been hugely successful, producing $100,000 in subscriptions and $60,000 in collections. As a result, he advised KORIC to authorize the KNA to continue its collection of the Patriotic Funds and to sell the Liberty Bonds only after the collection of the Patriotic Funds had been completed. Lee added that Korean residents on the mainland "sympathize [with] us," and so in the interim, the Commission could still obtain its operating funds from the monies raised by the Patriotic Funds. Lee also informed Rhee that KNA officials were upset that he had appointed his own local commissioners without KNA consultation and urged Rhee to stop such "private communications." Lee warned that the "local commissions will not be successful and meet attack." Given these circumstances, Lee urged Rhee to reauthorize the Patriotic Funds as he foresaw "trouble ahead."[19]

Rhee adamantly refused to withdraw his order, asserting that the Commission had already granted Lee "full power" to sell its Liberty Bonds and "to help organize local and district commissions." To ensure that no confusion would result from Lee's request for a reversal in KORIC orders, the Commission wired telegrams to each local commission, reiterating its directive to substitute the Patriotic Funds with the Liberty Bonds. However, Lee's ominous warning seemed to have worried KORIC officials enough for them to order the local commissions to send immediately to Washington all funds available, including the "Patriotic Funds collected or pledged for government purposes."[20]

Frustrated, David Lee resigned from his position with the Korean Commission, exclaiming he wanted "no more connection with [Rhee]."[21] Lee stated that he could no longer go against "the majority will of our Pacific Coast people," who unequivocally supported the Patriotic Funds. Lee once again warned that the Korean Commission's policies would ultimately lead to the complete loss of any potential funding from KNA members.[22]

KNA headquarters also sent KORIC an urgent plea to rescind the order to cease the Patriotic Funds. KNA officials explained that the Patriotic Funds program had raised $100,000 and any changes at this point jeopardized future collections. KNA assured KORIC that it would send necessary funds to Washington, D.C., from the collection of Patriotic Funds in compliance with the KPG's orders. "Since Shanghai and Washington need money very badly," KNA insisted that KORIC "should not lose this opportunity" to receive financial support.[23]

KORIC officials refused to revise its policies, asserting that the Patriotic Funds had already been "abolished" and replaced with the Liberty Bonds. Declaring that it had "full power from KOPOGO to solely handle all governmental affairs" in the United States and that "all must co-operate for common end," it suggested KNA noncooperation constituted an act of disloyalty and a betrayal of the cause of Korean independence.[24] KORIC once again pressed Shanghai to instruct the KNA to comply with the orders of the Commission and to send all available funds to Washington, reiterating its pledge to send all the money to the KPG after the necessary amounts had been subtracted to cover the operating expenses of the Commission. KORIC stressed the urgency of the situation and implored the KNA to obey orders from Washington. Otherwise, the Commission's work would be severely "handicapped."[25]

In what he described as a "very chaotic situation," the KNA president in San Francisco, E. K. Paik, sent KORIC a proposal on September 28 in an attempt to break the "deadlock." Paik despondently reported that the KNA was unable to collect or sell both the Patriotic Funds and Liberty Bonds due to the confusion caused by KORIC's orders. He proposed a compromise in which he would agree to implement KORIC's order to substitute the Patriotic Funds with Liberty Bonds on the condition that KORIC terminate all of its local commissions west of Chicago and prove that the order to repeal the Patriotic Funds had been issued directly from the KPG in Shanghai.[26] Proposed as "the only solution," Paik stressed that KORIC needed to make "some adjustment" to its policies "no matter how good the Commission may be" or else the "entire program will be a failure."[27] In a final attempt to persuade KORIC officials to accept his proposal, Paik informed them that they "should know" KNA members who had "pledged a big sum" had vociferously insisted that one-fifth of the total amount collected through the Patriotic Funds be sent directly to Washington and the remaining four-fifths to the KPG in Shanghai.

Kiusic Kimm, who worked alongside Rhee in Washington as chairman of the Korean Commission, curtly responded that KORIC policies had been clearly delineated in repeated messages, and further changes were not possible. Kimm once again urged "patriotic cooperation" from the KNA, emphasizing that any contrary actions jeopardized the cause for independence.[28] In a longer telegram, he explained that Koreans on the West Coast had the right to be represented by the KNA rather than the KORIC, if KNA headquarters could provide incontrovertible proof that it enjoyed majority support. Regardless of the outcome, Kimm stressed that the KNA would still fall under the jurisdiction of KORIC since the Commission was the direct representative of the KPG in the United States. Kimm added that the arrangement to channel a portion of the funds from the Patriotic Funds directly to the Korean Commission was only "a private agreement" between the KNA headquarters and its members. Accordingly, such an agreement could not be implemented as an official governmental policy since it had not been issued by the Commission or the Provisional Government.[29]

The deadlock between KORIC and the KNA appeared to be more than solely a power struggle over the control of fundraising activities, but part of a larger struggle to determine which group had the legitimate right to represent the national constituency of Koreans in the United States and Hawaii. While both the KNA and KORIC were wholly dedicated to the independence movement, their abilities to lead rested on different bases.

HENRY CHUNG.   KIUSIC KIMM.   SOON HYUN
THE MEMBERS OF THE KOREAN COMMISSION TO AMERICA AND EUROPE

Figure 4.2.
Members of the Korean Commission, 1920.
Source: K. W. Lee.

Syngman Rhee claimed his authority as the lawfully elected president of the newly created KPG and its ancillary in Washington. In his capacity as head of state, Rhee defined the national interests of the state to include not only the diplomatic activities of the Commission but also the mobilization of the national diaspora. He sought to achieve this mobilization by replacing the KNA's local structures of governance with KORIC's own apparatus through what he considered a democratic process in which "government and people can co-operate directly [in] centralizing affairs."[30]

While KORIC spoke structurally and ideologically as the most effective organization to mobilize the national diaspora, the KNA claimed its authority from its long-standing knowledge of local communities and ability to draw on immediate, personal loyalties. It saw itself as the legitimate representative of Koreans living in the United States and Hawaii, dating back to its roots at the beginning of Korean immigration to the United States in 1903 and its function as the de facto diplomatic representative for this population. Soon after the March First movement in Korea, KNA leaders had mobilized the Korean populace in the United States to aid the cause for Korean independence, and conference delegates had passed a series of resolutions vesting "executive authority of the independence movement in America" to the Central Headquarters of the KNA in San Francisco and the Regional Headquarters of Hawaii. In this capacity, both KNA headquarters were authorized to direct and oversee "patriotic contributions of Korean residents in the United States, Hawaii, and Mexico," which were to "be paid at the offices of the Korean National Association in San Francisco and Honolulu."[31] The KNA refused to relinquish this administrative jurisdiction over local Korean communities in the United States. Its effectiveness in raising and collecting funds for the KPG was based on its ability to mobilize the diaspora at the local level. When Rhee attempted to place its authority under the state apparatus of KORIC, he undermined the ability of the KNA to operate effectively as it was unable to collect any revenues from its members, putting the entire political system in jeopardy.

Given the urgency of the situation, the KPG took action to break the deadlock. To the chagrin of the Commission, the KPG ordered the continuation of the Patriotic Funds program to run concurrently with the sale of KORIC's Liberty Bonds. In addition, it informed KORIC that the Minister of Financial Affairs planned to appoint his own financial agent in the United States to oversee all subsequent financial matters.[32] Receiving the same message from KPG, KNA headquarters in San Francisco promptly cabled KORIC informing them that the KPG had directly authorized the KNA to continue the collection of Patriotic Funds.[33]

Upset by Shanghai's decision, KORIC defiantly responded that it intended to continue its activities regardless of the wishes of the KPG.[34] The Commission also denounced the KPG's plan to establish a financial office in Washington, D.C., claiming its sole authority to administer financial affairs in the United States. KORIC officials insisted that the national interest of the Republic of Korea depended on the KPG's unequivocal support for KORIC activities in the United States. If the KPG continued to interfere with those activities, KORIC avowed, it would bear full responsibility for "spoiling our cause abroad."[35] The Commission ordered KNA officials to disregard the KPG's recent decision and to await the arrival of Kiusic Kimm.[36]

While Kimm was en route to San Francisco, KNA headquarters released a scathing statement against the Korean Commission published in the widely circulated *Sinhan Minbo*. It specifically denounced Syngman Rhee and his attempts to override the authority of the KNA, proclaiming that "the Association will oppose any attempt by the Korean Commission to abuse the power of government or any attempt to ignore the will of the people." The statement added that "all activities of government offices must conform to the Constitution of the Government," and declared that Rhee's actions were in "clear violation of the basic principles of a democratic State." As a result, the KNA concluded that Rhee's actions were fundamentally undemocratic and illegitimate.[37]

On a broader level, the conflict between the KNA and KORIC exemplified the tensions in the dynamics of a civil society/state relationship. When Syngman Rhee sought to subsume the local chapters of the KNA under the central authority of KORIC, KNA members took an oppositional stance to the state-making activities of KORIC. As head of state, Rhee believed that he had issued his executive order under the rule of law through the legitimate administrative state apparatus of KORIC and thus expected full compliance from the KNA. In this light, KORIC officials repeatedly requested that KNA members act patriotically in the national interests of the state, suggesting their continued intransigence constituted acts of disloyalty. Operating in the realm of civil society as a self-regulating voluntary association, the KNA resisted what it perceived as the excessive concentration of political power in KORIC's undemocratic attempts to supplant the autonomy and self-governance of the KNA.[38] In its public critique of KORIC, the KNA forcefully articulated the primary function of civil society to check state power by seeking to hold Rhee accountable to democratic principles and processes on which the new Korean state had been founded. The KNA denounced what it described as Rhee's flagrant abuse of state authority in "the claim that 'Syngman Rhee is the government and his order is the law,'" which constituted "a clear violation of the basic principles of a democratic State." As a result, the KNA refused to consent to the authority of Rhee and the Korean Commission, declaring that "the Korean Commission is not the government, but an agent of the government for diplomatic and propaganda services."[39]

Civil society groups, however, do not operate solely in opposition to the state. Besides its role in curbing state power, civil society also legitimates state authority when that authority is based on the rule of law and legally guarantees the self-governance and autonomy of civil society. This legitimizing function of civil society is based on the premise that the power of the state is only legitimate when it holds the trust of its citizens.[40] The KNA's recognition and support of the legitimacy of the KPG were firmly grounded in its fundraising arrangements established with the KPG that enabled the KNA to maintain its local control and self-governing structures. KNA headquarters repeatedly refused to comply with Rhee's orders, contending that the KPG had already authorized the KNA to collect funds on behalf of the Republic of Korea and that KORIC did not have the authority to override direct orders from the KPG, asserting in its public critique that "the [Korean National] Association deems it illegal that the bonds of the Republic of Korea were issued by President Rhee without approval by the legislature of the Provisional government."[41]

Upon Kiusic Kimm's arrival in San Francisco, KORIC officials in Washington informed him of the recently published public attack on the Commission in the *Sinhan Minbo*. "Unless we answer them," they feared, "people might think of us fools."[42] Kimm urged them not to reply to the charges leveled against the Commission, stressing the need to demonstrate a "friendly attitude" and "readiness for any possible compromise" in his discussions with KNA headquarters. He assured KORIC that the situation was "not altogether hopeless" and emphasized the need to "keep cool" to prevent an "open fight" that could spoil the possibility of any compromise.[43]

A few days later, Kimm sent Rhee a possible compromise worked out with KNA officials, who had proposed that the KNA would sell the KORIC-issued Liberty Bonds to KNA members while continuing the KNA Patriotic Funds program. All funds collected through both programs would be deposited in a KNA bank account in San Francisco. KORIC could withdraw the funds necessary to cover its operating expenses in Washington, D.C. All remaining funds would be remitted to the KPG in Shanghai. In exchange, KORIC would agree to withhold establishing its permanent local commissions until the "Government (KPG and KORIC) adopts a definite internal policy" regarding KORIC activities in the United States.[44]

Rhee rejected the proposal outright. He demanded that the Patriotic Funds be discontinued immediately, with the exception of the collection of the funds already pledged. He also ordered that KNA headquarters send one-third of the total proceeds collected from the Patriotic Funds to the Commission in Washington. With respect to the local commissions, Rhee instructed that each local KNA chapter should decide by majority vote whether it wanted to maintain the local commissions established by KORIC. Before making any final commitments to the local commissions, Rhee requested that Kimm "study conditions" of other localities with KNA chapters in California to get a general sense of support for KORIC representation at the grassroots level.[45]

On the same day, KORIC received a belated response from the KPG regarding Rhee's earlier communication to defy the KPG's order for the continuation of the KNA Patriotic Funds program. Asserting that they did not intend to cause any discord, KPG officials explained that they had empowered the KNA to collect funds through the Patriotic Funds before the Liberty Bond program had been authorized. As a result, abolishing the Patriotic Funds without KPG approval was "improper." In order to "secure unity," the KPG stressed that all financial matters fell absolutely under the centralized authority of the Finance Minister in Shanghai and that KORIC was authorized only to issue bonds and not collect funds. KPG officials warned that Rhee's position was "too extreme" and would cause great dissension.[46]

Back in California, Kimm urged Rhee to accept the KNA proposal in its entirety. In consenting to the plan, he explained, KORIC would "concede only outwardly but gain materially [and] morally." According to Kimm, the proposed plan would give KORIC immediate and discretionary access to a steady source of funds as well as the opportunity to continue its "centralizing work" in a climate of harmony and cooperation rather than the "permanent discord" that would result if the full plan was not accepted. Kimm insisted that KORIC had little chance of gaining mass support for its plan to centralize its authority among Koreans in America given the widespread feelings of distrust and hostility toward the Commission. As a result, Kimm advised Rhee that "totally accepting present proposition" was the "wisest procedure" to ensure the survival and maintenance of the Commission.[47]

Rhee agreed to accept the proposal with the exception of withholding the local commissions, claiming that KORIC could not withdraw them "without [the] trouble" of adopting a new government policy.[48] Kimm reiterated his view that accepting the proposal in its entirety was the "only safe solution for continuing [the] work" of KORIC. He stressed that acceptance would demonstrate to KPG officials that KORIC had "conceded for common good" and thus give it valuable leverage to gradually "adjust" KPG policies in KORIC's favor. Otherwise, Kimm warned that all the work of the Commission would "collapse," with "all blaming" KORIC for "wrecking everything causing permanent discord."[49]

Nevertheless, Rhee refused to compromise over the local commissions. In a prepared but unsent telegram intended for Kimm, Rhee questioned exactly what "common good" was being served in consenting to the entire proposal. He claimed to serve the national will of the Korean people, not the will of the KNA. In his capacity as president of the KPG and in his work with the Commission in Washington, his responsibility was to obtain international recognition of the government of the newly formed Republic of Korea, not the KNA. Thus, Rhee rhetorically asked, "whether [the] Commission or the Gukminhoi (KNA) is the government agency in America."[50]

Expressing similar views in his response to the KPG, Rhee stated that the Commission had always sought to foster harmonious relations with the KNA. He blamed the KPG's "inconsistent and imprudent actions" for causing the present ordeal. He particularly criticized the KPG for disregarding his authority by "consulting Gukminhoi (KNA) only" on government affairs without any consultation with the Commission. Rhee asserted that this recognition of a "private organization as official agency" over his authority as KPG president violated his legal right to govern, which had been legitimately bestowed on him by the will of the Korean people. The plan to create a branch office of the Ministry of Finance in the United States would only cause further tension and confusion. Stressing that "any change or friction will hurt cause," he urged the KPG to cooperate with KORIC so that they could together work toward the national cause of international recognition of the KPG and Korean independence.[51]

A greatly disappointed Kiusic Kimm informed Rhee that any resolution was unlikely before his return to Washington. A few days later, however, Rhee inexplicably asked Kimm to make preliminary arrangements for a final settlement with the KNA and said that it was "absolutely necessary" for Kimm to return to Washington immediately to implement the changes in government policy.[52] Although the cause of Rhee's sudden reversal is unclear, desperate financial conditions in Washington seem to have played a major role. A few days earlier, Rhee had sent mass telegrams to KORIC-sponsored local commissions on the U.S. mainland and KNA headquarters in Honolulu, ordering them to send money immediately because KORIC was "in danger having no money."[53]

Back in Washington, Kiusic Kimm notified the KNA headquarters that KORIC would accept its entire proposal with the addition of two stipulations. First, KNA central headquarters would officially serve as a district commission of KORIC to oversee the local commissions throughout the continental United States. Second, all checks were required to be signed by the Commission Treasurer in Washington, D.C., and countersigned by KNA headquarters under the official title of district commission of North America.⁵⁴ Though these stipulations would not alter the KNA's jurisdiction, they most likely eased Rhee's concerns, skillfully creating a semblance of KORIC's authority over the KNA while simultaneously allowing the KNA to maintain its local autonomy.

KNA officials deliberated over Kimm's proposal for several weeks, while worried over the urgent need for funds to maintain the daily operations of KORIC in Washington, D.C., and its branch offices in Philadelphia, Paris, and London.⁵⁵ On December 19, KNA officials finally sent Kimm their final terms of agreement. They explained they had been waiting for a presidential proclamation that publicly announced the terms of the resolution. Nevertheless, KNA officials decided to guarantee KORIC $3,000 a month for a period of six months. While KNA officials agreed to act as a district commission of KORIC, they sought to ensure KNA's local control by stipulating that President Rhee officially authorize the KNA to handle all monetary collections from Koreans on the U.S. mainland, while KORIC maintain its diplomatic activities in Washington.⁵⁶ Kimm accepted the final terms, but asserted that the jurisdiction of KNA headquarters in San Francisco was confined only to Koreans residing on the U.S. mainland and the agreement must hold regardless of what happened in the next six months, after which a renewal of the funding arrangement could be discussed.⁵⁷ On December 31, KORIC acknowledged the receipt of $1,500 from the KNA, the first installment of financial support from the KNA.⁵⁸

This transfer finally brought an end to the feud between the two organizations. According to several sources, the Korean Commission received sizable amounts of funding after the final agreement. On December 29, 1919, the KNA central headquarters reported its total revenue to be $88,030.50, of which nearly half was dispensed to the KPG and Korean Commission. According to a Korean Commission financial report, it collected $70,190 between December 1919 and November 1920. During this time, Koreans in the United States and Mexico also purchased a total of $46,404 in Liberty Bonds.⁵⁹ Another source estimates that the Korean Commission collected approximately $45,000 between September 1919 and May 1920, none of which was sent to Shanghai.⁶⁰ Yet another report estimated that the Korean Commission had raised $50,000 to $60,000 between 1919 and 1924, of which $10,000 may have been sent to Shanghai.⁶¹

Despite the uncertainty over actual amounts of money raised and sent to Washington, D.C., and Shanghai, the KPG remained in deep financial trouble. In March 1920, KPG officials in Shanghai began to clamor for Rhee to come there to answer his critics who blamed him for the financial crisis afflicting the KPG.[62] These growing demands for Rhee's recall to Shanghai made clear that his actions remained controversial in light of his continual attempts to supersede the administrative authority of KPG officials.[63]

As money became scarcer, tensions among KPG officials began to mount. Strategic differences between Yi Tong-hwi and Syngman Rhee intensified and created further factional strife within the KPG. Divergent policies perhaps could have been pursued simultaneously had sufficient resources been available. However, most of the limited funds available had already been allocated to diplomatic activities in the United States. Yi criticized the continued diplomatic emphasis despite its failure to produce any substantive results in terms of either diplomatic recognition or financial support from the United States. Yi pressed for a shift in government policies that utilized KPG resources for military purposes, such as mobilizing Koreans in Manchuria and Siberia in preparation for a war of independence against the Japanese.[64]

Such conflicts over government policies and strategic plans had plagued the KPG from the outset. On assuming his post as premier of the KPG in October 1919, Yi vehemently criticized the KPG strategy of solely appealing to the United States and other Western powers, which had tepidly responded to Korean independence. He argued, instead, that developing ties with the Russian Bolsheviks represented a more expedient strategy for the independence movement, indicating that the Bolsheviks had shown a willingness to support Korean independence dating back to the Russian Revolution. With Soviet financial and military assistance, Yi sought to mobilize the large number of Koreans living in Siberia and Manchuria for a full-scale military attack on the northern part of Korea. Yi and his supporters believed that such an attack would kindle a revolution to overthrow Japanese colonial rule.[65]

Yi was initially successful in garnering support from the Soviet government. In May 1920, he secretly dispatched a KPG representative, Han Hyong-gwon, to Moscow to seek Soviet financial and military assistance. Han was well received by the Bolsheviks in Moscow and met with Vladimir Lenin. Lenin was favorably inclined to support the Korean cause as Japan represented a common enemy for both the Soviet Russians and Koreans. At the time, the Bolsheviks were caught in their own struggles against Japanese military forces that had been sent to the Russian Far East to support the anti-Bolshevik White Russians. In need of military allies against the Japanese and others in Siberia, Lenin promised two million rubles for the cause of Korean independence once the Bolsheviks were able to gain control of the chaotic political situation in Siberia. In his pledge of support, Lenin gave Han an initial payment of 400,000 rubles, with the remaining portion to be dispensed later.[66]

The Soviet funds would have certainly helped ease the financial crisis facing the KPG, but it never benefited from the arrangement made with the Soviets. By the time of the Russian pledge of support, the KPG had become embroiled in serious factional disputes. In the months prior to the agreement with the Soviet government, Yi Tong-hwi and other KPG officials submitted several different proposals for enhancing the military capabilities of the KPG, all of which were rejected as financially and strategically unfeasible. Disenchanted, Yi Tong-hwi decided to withhold the Russian funds from the KPG and left Shanghai to organize military troops in Manchuria.[67]

While conditions within the KPG were rapidly deteriorating, the military activities of armed struggle groups in Manchuria and Siberia were flourishing. Having organized themselves into several different independence armies, these groups were staging frequent guerilla attacks inflicting severe damage and casualties on Japanese forces stationed along the Korean border. Between March and June 1920, the independence armies engaged in 32 border battles that destroyed numerous Japanese police and administrative buildings and inflicted numerous Japanese casualties.[68] Though the Japanese launched several counterattacks against the independence armies in Manchuria between May and October, the Korean militia groups not only withstood the offensives but also scored some remarkable victories over the vastly superior Japanese military forces. At the height of their success in the fall of 1920, the Korean independence armies commanded 3,500 troops.[69]

The unlikely success of the Korean independence armies humiliated and infuriated Japanese military authorities. The Japanese were particularly incensed when a much smaller Korean contingent crushed a massive Japanese assault on independence forces in Manchuria in October. In what is known as the "Ch'ingshan-li Battle," Korean independence fighters killed over 1,000 Japanese soldiers while sustaining minimal casualties of their own. The Japanese retaliated by launching a full-scale attack on the large Manchurian settlement of Korean émigrés in Chientao on the pretext of eliminating "recalcitrant Koreans."[70] During the "1920 Massacre," Japanese troops committed brutal atrocities against Korean residents, indiscriminately arresting, killing, and raping thousands of Koreans and burning scores of Korean-owned homes, churches, and schools. The attack forced the independence armies to retreat from their sanctuaries in Manchuria to interior regions of the Russian Maritime Province. Earlier, in April 1920, Japanese military forces stationed in the Russian Far East under the auspices of the Allied Intervention had launched a series of similar offensives against "recalcitrant Koreans" in areas of the Maritime Province with large Korean settlements. These assaults forced Koreans to seek refuge in the inner regions of Siberia. By the end of 1920, the Japanese military had successfully knocked out the major bases of operation for the Korean armed struggle movement in the border regions of Manchuria and the Maritime Province (see Fig. 4.3., p. 91).[71]

Though largely removed from the bloody battlegrounds of Manchuria and Siberia, the KPG in Shanghai suffered grave repercussions from the brutal destruction of the major operational bases. After the October massacre in Chientao, Koreans in and out of the KPG denounced the government for its failure to protect innocent Korean lives and property. These events created even greater KPG internal strife as officials argued over how to respond to the Japanese military assaults on Korean communities, further intensifying preexisting conflicts over strategies for achieving Korean independence. The most vocal criticism came from Yi Tong-hwi, who urged the KPG to declare immediate war against Japan. Yi had been actively involved in anti-Japanese activities in the Chientao region long before the formation of the KPG in Shanghai. He demanded that the KPG reorganize the dispersed Korean troops under the single command of the KPG and wage full-scale war. Without direct authority over most of the armed struggle groups based in Manchuria and Siberia, more moderate KPG leaders asserted that a war of independence would be considered a last resort for the government, arguing such drastic action was premature and akin to asking "the crippled to run."[72]

Amidst these heightened tensions, Syngman Rhee suddenly decided to respond to the ongoing demands from KPG officials to come to Shanghai. While his arrival shifted attention away from the bitter internecine conflicts, his presence deepened the existing tensions and divisions in the KPG. Commencing on January 5, 1921, KPG officials organized a series of cabinet meetings to review Rhee's past actions with the hope of implementing reforms in KPG policies with the approval of President Rhee. Yi Tong-hwi and other officials harshly denounced "President Rhee's confused policies" that had created a situation in which "the position of the government was unsteady." Cabinet members proposed several different plans that would reallocate decision-making authority from President

Rhee to a collective body of various cabinet members in Shanghai. Rhee, however, adamantly refused to make any changes to his presidential power or his policies.[73]

Exasperated with Rhee's intransigence, Yi Tong-hwi officially resigned from the KPG on January 24, 1921. A wave of resignations soon followed. The most notable departures were those of Ahn Chang-ho, who had been so instrumental in brokering and maintaining unity within the government, and Kiusic Kimm, who had been Rhee's close associate in the Korean Commission and supported him throughout the fundraising controversy.[74] In a collective public statement, the cabinet members who resigned explained that they had "hoped to correct the faults of the past" by cooperating with President Rhee "to improve the administrative structure [of the KPG] without changing the membership of the cabinet." However, Rhee "refused to admit the errors of the past, and insisted upon following his temporary decisions.... Since the will of the majority was not followed and no policy for improvement was adopted, nothing but conflict has resulted." The cabinet members asserted that if they "were to maintain the *status quo* [emphasis in original], this in effect would be an act of assisting the dubious policies of Syngman Rhee."[75]

Despite this, Rhee managed to retain his presidential authority and keep the government intact. In March 1921, some 45 members of the KPG, including the few remaining cabinet members, pledged their commitment to support President Rhee and the KPG and vowed to uphold the policies and activities of the Provisional Government. Rhee appointed several of his supporters to fill the vacancies in the cabinet and hastily departed for Honolulu in May 1921.[76]

The withdrawal of the Korean Socialist Party from the KPG marked the dissolution of the united front between the "American group" of nationalists and the "Siberian-Manchurian group" of socialists. The KPG could no longer claim to be the central organ of the independence movement. It would never fully regain the support of Korean military and political organizations in Manchuria and Russia.

Following his resignation from the KPG, Yi Tong-hwi and his supporters from the "Siberian-Manchurian group" left Shanghai and channeled all of their energies into the Communist movement using the initial funds procured from Lenin earlier in 1920. In February 1921, he changed the name of the Korean Socialist Party to the Korean People's Communist Party and established its headquarters in the Siberian capital of Chita. With approximately 6,000 members, the Korean People's Communist Party became known as the Shanghai-Chita group. Declaring the Korean

People's Communist Party the only true Korean government in exile, Yi claimed authority over all Korean Communist groups.⁷⁷

Yi's Shanghai-Chita group, however, encountered immediate opposition from another Korean Communist group in Russia. With a membership of 4,500, the Communist Party of All Koreans in Russia also claimed to be the central representative body of all Korean Communist organizations. Initially formed by a group of Koreans in Irkutsk in January 1919, the Communist Party of All Koreans in Russia, often referred to as the Irkutsk group, were mostly long-time Russian residents whose families had migrated to areas of the Russian Far East in the late nineteenth century. Many of these Koreans were naturalized Russian citizens and were thoroughly "Russianized" in cultural and political outlook.⁷⁸

In contrast, the Shanghai-Chita group consisted primarily of nonnaturalized foreign Koreans, who had immigrated to the Maritime Province in large numbers following the annexation in 1910 and soon thereafter made up the overwhelming majority of the Korean population in the Russian Far East. While their Russianized counterparts held rights equal to other Russian citizens, the more recently arrived foreign Koreans were often subjected to government discrimination and repression, such as the denial of Russian citizenship and the imposition of numerous burdensome taxes. Without a stable legal status in Russia, the great majority of these Koreans remained mired in poverty. Stateless and landless, many maintained strong cultural and political ties to Korea.⁷⁹

The Irkutsk and Shanghai-Chita groups quickly emerged as rivals for support from the Comintern in Moscow and control of the Korean Communist movement. The Russianized Koreans of the Irkutsk group were committed to becoming an integral part of the Communist movement within the Soviet Union. Members of the Shanghai-Chita group, though professedly dedicated to Communist ideology, saw themselves primarily as Korean nationals and sought Soviet assistance in securing Korean independence. Unlike their Irkutsk counterparts, they perceived Communism as a means to achieving victory against the Japanese rather than an end in itself.⁸⁰

Hostilities between the two groups erupted into violence in the summer of 1921 as they fought for control over the Korean militia groups that had been forced to retreat from their bases in Manchuria and the Maritime Province following the Japanese offensives in 1920. By March 1921, these dispersed military troops had gathered in the Siberian city of Alekseyevsk in the Amur province, preparing to help the Bolsheviks fight the White Russians and their Japanese allies, in exchange for Soviet aid for Korean independence. From approximately 36 different militia groups, these forces, most of whom were loyal to Yi Tong-hwi, reorganized themselves under the banner of the Greater Korean Independence Corps. In June, the Irkutsk faction, with the support of the Far Eastern Secretariat of the Comintern under the leadership of Boris Shumiatsky, formed its own military contingent under the name of the Korean Revolutionary Military Congress and proclaimed that all Korean military forces in Siberia were to be united under its authority. Frustrated by the pro-Yi Greater Korean Independence Corps' continual refusal to recognize their authority, the Irkutsk-led military group and their Russian allies surrounded the troops of the Greater Korean Independence Corps stationed at Alekseyevsk and demanded that they disarm. The confrontation quickly escalated into what became known as the Free City Incident. With the aid of the Red Army, the Irkutsk group emerged victorious. Hundreds of their Korean rivals were killed or wounded, and they captured approximately 1,000 soldiers, who were executed, imprisoned in Irkutsk, or incorporated into the Bolshevik army. The remaining troops from the Greater Korean Independence Corps retreated into southeastern Manchuria.[81]

The Free City Incident brought about a precipitous decline in Yi Tong-hwi's political power and influence among Koreans in the Russian Far East and Manchuria. Though the Comintern condemned both Korean factions, Boris Shumiatsky used his influence with the Comintern to bolster the status of the Russianized Irktusk group with the Soviet government and to discredit Yi and his Korean People's Communist Party. In April 1922, the Comintern ordered Yi to return the remaining portion of the initial 600,000 rubles given by Lenin and declared that he would no longer receive the remaining 1.4 million rubles pledged by the Soviet government. In this aftermath of the Free City Incident, many Korean nationalists who had seen Communism as a means of achieving Korean independence became disillusioned. Many of Yi's supporters fled the ranks of the Shanghai group, leaving the Korean national liberation movement in Manchuria and the Russian Far East divided and in disarray. Unable to reconcile their differences, the "Siberian-Manchurian group" of nationalists remained largely inactive throughout the remainder of the 1920s.[82] Nevertheless, Koreans in the Russian Far East had played an instrumental role in the development of Korean diasporic nationalism through their active involvement with the Bolsheviks and dissemination of Communist ideology into other parts of the Korean diaspora, ensuring that Communism would remain a significant ideological force in the national liberation movement.[83]

During this retrenchment of nationalist activities in Manchuria and Siberia, Syngman Rhee and his supporters in the KPG continued to conduct their diplomatic appeals to the West. The government had lost its leadership over the overall national liberation movement, but members of the American group clung to the belief that the KPG could attain diplomatic recognition from foreign powers and once again become the center of the Korean nationalist movement. The realization of their objectives seemed within reach with the announcement of an unprecedented meeting of the world's major powers at the Conference of Limitation on Armament to be held in Washington, D.C., from November 1921 to February 1922.

Initiated and organized by the United States, the Conference of Limitation on Armament brought together the United States, Great Britain, France, Japan, and China to discuss and formulate policies to limit naval construction among the leading powers to prevent the possibility of war. As part of these discussions, the political situation in East Asia had been designated a primary topic for the Conference. Consequently, Syngman Rhee saw the upcoming conference as a critical opportunity to present the Korean cause for independence before an international stage. Rhee temporarily changed the name of the Korean Commission to the Korean Mission to the Conference on Limitation of Armament. Reportedly spending nearly $12,000, the Korean Mission organized a publicity and lobbying campaign to ensure that the "Korean Question" be included on the conference agenda. On October 1, the Korean Mission submitted an official appeal to the U.S. delegation to the Conference requesting the opportunity to address the Korean cause at the conference.[84]

The appeal contained previously presented arguments that detailed Japan's coerced occupation of Korea and the international community's responsibility to assist Korea. The lengthy appeal also included a 44-page document, entitled "Brief for Korea," written by Fred Dolph, a Washington attorney who served as legal advisor to Rhee and the Korean Commission. Rather than highlighting the moral, humanitarian aspects of the Korean situation under Japanese colonization, Dolph focused on the "purely legal standpoint" of Korean sovereignty, claiming the case of Korea represented an infringement of the international sovereignty rights of the Korean nation that "rests almost entirely on conceded facts and principles of international law."[85]

Dolph built his legal arguments around the 1882 Treaty of Amity and Commerce between the United States and Korea. According to him, the United States had already recognized Korean independence and its territorial integrity by entering into the treaty agreement with Korea, which had been a sovereign nation at the time of its signing. Claiming that Japan's annexation of Korea violated basic tenets of international law, Dolph provided a lengthy narrative of historical events that indicted Japanese subterfuge and coercion in establishing its protectorate and annexation agreements over Korea. Throughout his narrative, Dolph maintained that the Korean government and the Korean people never consented to Japanese rule and that the Japanese had brutally suppressed any Korean attempts to protest the Japanese presence in Korea. As a result, Japan's claims to Korean sovereignty had no legal standing, and therefore, "The nations of the world who made Treaties with Korea, including the United States, must still regard Korea as a separate entity and the Treaties in force, irrespective of Japan's claims to the contrary."[86] Dolph therefore concluded that "the United States is bound to interpose its 'good offices' in protest to Japan, against the oppression of Korea, and it should in good faith use all of its powers of persuasion and argument to induce Japan to remedy the wrong that she has done to Korea."[87]

The Korean Mission's appeal further declared that the situation in Korea was not solely an internal matter for the Japanese empire as presumed by the Conference delegates, but rather an international question that merited wider attention. It pointed out that the Conference delegates had gravely neglected to consider the significance of Korea in their extensive deliberations about the situation in China.[88] Arguing that any discussion involving China must first begin with an examination of the "Korean Question," the appeal forcefully asserted:

> If the observance of this pledge be now essential to the preservation of China, it is the more essential for the restoration of Korea, which presents in concrete form the fruitage [sic] of every policy which threatens China's economic or political integrity. The processes involving China are those which submerged Korea. They are identical in origin, in purpose and in result. They cannot be thwarted in China if they are to be disregarded in Korea.[89]

The Korean Mission also submitted a letter from the League of the Friends of Korea addressed to Secretary of State Charles Evans Hughes, who chaired the U.S. delegation to the Conference. Proclaiming a membership of 25,000 individuals, all citizens of the United States, the appeal from the League of the Friends pledged its full support for the cause of Korean independence and requested that the Korean Mission be granted a hearing at the Conference.[90]

The lengthy appeal concluded with the presentation of a petition for a hearing, translated into English, which had been composed and signed clandestinely in Korea by a diverse cross-section of the Korean populace, including "the presidents and secretaries of fifty-two national organizations of various descriptions, educational, religious, commercial, industrial, historical, including the members of the Imperial family and the Nobility Club."[91] The petitioners pledged full support for the Korean Provisional Government, declaring it the sole and authentic government of the Korean nation and its people. The Korean Mission dramatically emphasized the extraordinary risks taken by the authors and signatories in light of Japan's close surveillance, and extreme intolerance, of any signs of organized resistance in Korea.

Nonetheless, the Korean Mission had not received an official response from the conference organizers by January 1922. It did get a private hearing from U.S. Secretary of State Hughes, but he offered no public recognition of the meeting or the Mission's appeal.[92] On January 25, the Korean Mission submitted a supplementary appeal to the Conference, reasserting the significance of Korea to the overall peace and stability in East Asia and once again pleading for a chance to present its case more fully to the Conference delegates.[93] When the Conference ended in February with several new agreements signed by the participants, the Korean situation was not included in any of those final agreements, nor was it addressed by any of the delegations during the conference proceedings. Moreover, the Korean Mission and their supporters never received a single acknowledgment of their multiple appeals, shattering the faith of even the most ardent supporters of Syngman Rhee and the KPG. For many involved with the Korean Mission, the humiliating experience indicated the international community's lack of interest in the Korean struggle for independence and hence a de facto recognition of Japanese claims over Korean sovereignty.

The situation within the KPG deteriorated rapidly soon thereafter. In the months following the Washington Conference, the activities of the Provisional Government came to a virtual standstill. On April 17, 1922, the Provisional Legislative Assembly of the KPG cabled Syngman Rhee in Washington, D.C.: "Situation of the government is urgent. Please instruct us as to your policy for maintaining the government and correcting the situation." Rhee responded with an order to appoint No Paek-rin as premier and to reorganize the cabinet. A few weeks later, the KPG frantically demanded Rhee take immediate action to end the crisis in the government. "No Paek-rin is not available for the premiership and there are no officers in the government. It is virtually in a state of anarchy. Please carry out your responsibilities immediately and instruct us within five days."[94] Rhee chastised KPG officials for letting the situation get out of hand and demanded that they promptly take appropriate measures to restore order within the government.

Conditions only worsened as strife within the government mounted. By the summer of 1922, the KPG at large had lost all faith in President Syngman Rhee. On June 17, 1922, the members of the Provisional Assembly passed a no-confidence vote against Rhee, accusing him of failing to fulfill his administrative duties. Rhee adamantly denied the charges and ordered the election of new leaders to the government. The KPG lay dormant for the next several years as the government experienced numerous turnovers in both the cabinet and assembly positions.[95]

In July 1924, Rhee decided to stop sending money to the KPG in Shanghai, asserting that the government was no longer operational. He put the Korean Commission in Washington, D.C., in full control of the affairs of the KPG. In response, the Provisional Assembly in August declared that the premier in Shanghai should serve as acting president, due to Rhee's continual residence in the United States and failure to fulfill his duties to the government.[96]

Both sides, though largely powerless, continued to contest the right of supreme authority. On March 10, 1925, the KPG cabinet abolished the Korean Commission in Washington, D.C., claiming it to be an illegitimate organization that was not endorsed by the Provisional Government. It further asserted that the Commission had misappropriated state revenues collected from Koreans in the United States and Hawaii. A few days later, members of the Provisional Assembly issued a resolution for the impeachment of President Syngman Rhee, which was adopted on March 18 and passed with a 75 percent majority vote in the Assembly on March 25.[97]

The impeachment of Rhee and abolishment of the Korean Commission officially severed the ties between Rhee and the KPG. The charges against the ex-president echoed the funding ordeal involving Rhee and the KNA in 1919. In many ways, the nationalist movement had come full circle. The political mobilization of the Korean diaspora in the aftermath of the 1919 March First protests had broadened the scope and nature of the movement with the addition of new resources and new organizations. This expansion in nationalist activities abroad gave rise to a campaign to create a national state in the form of the KPG in Shanghai. At the same time, an active armed struggle movement emerged in Manchuria and the Maritime Province that maintained some connection to the KPG. However, both movements were dead by the mid-1920s.[98] With the breakdown of the KPG in Shanghai and the suppression of the armed struggle movement, the national liberation movement throughout the diaspora was in disarray and largely inactive.

The decade of the 1920s thus ended much as it began, with nationalist activities abroad operating largely independent of one another.

The locus of nationalist activities shifted to the Korean peninsula, marking the start of the second period of the nationalist movement from 1925 to 1930.[99] The efforts to create a united front continued during this period in the form of a movement to create a single national party within Korea, culminating in the formation of the Sin'ganhoe (New Korea Association) in 1927. The Sin'ganhoe represented a coalition of moderate nationalists and radical leftists, led by the Korean Communist Party, that emerged in Korea during the 1920s. In 1931, however, the Sin'ganhoe was forced to dissolve when its leftist elements voted to withdraw due to continual internal factional strife and increasing Japanese restrictions on its organizational activities.[100]

After the KPG in Shanghai lost its leadership, Koreans in and out of the homeland had no supreme authority to mobilize and direct their nationalist activities. As a result, struggles for political power from abroad became highly localized as nationalist activities began to reemphasize local issues.

Figure 4.3.
Major sites of Korean settlements and political activities in Manchuria and Siberia.
Source: Map by Elizabeth Lee with additional assistance from Jennifer Giang.

CHAPTER 5

Local Struggles and Diasporic Politics

The 1931 Court Cases of the Korean National Association of Hawaii

With the collapse of the KPG and the subsequent period of retrenchment, there was no longer a supreme authority to coordinate activities within the diaspora. Nevertheless, questions of state power and its uses continued to dominate the political concerns of all Koreans abroad. By 1931, these questions assumed a greater local significance rather than a diasporic one. The factionalism that led to the breakdown of the Shanghai Provisional Government in the early 1920s created deep fissures among Koreans in Hawaii and the U.S. mainland. From the start of the fundraising conflict, the Korean National Association (KNA) of Hawaii had unfailingly complied with Syngman Rhee's orders to send KNA monetary collections directly to the Korean Commission in Washington, D.C., rather than the Korean Provisional Government (KPG) in Shanghai. In so doing, the Hawaii regional headquarters had failed to cooperate with the KNA Central Headquarters' refusal to comply with Rhee's plan. The controversy created a rift in the relationship between the Hawaii regional headquarters and the Central Headquarters in San Francisco.

Amidst these tensions, the KNA of Hawaii, under the direction of Syngman Rhee, severed its relationship with the KNA Central Headquarters in January 1921. In March 1922, the KNA of Hawaii dissolved itself and changed its name to Taehan'in Kyomindan (Korean Residents Association) under the sanction of the KPG in Shanghai. The change was largely in name only, with almost all the KNA bylaws of self-governance left intact, except that the offices of president and vice-president were to be chosen by the chairman of the Korean Commission in Washington, D.C. Rhee thus ensured direct control over the Kyomindan. Earlier in the year, the Central Headquarters of the KNA in San Francisco had also been dissolved and reorganized as the Korean National Association of North America. With these changes, the organizational activities of Koreans in America essentially returned to their separate localized status prior to the unification of the KNA.[1] Koreans in Hawaii were further divided into factions based on disputes dating back to 1915. Given the division and retrenchment within the overall Korean nationalist movement during the 1920s, the self-governing functions of the KNA gained heightened importance and groups competed over who had the legitimate authority to lead Koreans in Hawaii.

These struggles for leadership led to a highly contentious legal battle that lasted for almost one year. The judicial proceedings commenced in early February 1931 between opposing sides of the "regular" and "irregular" factions within the KNA of Hawaii.[2] Initially, the dispute between the two groups of litigants revolved around administrative affairs of the KNA, but it exposed multiple irreconcilable differences in interpretations of the constitution and bylaws of the KNA of Hawaii. Unable to resolve these differences through its own procedural processes, the two groups turned to the U.S. judicial system.

As the litigation continued, both sides would bombard the court system in Hawaii with multiple, often repetitive charges and allegations against each other as they told and retold their own versions of the tumultuous events that occurred at the KNA building in January 1931. At first glance, the court records presented over the course of nearly one year seem to document nothing more than a feud over procedures, bylaws, and charters, devoid of any significant ideological content. Upon closer examination, however, each successive hearing before the court reveals a new layer of complexity for the issues, showing that these local disputes were intricately linked to a larger chain of events within the Korean independence movement. Ultimately, the protracted legal battle of 1931 represented a battleground in the struggle for local leadership to determine the right of governance and the control of organizational resources in representing Koreans of Hawaii in the diaspora.

On January 5, 1931, the KNA of Hawaii opened its annual delegate convention to determine its activities and budget for the coming year. A group of twenty-one delegates from various localities arrived at its headquarters in Honolulu to take part in the annual meeting, but officials at the door refused to let them enter. Citing provisions from the KNA bylaws, officials claimed that the delegates were not qualified to participate in the convention due to their failure to pay their previous year's membership dues. A boisterous argument soon erupted into a physical altercation. KNA officials were forced to postpone the convention until the following week.[3]

On January 12, KNA officers tried to reconvene the meeting. During the adjournment, officials had distributed admission badges to those delegates deemed qualified to participate in the convention. Officials also posted guards at the entrance of the KNA building in anticipation of another altercation. When the disqualified delegates returned, the guards blocked their entrance. The delegates protested vehemently, prompting the guards to expel them from the premises. After the minor scuffle, the delegates inside began their proceedings.[4] At the end of the day, KNA President Shon Duk-yin was notified that the excluded delegates had threatened to take over the KNA building by force.[5]

The following day, the excluded delegates, with a group of some 40 supporters, stormed the building while the assembly was in session and forcibly expelled the members with passes from the building. The disgruntled delegates and their supporters then barricaded themselves inside the building and refused to admit the ousted members.[6] A large part of the Honolulu police force was called in to restore order.[7]

The excluded delegates occupied the KNA building for two weeks. During that time, they conducted their own assembly, appointing Chung Tai-wha as the new chairman to preside over the annual convention. In the meantime, the police maintained watch over the KNA premises to prevent the ousted members from reentering the building, while those inside continued with their assembly meeting.[8]

The violent altercation and subsequent police action received widespread local press coverage in Honolulu. Chung Tai-wha informed reporters that the delegates holding the present convention believed that President Shon and his officers had misappropriated KNA funds, which constituted a serious violation of the KNA constitution and bylaws. More specifically, Chung stated that the ousted officers had transacted a mortgage on KNA property with the Bishop Trust Co. on December 24, 1930, for $1,050 without proper authorization from KNA membership. According to Chung, Henry Kim (Kim Hyon-gu), treasurer of the KNA, had refused repeated requests to release the organization's financial records for an official audit, which prompted the seizure of the building. The delegates inside the convention, Chung noted, were deliberating on whether to take legal action against Henry Kim and the other officers in order to gain access to the financial records of the KNA that Kim and other officers had moved to another location just days earlier.[9]

Chung also informed the press that President Shon's refusal to admit qualified delegates who were entitled to participate in the annual convention constituted yet another violation of the KNA's constitution and bylaws.[10] As such, Shon's leadership and any decisions passed during the meeting on January 12 should be nullified. According to Chung, the assembly in progress had voted to impeach and discharge KNA President Shon and his officers for violations of the KNA constitution and bylaws. He announced that new elections to replace the dismissed officers would take place on January 31, 1931. Pending the results of the elections, the delegates appointed Kim Chung-hyun as temporary president, Choy Baik-yurl as secretary, and Chung Tai-wha as manager, all of whom were in attendance at the convention in question. Chung also notified the press that the temporary officers had decided to retain the legal services of Honolulu attorney Fred Patterson in order to force Henry Kim and the other ousted officers to release the KNA financial records for an official audit. Further legal action, according to Chung, depended on the outcome of the audit.[11]

On January 24, the ousted officers and delegates, who described themselves in the local Honolulu press as the "regular" faction, filed charges in police court against those involved in the takeover. The regular faction declared that they themselves were the lawful owners of the KNA building

Figure 5.1.
KNA headquarters building in Honolulu. Site of the 1931 fracas involving competing KNA factions.
Source: University of Hawai'i Press.

and proclaimed that the "irregular" group had illegally trespassed on and seized private property. They also charged their opponents with assault and battery committed during the forcible seizure of the building.[12]

Later that day, Judge Francis Brooks ruled that his police court was not the proper place to settle internal factional disputes among the Koreans. Brooks dismissed the charges and ordered the disputants to take their grievances to the circuit court. He exclaimed that "pulling down doors, rushing halls, and flourishing firearms was not the recognized method of settling factional disputes in this country" and that any decision on his part "would merely fan the flames again."[13]

Informed that another violent altercation at the KNA building between the two feuding factions was set to occur on January 26, Honolulu Sheriff Patrick Gleason closed the KNA building indefinitely and maintained a police watch over the premises. Despite his efforts, the two factions opened hostilities elsewhere in the city that night. According to police reports, the newly appointed officers of the KNA were conducting a meeting near Liliha and School streets when members of the ousted "regular" faction arrived. A boisterous argument quickly escalated into violence. A Japanese man, who was an innocent bystander, suffered a gunshot to the leg from a revolver fired during the melee. A Korean man sustained a deep laceration on the head after being hit with a wrench by two assailants. Both men were taken to the hospital. Responding to a riot call, the police arrested fourteen men and one woman, all of whom were booked for investigation and taken to the county jail for the night.[14]

The next day the combatants once again faced Judge Francis Brooks in police court. Brooks denounced the fights as "utterly alien to the spirit of American lawfulness," proclaiming that they constituted a felony of unlawful assembly.[15] He strongly recommended that the district attorney investigate the matter. The factional strife "has become too serious to be tolerated any further. The police court is no longer the place to bring these bickerings. While I have no knowledge one way or the other as to which side is responsible, the manner in which the dispute is being conducted has become a criminal matter and should be investigated by our prosecuting authorities."[16]

A few days later, Sheriff Gleason brought together members from both factions for a meeting. Gleason forcefully explained that all the disputants had violated the law in their unlawful assembly and rioting. His office had gathered sufficient evidence to request that federal authorities deport the parties responsible for the recent rash of violence. Demanding that the feuding factions end their attacks on each other, he insisted they settle their differences in the court of law. Gleason told those present, "I warn you not to hold any more meetings, to stop gathering around street corners and in homes, and to cease threatening to 'get' certain members of the opposing factions.... You are living in an American community, are bringing your children up to American standards, and must abide by the laws of the United States."[17] He further warned the group at the meeting that if the police had to respond to any more incidents of violence between the two factions, he would take the necessary steps to deport all those involved. Chung Tai-wha explained to the sheriff that the dispute could be settled peacefully without resorting to legal action if only the leaders of the "regular" faction were willing to negotiate some sort of compromise. Members of the "regular" faction immediately countered Chung's claims and accused his group of inciting violence.[18] The meeting ended with both sides arguing over who was to blame for the present problems afflicting the Korean community.

On February 3, 1931, the "irregular" group, including Pai Yil-chin, Choo Char-moon, and Choi Bong-cho, filed a writ of mandamus against KNA officers Shon Duk-yin, Ahn Young-chan, Henry Kim, and Warren Y. Kim (Kim Won-yong) in the First Circuit Court of Hawaii.[19] The petition sought to gain access to the financial records of the KNA in order to determine whether Shon, et al. had committed any financial wrongdoing. The plaintiffs charged Shon and his officers with committing "gross irregularities in the books of account" by raising large amounts of money from members of the Association and then deliberately failing to deposit the funds into the KNA bank account and to record the amounts properly in the accounting books.[20] The plaintiffs also accused Shon, et al. of covertly mortgaging KNA property on December 24, 1930, and using the funds "for purposes other than contemplated by the by-laws and charter of the Society."[21] Pai, et al. further charged the defendants with repeatedly refusing their requests to submit the financial records of the KNA for an official audit, which constituted a conspiracy to keep the books concealed from KNA members. Lastly, the plaintiffs accused the defendants of failing to hold the annual delegate meeting in accordance with the KNA constitution and bylaws by refusing to recognize legitimate members and delegates as participants in the meeting. The plaintiffs concluded that the charges against Pai, et al. constituted grievous violations of the bylaws and constitution of the Korean National Association and provided sufficient grounds for their removal from office.[22] The presiding judge, Albert M. Cristy, ordered Shon, et al. to appear in court on February 17, 1931, to explain why the contents of the books should remain undisclosed to the plaintiffs.[23]

On February 17, Shon, et al. denied all allegations of wrongdoing. Referring to Section 9 of the KNA bylaws, the respondents acknowledged that the delegate assembly had the power and authority "to make the annual budget, to audit and examine accounts of the past year, to appropriate expenditures for the year and the sole power to examine and inspect the books, records and accounts of said Society at any time upon request."[24] The respondents affirmed that they had abided by this provision in a meeting on January 10, 1931, where the delegate assembly had examined and audited the financial records for 1930 and determined the accuracy of the information. They emphasized that the assembly did not voice a single complaint about any inconsistencies or errors in the bookkeeping.[25] After hearing both sides, Judge Albert Cristy decided in favor of the petitioners, Pai, et al. He ordered that the respondents surrender all the financial records of the KNA for 1930 with the courthouse, where the petitioners could examine and audit them from March 4 to 6, 1931.[26] Despite the ruling, the case was far from over. A few days later, attorney Ray J. O'Brien, representing Shon, et al., filed an appeal contesting the ruling.[27]

The irregular group's February 3, 1931, petition would be the first of numerous pretrial motions filed by both sides over the next several months. On that same day, members of the "regular" faction, comprised of Shon and other KNA officers, filed their own court action against their antagonists. They filed a writ of quo warranto with Judge Cristy challenging Kim Chung-hyun and Choy Baik-yurl's election to the positions of temporary president and secretary, respectively, during the delegate assembly conducted by the "irregulars."[28] For the next several months, the case revolved around multiple interpretations of the "takeover" of the KNA building. Both sides repeatedly gave their own accounts of the events, attaching to them completely different meanings and significance.

Shon, et al. claimed that they had been lawfully elected to their offices for two-year terms based on the results of KNA elections held on December 18, 1929. They listed their elected posts as Shon Duk-yin, president; Ahn Young-chan, vice-president; Kim Kyung-choon, manager; and Henry Kim, secretary/treasurer. Park Yern-sho, Char Shin-ho, Lee Chun-kun, Park Sung-kun, and Cho Moon-chil, who had all been appointed directors by President Shon, were also listed as plaintiffs in the suit.[29] They charged that the defendants, Kim and Choy, had no legal authority to their claims of leadership in the KNA. In support of their allegations, Shon, et al. recounted their version of the takeover, charging Kim and Choy with breaking in and usurping the offices of president and secretary/treasurer.[30] From that day on, the defendants had "unlawfully and without right and contrary to law and contrary to the rights and interests of plaintiffs herein attempted to exercise and hold the aforesaid office of said corporation and association and withhold the same from the plaintiffs herein who are duly elected and qualified officers of said corporation and association...."[31] When informed that further violence would ensue at the KNA headquarters, Sheriff Patrick Gleason ordered the KNA building to be closed indefinitely, preventing the plaintiffs from fulfilling their duties and responsibilities as the legitimate officers of the KNA.[32]

The plaintiffs requested a writ of quo warranto, requiring the defendants to appear before the court to demonstrate "by what authority and right they and each of them attempt to claim, hold, or usurp offices in said corporation and association and by what authority to exercise and exercised the functions, duties, and powers of any office of said association."[33] Judge Christy granted their request and ordered Kim Chung-hyun and Choy Baik-yurl to appear before the court.[34] Citing legal technicalities, attorney Fred Patterson managed to delay his clients' appearance for several weeks. On March 6, the defendants finally submitted an answer to the court, denying the charges that they had usurped offices held by the plaintiffs and providing their own version of events. While their account did not dispute the actual "takeover" of the KNA building, it departed significantly from the one presented by their adversaries.[35]

The defendants claimed that 21 delegates from 19 local associations arrived at KNA headquarters on January 5, 1931, and were unlawfully refused entry to the meeting. Due to the confusion, KNA officials decided to postpone the meeting for one week. When the defendants came back a week later on January 12, they were again turned away and eventually chased off the KNA premises. On the following day, they returned, occupied the KNA building, and opened the proceedings of the convention among themselves. They first collected $526 in membership dues from those in attendance and then elected Chung Tai-wha as chairman, Lee Chong-kwan as vice-chairman, Shin Choong as secretary, Chung Do-won as correspondent secretary, and Kim Kio-hyun as assistant secretary to preside over the convention. On the first day, the assembly voted to issue an order for KNA President Shon Duk-yin to turn over the financial records of the KNA for the entire year of 1930. They then formed a committee to inspect and audit the records. For these purposes, the delegate assembly hired Fred Patterson as legal counsel to obtain the financial books of the KNA from Shon, et al.[36]

During the next several days, the delegates voted to impeach and expel President Shon and his officers from the Central Association of the KNA on five counts of violating KNA bylaws. They nominated the following individuals to replace the ousted officers: Lee Chong-kwan and Kim Kwang-chai for president of KNA Central Association and Chung Yin-soo and Ahn Hyun-kyung as vice-president. Until the new officers were officially elected by the KNA membership at large, the delegate assembly appointed Kim Chung-hyun, Choy Baik-yurl, and Chung Tai-wha as temporary president, secretary, and manager, respectively. These temporary officers announced news of the impeachment and dismissal of President Shon and his cabinet to all chapters of the KNA throughout the Hawaiian Islands and set new elections for January 31, 1931.[37] The respondents answered that the petitioners had been impeached through legitimate means.[38]

Dissatisfied with the arguments and evidence provided by both sides, Judge Cristy continued pretrial hearings. On April 28, 1931, Pai Yil-chin, Choo Cha-moon, and Lee Kun-koo filed a new petition against KNA President Shon Duk-yin and his officers, alleging financial wrongdoing. Represented by new attorneys from the firm of Thompson, Beebe, & Winn, Pai, et al. requested that the court issue a temporary restraining order directing the respondents to submit all KNA financial records for 1930 to the court. They also petitioned the court to find Shon Duk-yin and Ahn Young-chan unfit to preside over their respective offices as president and vice-president, and requested that the court replace them with new members in good standing.[39]

Pai, et al. alleged that Shon and his cabinet had (1) expended money other than that in the budget; (2) failed to spend money as called for in the budget; (3) mortgaged KNA property without authority; (4) excluded accredited members from the right to participate and vote in the annual delegate assembly; and (5) allowed nonmembers to participate in KNA affairs. The petitioners claimed that each charge violated KNA bylaws and gave sufficient grounds for dismissal from office. They claimed to want to recover damages for their own behalf, as well as for the general good of the KNA.[40]

Yet again, the petitioners detailed the events that led directly to the forcible takeover of the KNA building. On January 13, 1931, KNA officers held their annual delegates' meeting. However, the petitioners claimed that the meeting was unlawful because Shon and his officers deliberately denied the admission and participation of qualified members and delegates. In doing so, Shon, et al. had committed a gross violation of the KNA bylaws and the meeting should, therefore, be invalidated. According to the petitioners, only those who supported President Shon were issued admission passes, while all others were forcefully excluded. Pai, et al. contended that some of those allowed to enter the meeting were not even members or delegates of the KNA. Had the meeting been lawfully organized with all eligible members and delegates permitted to enter, Shon and his officers surely would have been ousted from office due to widespread discontent among the membership concerning their misappropriation of KNA funds.[41]

According to the petition, Shon, et al. were well aware of this discontent among the delegate body and were in the process of preparing a new set of financial books that would absolve them of any wrongdoing.[42] Pai, et al. believed that the respondents were planning to complete this new set of books by April 29, 1931, and then to destroy the true books and records, as part of a conspiracy to deceive KNA membership and gain control of the KNA. They concluded that the constitution of the KNA stated that officers who committed "actions deliberately contrary to the Constitution and by-laws and embezzlement of public money" were to be discharged from office.[43]

On April 29, 1931, Judge Cristy ordered Shon, et al. to "restrain from destroying, concealing, or tampering with the books, data and records of the Korean National Association of Hawaii" and required them to turn over all financial records to the court. He also summoned all the defendants to appear before him on May 2, 1931, to answer the charges enumerated in the petition. KNA Secretary/Treasurer Henry Kim complied with Cristy's order and submitted KNA's financial records to the court clerk. As for their appearance before the court, Ray O'Brien, representing Shon, et al., successfully motioned the judge to order the petitioners to amend and resubmit their lengthy petition on the grounds of improper legal procedures. After nearly three months of haranguing over legal technicalities, the respondents finally submitted an extensive answer on July 21, 1931.[44]

Shon, et al. denied that they had misappropriated any funds by mortgaging KNA property without proper authority, because the bylaws gave them as officers of the KNA the power to mortgage property belonging to it. Nevertheless, the property in question was already under a mortgage transacted by their predecessors in office, which had been approved at the annual delegates' convention in January 1914. Moreover, the respondents claimed that all funds collected through that mortgage had been spent on behalf of the KNA.[45]

Shon, et al. also refuted charges that the annual meeting was unlawful. Moreover, the respondents asserted that petitioners Pai Yil-chin and Choo Cha-moon had been determined to be qualified delegates and were accordingly admitted to the annual convention, but had left on their own volition shortly before it began. According to Shon, et al., this fact demonstrated that they had not refused admission to any qualified delegate or prevented the entry of any qualified member by using force.[46]

The respondents admitted that they had issued admission passes to qualified delegates in order to keep out nonmembers and ineligible delegates. More specifically, they charged that:

> Syngman Rhee, who was not a member of the KNA, but seems to have had influence among certain Koreans living in the Territory of Hawaii, had laid plans to commit violence against the officers of the Korean National Association, take possession by force the books and property of said association, cause said meeting to be interrupted, and endeavor to secure control of said Korean National Association for his personal gain.[47]

This situation necessitated a formal method to identify those delegates who were duly qualified to attend the annual convention. Despite this slight departure from normal procedures, they asserted that the meeting was lawfully organized and attended by only qualified participants.[48] Finally, the respondents denied charges that they had either tampered with the financial records or prepared new ones. Shon, et al. declared these claims as "absurd, without foundation and an endeavor by the petitioners to create some ground upon which to bring respondents into court and to harass and annoy them."[49] In all instances, the respondents claimed that they had acted within the bounds of the KNA constitution and bylaws, and asked the court to dismiss all charges.[50]

Astoundingly, this was the first mention of Syngman Rhee in the proceedings of the case though it was undoubtedly a direct outgrowth of the bitter factional strife between Rhee's personal organ, the Tongjihoe (The Comrade Society), and the KNA. In July 1930, Rhee organized a Tongjihoe Representative Conference in Honolulu as part of ongoing efforts among Koreans in Hawaii to unify the deeply splintered community of Korean political organizations under the authority of the Tongjihoe, which had been largely inactive in the last several years.

The conference instead created even greater dissension, especially between the Kyomindan and the Tongjihoe. Ironically, both organizations had been established under the direct authority of Rhee in the early 1920s. Upon his return from Shanghai in July 1921, Rhee had formed the Tongjihoe in Honolulu as his own personal political organization to solidify his base of support in Hawaii. Consisting of his most ardent supporters, the primary goal of the Tongjihoe, according to Rhee, was to "enforce severe punishment on those who worked against the provisional government [in Shanghai]" and to be the self-appointed law enforcement agency to keep peace in the Korean community.[51] Like the Tongjihoe, the Kyomindan was created in March 1922 to support the KPG and Rhee's own activities. Both organizations were nearly indistinguishable from each other in their memberships and activities from the start, even sharing the same office in the former KNA, now Kyomindan, building until their schism in 1930.[52] Kyomindan members were particularly incensed that Rhee so vigorously sought to revive the declining Tongjihoe, even though the Kyomindan had remained active. They asserted that their organization was the legitimate representative of Koreans in Hawaii since it had been sanctioned by the KPG, whereas the Tongjihoe was a private organization with no official status.[53]

Shon, et al. viewed the case as a last-ditch effort by Syngman Rhee to gain control of the KNA. They claimed Rhee had first tried to sell off the KNA building in August 1930 without the authorization of KNA officers, only to be thwarted by the newly elected KNA President Shon Duk-yin. Rhee then tried to oust Shon from office but failed. Finally, he turned to Henry Kim, secretary/treasurer of the KNA and editor of the *Korean National Herald*, the official organ of the KNA of Hawaii. Rhee repeatedly insisted that Kim publish exclusive endorsements of the Tongjihoe plan for unification while repudiating the KNA, but Kim refused to comply. Rhee, under his self-proclaimed authority as president of the KPG, ordered Kim to resign, which he did to avoid further conflict with Rhee. Meanwhile, Rhee issued public statements asking the Koreans of Hawaii to accept Kim's resignation and to turn over the secretary/treasurer and editor positions to him. The situation created a stir within the KNA when members claimed that a nonmember could not dismiss a regular member from office. The local chapters of the KNA took a vote on the matter and overwhelmingly voted to retain Henry Kim, who promptly returned to his posts.[54]

Unable to sway the KNA, Rhee resorted to more aggressive methods. Claiming that the KNA was the "common property" of all Koreans in Hawaii regardless of whether they were dues-paying members, Rhee publicly called for the "forceful occupation" of the KNA.[55] According to Shon and his officers, Rhee then invited to the 1931 annual delegates' assembly in January "all sorts of delegates from where there are no local associations, from local associations which have no required number of members for their own legal status, from local associations deprived of a delegation, from local associations of which no member paid a membership fee, from local associations installed by the worst methods of Gambetta,—all contrary to customs and by-laws of the Association."[56]

These "unqualified" delegates demanded entrance to the annual conference on January 4, 1931, creating mass confusion and leading to a postponement of the meeting. KNA officials issued admission passes to identify those delegates who were qualified in accordance with the bylaws. The following week, Rhee's supporters, accompanied by a group of "roughnecks" hired by Rhee, returned to KNA headquarters and took over the building by force. They refused to vacate, arguing that they were the rightful proprietors, reoccupying a building that had been taken illegally from them. According to Henry Kim and others, the legal suits to determine the legitimate leaders of the KNA began soon thereafter. However, because Rhee was not a member of the KNA, the suits were filed by KNA members Pai and others, who supported Rhee's plan to abolish the KNA in favor of the Tongjihoe. Shon, et al. maintained that these suits were intended to benefit Rhee and the Tongjihoe, not the KNA, and were ultimately part of an extensive Tongjihoe plan to gain control over the KNA.[57]

Naturally, the opposing side had its own interpretation of the origins of the disturbances that had left the Korean community of Hawaii "paralyzed and helpless."[58] In a press statement released shortly after the court proceedings began in February 1931, the faction in support of Pai, et al. stated that they were baffled by the sudden occurrence of violence, which was neither a renewal of old hostilities or the beginnings of a new factional rift. They reported that internal divisions among Koreans in Hawaii had been rapidly declining in recent years as all organizations were working toward the common goal of unification. As evidence of the prosperous and self-reliant community Koreans in Hawaii had created since their arrival, they listed their properties and institutions: the KNA on Miller St. worth $20,000; the Korean Old Men's Home on School St. near Liliha worth $10,000; the Korean Christian Church near Palama Settlement with a one-acre lot worth at least $17,000; the Korean Christian Institute in Kalihi Valley, which owned 27.5 acres of land worth about $100,000; and the Dongji Investment Co., which held some 90 acres of farmland in Olaa, worth another $100,000.

These institutions and properties, worth nearly $250,000, were collectively owned and maintained by the Korean community of Hawaii.[59] However, a group of "educated" Koreans from the mainland had sought control of these valuable community resources for their own purposes. The press singled out four men in particular: Henry Kim, Warren Y. Kim, Choy Young-ki, and Reverend William Y. Lee (Yi Yong-jik), all of whom had managed to acquire positions of authority in the KNA and the Korean Christian Church.[60] With the support of a few local Koreans, Pai's group claimed, these men "declared war on us with the weapons which we placed in their hands... endeavoring to get rid of some of our outstanding leaders, who they believe to be standing in their way...."[61] When the 21 delegates representing various local associations arrived in Honolulu in early January for the annual convention, they discovered that their entrance to the KNA building had been blocked by these "outsiders." The statement to the press declared that this moment signaled the beginning of the "Korean riots" and how they came to be known unfairly as the "irregular" faction.[62]

Judge Cristy finally set a trial date for October 3, 1931. Filing suit against Shon, et al., Pai, et al. presented their arguments and evidence to the judge, outlined in a brief presented by their attorneys, Thompson, Beebe, and Winn. Their case against Shon and his officers revolved around two basic issues: "Have the respondents, the officers and directors of KNA, exceeded their authority, not under honest mistake, or have they been guilty of fraud and negligence in management of the affairs of the corporation, threatening or causing loss to the corporation?"[63]

On the first issue of exceeding their authority, Pai, et al. accused Shon, et al. of violating multiple provisions of the KNA constitution and bylaws in organizing the annual delegates' convention. They argued that the respondents had deliberately waived or amended certain provisions of the bylaws so that they could hold the annual convention with only delegates who favored their policies. Many of these delegates were delinquent in their membership dues and thus ineligible to attend and vote in the assembly. The petitioners asserted that these "handpicked" delegates participated at the expense of qualified members and delegates who were denied entry to the meeting. For these reasons, the convention was unlawful and invalid.[64]

Next, Pai, et al. turned to charges of financial wrongdoing, singling out KNA Secretary/Treasurer Henry Kim for unlawfully transferring the KNA bank account into his own name.[65] Attorneys for Pai, et al. then discussed numerous discrepancies in the financial records of the KNA. They dwelled on expenses that exceeded the KNA annual budget and Kim's questionable bookkeeping practices, pointing out his failure to record accurately and honestly the expenses in question. The petitioners concluded that Henry Kim and the other respondents were guilty of concealing their unauthorized use of the public funds of the KNA for their own personal advantage.[66]

Pai, et al. determined that the evidence overwhelmingly indicated that the respondents were guilty both of exceeding both their authority without honest mistake and of fraud and negligence in the management of administrative affairs, thereby threatening or causing loss to the KNA. Citing a well-known legal precedent, the petitioners' attorneys argued that officers of a corporation found guilty of the aforementioned offenses were subject to immediate removal from office and could be sued by individual members of the corporation, on behalf of the majority, to recover any financial losses. Given the evidence, Pai, et al. argued that they were entitled to relief on both counts.[67]

The respondents' testimony provided a completely different interpretation of the events when their attorney, Ray J. O'Brien, submitted a brief of their case to Judge Cristy. Extremely lengthy, their brief not only refuted each and every fact alleged by the petitioners, but also drew on an exhaustive docket of legal precedents to challenge the legal reasoning of their opponents. The testimony and arguments of Shon, et al. revolved around several assertions. First, they claimed that the petitioners had failed to establish the allegations of financial wrongdoing contained in their bill of equity. Second, there was no proof that the petitioners had sought or gained the consent and support of KNA membership at large to file their case on behalf of the majority. Finally, the petitioners could not bring suit upon the respondents on behalf of the KNA because Pai, et al. were not members of the KNA in good standing at the time of the trial.[68]

On the charges of financial misappropriation, Shon, et al. challenged the validity of the audit on the grounds that the auditor was not a certified public accountant and was an employee of an accounting firm hired by Syngman Rhee, described by O'Brien as "the enemy of the respondents."[69] As such, the results of the audit could not be considered reliable or objective. O'Brien brought Henry Kim to the witness stand to account for each of the alleged bookkeeping discrepancies, with O'Brien noting that most errors were committed by the auditor.[70]

Henry Kim also testified that he only put the KNA account under his own name due to widely circulating rumors that Syngman Rhee intended to appropriate KNA funds. As a result, the KNA board of directors had allowed him to transfer the account to safeguard their assets. Given the multiple disturbances caused by Syngman Rhee dating back to September 1930, Shon, et al. argued that such measures were reasonable and necessary.[71]

The respondents then turned to the charges of holding an unlawful delegates' assembly on January 12, 1931, one day before the "ouster." O'Brien asserted that there was no evidence that showed his clients had refused admission to any duly qualified delegate or that they prevented anyone's entry by force, citing the voluntary decision of petitioners Pai Yil-chin and Choo Cha-moon to leave. Petitioner Lee Eun-koo was denied entry because KNA records revealed that his district association from Maui was no longer eligible for representation at the annual convention.[72]

Given the confusion caused by the factional disputes at the time, Shon, et al. explained the pragmatic measure of issuing admission passes and denied blocking any qualified delegate, even if that individual was unfavorably inclined toward their policies. O'Brien stated that petitioners Pai Yil-chin and Choo Cha-moon were indisputably opposed to the actions and policies of President Shon and his cabinet, yet they had been given passes.[73] For those denied entry to the meeting, O'Brien provided detailed records showing that such individuals had either failed to pay their member dues for 1930 at the time of the meeting or represented local associations that were no longer eligible to participate. Records clearly indicated that the petitioners had failed to pay their dues for 1931 and were therefore no longer members in good standing, and thus could not sue the respondents for damages.[74] On the latter point, O'Brien cited specific provisions from the KNA bylaws that authorized the president and his cabinet to determine the status of local associations for representation at the annual delegates' assembly.[75] Based on the evidence presented, O'Brien concluded that Shon and his officers were fully entitled to complete their two-year terms, and there was no need for new elections or new appointments as requested by the petitioners.[76]

On December 19, 1931, after hearing the exhaustive arguments from both sides, Judge Cristy ruled in favor of the respondents. Shon, et al. were cleared of all charges involving the embezzlement and misappropriation of public funds, organizing and holding an unlawful delegate convention, and tampering with KNA financial records. Basing his decision on a close reading of the KNA constitution and bylaws, Cristy found that the plaintiffs, Pai, et al., had failed to provide conclusive proof to support their multiple allegations.[77] Dismissing the case on the grounds of lack of evidence, Judge Cristy declared:

> The record in this case shows that the officers have been through a very trying period, beset by hasty and unfounded accusations and by the efforts of persons who apparently were either misinformed or who were seeking to disrupt the organization. The record shows that the officers have made a bona fide effort to carry on the association within the spirit of the Constitution and By-laws. Whatever temporary enlargement of the By-laws may be indicated by the evidence appears from the record to have been reasonable and for the purpose of *preserving the corporation* [emphasis added in original text], rather than preserving the power of the respondents.[78]

In particular, Cristy's decision gave credence to the respondents' claims that the petitioners were acting as part of a faction led by Syngman Rhee.[79]

The battle over the interpretation of the KNA constitution and bylaws was essentially a battle over who had properly upheld the laws of the state and were thus entitled to the right of governance. The KNA faced the challenge of trying to perpetuate its legal status within the diaspora without a central authority such as the KPG to arbitrate such disputes. The diasporic political movement bred conditions for the emergence of multiple and at times contradictory positions, as a host of exile organizations each claimed to represent legitimately the national will of Koreans at home and abroad. By appealing to the U.S. state, the KNA demonstrably affirmed its civil society status. KNA leaders lacked the coercive power as a state entity to force dissenters to comply with their orders. Moreover, Syngman Rhee, proclaiming his authority as the head of state, was once again powerless. Instead, Rhee and the KNA both had to turn to the U.S. state to adjudicate disputes within the Korean nationalist movement, foreshadowing their reliance on another party to achieve the goals of Korea's national liberation.

The outcome of the 1931 court case had significant consequences for Koreans living in Hawaii. The KNA now had a legal mandate to restore its original name and political functions, which had been dissolved by Rhee and appropriated under his control as the Kyomindan in 1922. The court case had taken a huge toll on the financial resources of the Korean community in Hawaii as both sides paid legal fees that amounted to nearly $50,000.[80] Ultimately, Judge Cristy's verdict found Syngman Rhee to be the primary instigator of the disruptions within the KNA and the overall Korean community in Hawaii. This severely damaged Rhee's reputation and within six months he would leave Hawaii under duress. New developments on the international stage also contributed to Rhee's sudden departure. Japan's full-scale occupation of Manchuria in 1931, which elicited immediate international condemnation, renewed the activities of the Korean nationalist movement, including most notably the reorganization of the Korean Provisional Government with Kim Ku as president. Rhee hastily traveled to Geneva to petition the Korean cause before the League of Nations. These new circumstances ushered in significant changes for the Korean community of Hawaii—new voices, new alliances, new leaders, and new strategies emerging throughout the 1930s as Rhee was forced to relinquish his authority following the court's verdict in 1931.

CHAPTER 6

Kilsoo Haan and "Constructive Americanism"

The Ethnicization of Korean Immigrant Nationalism, 1931–45

As Syngman Rhee's political star faded, a relatively unknown figure named Kilsoo Haan emerged as a leading voice within the nationalist movement in the United States. Much like Rhee, Kilsoo Haan demonstrated a strategic understanding of U.S. foreign affairs and international developments. Also like Rhee, Haan ably exploited this "expertise" to establish his authority and prestige. Haan's outspoken demeanor and controversial views attracted considerable attention from U.S. government officials and the American public, at times drawing criticism of him as a self-serving propagandist. He nevertheless put forth a clear, pragmatic vision, skillfully accessing a wide variety of political channels in the U.S. government and military.

In the early 1930s, Haan became involved in the Korean independence movement, engaging in intelligence activities to combat the threat of what he called the "Japanization" of Hawaii. Through what he called "constructive Americanism," he believed Koreans in the U.S. mainland and Hawaii could serve as valuable allies of the United States in combating the Japanese threat at home and abroad.[1] He sought to use this "constructive Americanism" to claim the right of Korean participation in the U.S. public sphere.

Haan's rhetorical strategies and actions articulated a distinct U.S.-based ethnic identity as he endeavored to advance the interests of Koreans in the

United States and abroad simultaneously. As Korean liberation struggles became increasingly reconfigured by their localization in the United States, strategic visions within the movement began to change and increasingly reflected the realities of living and working within a U.S. environment. Haan not only lobbied for U.S. material aid for the nationalist cause of Korean independence: his organizing efforts conspicuously positioned the status of Koreans in the United States as a part of U.S. state structures and society. Korean nationalism facilitated the development of a collective identity as ethnic Americans. This identity was not solely rooted in cultural ties to the homeland or imagined notions of a Korean nation-state, but also emerged from the daily experiences of living in the United States. In other words, ethnicity was not an intrinsic cultural identification carried over from Korea that was to be preserved or maintained. Rather, it was an ongoing process emerging from the daily interactions between immigrants and the dominant host society as immigrants adapted to specific historical realities at particular moments in time.[2]

Though Kilsoo Haan's activities exemplified this shift toward the ethnicization of nationalist politics, his role is often obscured by the typical emphasis on Syngman Rhee's involvement in the independence movement. For much of the 1930s, Rhee remained politically inactive. Accordingly, most studies tend to downplay the important changes that occurred during that decade and resumed in the 1940s when U.S. entry into World War II created conditions favorable for Syngman Rhee to reassert his authority as diplomatic recognition of the Korean Provisional Government (KPG) once again became paramount for the nationalist movement.[3] A reexamination of Haan's significance provides a more complete view of the trajectory of the movement that unfolded in the 1940s.

In many ways, Kilsoo Haan seemed to be an unlikely successor to Syngman Rhee. Born in Korea on May 31, 1900, he arrived in Hawaii as a five-year-old with his parents who had immigrated as laborers. While his father returned to Korea in 1910, Kilsoo and his mother remained in Hawaii, where he attended the Korean Compound School and the Kaiulani School up until the eighth grade. In August 1920, he departed for San Francisco to spend a year preparing for the ministry at the Salvation Army Training School. When he returned to Hawaii, he was assigned to the island of Kauai to serve as a Salvation Army representative and rose over the next six years to the rank of captain. In 1926, Haan married Stella Yoon, a fellow Korean from Honolulu, and resigned from the Salvation Army, reportedly because his wife's religious beliefs conflicted with those of the Salvation Army.[4]

In the early 1930s, Haan became involved in the Korean independence movement first as a member of the Korean National Association (KNA) of Hawaii. Along with his colleague Chung Doo-ok, he formed the Korean Information Bureau, as part of the KNA, to obtain and collect information about political developments in East Asia following Japan's invasion of Manchuria and to regularly report this information to the U.S. government. KNA officers Henry Kim and Warren Kim opposed the existence of the group within the KNA and forced the Bureau's dissolution in the spring of 1932. Around this same time, Kiusic Kimm arrived in Hawaii from China and with Haan's aid established the Sino-Korean Peoples League of Hawaii to actively combat "Japanism" and to establish intelligence networks in Korea, Japan, and China to aid the Chinese against the Japanese. After Kimm returned to China, Haan continued his "intelligence" activities and soon drew the attention of government and military officials in Hawaii.[5]

In early 1933, Kilsoo Haan submitted a document entitled "A Survey of Public Opinion among the Japanese in the Territory of Hawaii" to U.S. military officials in Hawaii. Written under his pen name W. K. Lyhan, the survey declared that war between Japan and the United States was quickly approaching. The forcible occupation of Manchuria by the Japanese military in September 1931 provided the most recent evidence of Japan's aggressive plan to control the entire Pacific area. Stating that the United States was "the only remaining obstacle in their plan for consolidation of Contintential [sic] Asia to the Japanese Empire," Haan cautioned that Japan was preparing for "an attack without warning" on the Hawaiian Islands.[6] Given the American government's preoccupation with the Great Depression and the isolationist attitudes of the American public, Haan believed that the time was ripe for a Japanese surprise attack on the United States.[7]

Haan sought to convince U.S. officials that Japan had already established the groundwork for an attack targeting Hawaii. He claimed to have uncovered an array of espionage activities within the Japanese community in Hawaii, which made up nearly half of the total population in Hawaii.[8] Haan vividly described a scenario in which three groups of Japanese in Hawaii were working in conjunction with the Japanese military:

> On any one peaceful night many prominent American businessmen, plantation managers, army and navy officers will awake to discover with horror and suprize [sic] that their trusted cook, maid, yardman or chauffer has poisoned or mortally wounded some of the members of their family. . . .

> Simultaneously with the first attack on the homes of responsible citizens, every locality will be attacked by thousands of Japanese citizens with the aid of marines and sailors.[9]

Haan urged the United States to take immediate military action. Referring to the Stimson Doctrine, Haan asserted, "Uncle Sam is now an active participant in the Far Eastern politics" and should take more decisive action against Japan in East Asia to prevent such an attack on American soil.[10] In 1931, U.S. Secretary of State Henry L. Stimson had issued a statement condemning the Japanese military takeover of Manchuria as a violation of the Open Door policy, the Kellogg-Briand Pact, and the Nine-Power Treaty. According to the doctrine, the United States would refuse to recognize any territorial changes that had come about through conquest. For Haan, the condemnation of Japan in the Stimson Doctrine suggested that the United States had publicly declared Japan a dangerous threat to international peace.[11] Haan urged the United States to enforce the international treaties violated by Japan's occupation of Manchuria and forcibly oust Japan from Manchuria. By taking an offensive posture against Japanese aggressions abroad, Haan believed that the American military could safely protect the national security of the United States at home and prevent Japan from forcing America into a defensive war.

Haan's survey represented a new strategic approach among Korean nationalists in the United States. Departing from previous tactics that emphasized a diplomatic approach, Haan did not seek official recognition of the KPG from State Department officials. Instead, he directed his lobbying efforts toward gaining the support of the U.S. military. Depicting Japan as a militaristic nation "dominated by imperialistic aims knowing no bounds," Haan sought to link the domestic threat of a Japanese attack on U.S. soil with Japan's recent aggressions in Manchuria.[12] Haan argued that the international situation involving Japanese aggressions abroad was inextricably linked to the domestic security of the United States. Haan also drew attention to alleged anti-American activities conducted by Japanese within the United States, thereby localizing the Japanese threat. In denouncing all Japanese aliens and citizens as potential threats to the security of the American nation, Haan implicitly positioned Koreans as loyal to America and willing to stand by the United States in the event of war with Japan.

In "Korea's Appeal," Kilsoo Haan expanded his ideas in a lengthier document submitted to U.S. Secretary of War George Dern. Again emphasizing "the grave situation of the Far East," Haan repeatedly asserted that the United States had the power and influence to cease further Japanese aggressions and thereby prevent a costly war.[13] Seeking to convince American government officials to take military action against Japan, Haan highlighted the significance of the United States as a vital force in East Asian political affairs. Like previous appeals from Korean nationalists before him, Haan referenced the clause of the 1882 Treaty of Amity and Commerce between the United States and Korea concerning the obligation of either nation to exert its "good offices" to aid the other in cases of national crises caused by the belligerent actions of a third power.[14] However, he provided a more complex and nuanced analysis of diplomatic relations between the two nations. Rather than solely basing his appeal for U.S. intervention on the reciprocity clause of "good offices," Haan tried to underscore the larger historical significance of the treaty. He explained at length:

> In a sense, the U.S. as a result of the treaty of 1882 assumed a certain moral and legal obligation connected with the question of Korea's status as an independent power, and to the extent that the treaty upset the balance of power between China and Japan and later Japan and Russia. The U.S. was responsible in no small measure for the subsequent course of events, ultimately so disastrous to the course of peace in the Far East. If the United States had adopted a strong policy toward maintaining Korea's independence it could have eliminated the Sino-Japanese war of 1904–05, thus possessing the key to permanent peace in the Far East and the guarantee of the Open Door of Asia. It is safe to say if the U.S. had intervened in the early stages of the Sino-Japanese war, Japan could never had expanded her power, as she has done today and the Manchurian question would have been a myth.[15]

Stressing that Korea had always been the cornerstone to peace and stability in East Asia, Haan argued that the U.S. government's failure to fulfill its treaty obligations to Korea represented its larger failure to realize its role in East Asia, putting American soil at risk. Nevertheless, Haan maintained that the United States still had the power to prevent a direct attack through immediate military action against Japanese expansionism in Manchuria.

Haan declared that Koreans and Chinese were now part of the same struggle to liberate their respective lands from Japanese imperialists. As evidence of the new alliances created by Japanese aggressions abroad, he attached a formal declaration of support between Korean and Chinese nationalist groups in Hawaii to "unite the revolutionary forces of China and Korea in checking Japan's Imperialism out of the Asiatic continent."[16] Haan warned, "[Japan] will not only attempt to conquer China but she will make a desperate attempt to control the mastery of the Pacific Ocean."[17] Seeking to mobilize a tripartite alliance against Japan, Haan emphasized that Koreans could play an indispensable role in the fight against Japan. "We have the spirit and we have men ready to lay down their lives for this worthy cause. But we lack arms, ammunition and money to carry out our aggressive program on a major scale."[18]

Haan outlined Korean involvement in a variety of capacities, including armed resistance, military training, espionage, and propaganda work. In conjunction with the Chinese army, Haan believed his program involving Koreans in China, Manchuria, Korea, and Japan could successfully oust Japan military forces from occupied territories in Korea and Manchuria, and ultimately "overthrow the present militaristic Japanese Government."[19] To implement his plan, he requested from the Department of War a sum of $1 million annually, with the addition of arms and ammunition for a three-year period. Haan assured the U.S. government that this material aid would ensure that the war with Japan remained "localized in China, Manchuria, Korea and Japan" and would ultimately prevent "a major war with America."[20] Believing that Koreans first needed to demonstrate their usefulness to the United States, he proposed that the United States pledge its assistance by recognizing the KPG after the three-year "trial" period.[21]

Haan's plan entailed close coordination between U.S. military officials and Korean nationalists throughout the diaspora. Calling for the need for a new Korean organization that reflected his direct action tactics, Haan proposed the creation of A-K-R-O-N (Another Korean Revolutionary Organization is Necessary), which ostensibly referred to the Sino-Korean Peoples League. He likened the new organization to the U.S.S. *Akron*, a dirigible designed by the U.S. Navy that had been destroyed in a fiery crash off the coast of New Jersey in stormy weather on April 4, 1933. Rather than replacing the *Akron* with a new dirigible, Haan advised that the United States build "a slow moving and death giving war-tank" by mobilizing Koreans strategically located throughout the diaspora.[22]

In his call for A-K-R-O-N, Haan alluded to the inadequacies of existing nationalist organizations. The KNA was in a state of organizational malaise and inertia due to debilitating factional feuds during the early 1930s. The KPG was also in a state of inactivity and disarray. Given the lack of a legitimate state authority within the Korean diaspora, Haan astutely understood diplomatic recognition from the United States would have little value. Rather, he proposed that a new organization, presumably the Sino-Korean Peoples' League working under the aegis of A-K-R-O-N, should be responsible for directing military operations against the Japanese abroad.

In doing so, he sought to position himself and the Sino-Korean Peoples' League at the forefront of the Korean nationalist movement in the United States and abroad.

The movement had entered the 1930s in a dormant state due to repeated disappointments on the international front and debilitating factional strife, but the Japanese occupation of Manchuria in 1931 stirred the movement out of its inertia. Provoked by Japan's aggressions into Chinese territories, first into Manchuria and then into the northern parts of China proper, the Chinese government began to reach out to Korean nationalists in China to fight the Japanese as a common foe. Following the Japanese occupation of Manchuria, much of the Korean national movement in Manchuria moved to China, where it renewed and reorganized its activities with a new vigor.

Soon after the invasion of Manchuria, the KPG, under the leadership of Kim Ku, attracted the attention of Chiang Kai-shek, head of the Chinese Nationalist government. Chiang provided Kim Ku with monthly financial support to mobilize and train Korean officers who would work closely with the Chinese military. Kim, however, squandered the opportunity and failed to consolidate his leadership over the various groups affiliated with the KPG. As a result, the KPG remained deeply divided and largely ineffective throughout most of the 1930s.[23]

The inability of the KPG to capitalize on its alliance with the Chinese Nationalist government provided an opportunity for leftist groups to gain greater prominence. By the end of the 1920s, the left consisted of several different organizations, such as Comintern-oriented Communists in Siberia, nationalist-Communists in Shanghai and Manchuria, and moderate leftist nationalists with no specific organizational affiliation like former KPG Minister Kiusic Kimm. Like its counterparts on the right, the left was largely divided at the beginning of the 1930s, but Japan's invasions of Manchuria and China helped launch efforts to create a united front within the left.

Out of the various leftist groups, Kim Won-bong, a nationalist-Communist in the mold of Yi Tong-hwi, emerged as the most prominent leader in the early 1930s.[24] In the aftermath of the March First movement, Kim organized a small militia group in Manchuria called the Korean Righteous Fighters' Corps, which engaged in terrorist guerilla tactics against the Japanese. In the late 1920s, Kim became affiliated with the Korean Communist Party in Shanghai and helped organize Korean Communist groups in China.[25]

Japan's increasing aggressions into Chinese territory forced Kim Won-bong to retreat to Nanking, where he made contact with high-ranking officials of the Chinese Nationalist government. In May 1932, he proposed a Sino-Korean alliance to fight the Japanese. Apparently impressed with Kim's ideas, Chiang Kai-shek decided to assist Kim with a monthly stipend to support his military activities. He allowed Kim the use of Chinese military facilities to train Koreans for military and terrorist activities against the Japanese in Manchuria.[26] Kim also used Chiang's financial resources to propagate Communist ideology and activities in Korea.[27]

Kim Won-bong's arrival in Nanking coincided with Kiusic Kimm's attempts to create a new united front in the form of the Korean Anti-Japanese Front Unification League on November 10, 1932.[28] Under these auspices, Kiusic Kimm arrived in Hawaii between 1932 and 1933, where he helped to establish the Sino-Korean Peoples League with Kilsoo Haan.[29] For the next three years, Kiusic Kimm continued to recruit nationalist groups. However, he encountered great resistance from the KPG and its supporters, many of whom were unwilling to join the united front because doing so would require the dissolution of the KPG. Despite Kiusic Kimm's extensive recruitment, Kim Ku and his KPG supporters refused to participate in the united front. In the summer of 1935, Kiusic Kimm and other nationalist organizations from China, Manchuria, and Hawaii convened a plenary conference in the Chinese city of Nanking, where all participating groups dissolved their organizations and formed a single alliance called the Korean National Revolutionary Party (KNRP). The alliance consisted of members of Kim Won-bong's Korean Righteous Fighters' Corps, two major military groups in Manchuria, members of groups formerly associated with the KPG, and the Sino-Korean Peoples League of Hawaii. Owing to the organizational and numerical strength of his Righteous Fighters' Corps, Kim Won-bong and his close associates assumed leadership of the new organization. Although the participation of Kim Ku and the KPG was conspicuously absent, the Korean National Revolutionary Party represented a successful united front of most of the national liberation groups in China and Manchuria.[30] As a result, left-wing nationalist groups, which had advocated direct military action against Japan instead of diplomatic recognition from the West, gained ascendancy over their counterparts who supported the KPG. Haan's nationalist activities in Hawaii emerged from these changes abroad.

Haan's "Survey of Public Opinion among the Japanese in the Territory of Hawaii" generated considerable attention from American military officials and other government authorities at both the local and federal levels. The military intelligence division in Hawaii forwarded the document to B. H. Wells, the Commanding General of Headquarters, Hawaiian

Department, Fort Shafter, Territory of Hawaii, and S. B. D. Wood, the U.S. Attorney for the Territory of Hawaii.[31] From the beginning, government and military officials, such as Wells and Woods, approached the survey with some skepticism, doubting the veracity of some of Haan's more exaggerated statements. However, the survey did cause serious concern about the existence of espionage groups within the Japanese community in Hawaii. In early March 1933, both Woods and Wells requested that the Department of Justice conduct a formal investigation into Haan's allegations of organized espionage activity among Japanese residents of Hawaii. Haan's survey further prompted Major Wells to request that the Bureau of Investigation, predecessor of the FBI, appoint a special agent in Hawaii:

> Because of its location at the junction of world passenger routes, because of its strategic military value, and because of the many alien races strongly represented here and the cosmopolitan character of its society, Honolulu is and has long been a focus of intrigue.... There is a real need here at all times for a loyal, intelligent experienced operative of the Bureau of Investigation, who will work through the local United States attorney in co-operation with the Army authorities.[32]

The Department of Justice promptly appointed a special agent, James P. MacFarland, to investigate the facts and statements contained in Haan's survey.

MacFarland meticulously reviewed the entire survey paragraph by paragraph with Kilsoo Haan. He pressed him to provide further details and his sources for each paragraph of text.[33] Haan claimed that he himself and some 60 Korean agents working for him had gathered most of the information. Explaining that "the inevitability of war between the United States and Japan are matters freely discussed among the Japanese," Haan told MacFarland he had compiled the survey based on his conversations with Japanese residents in Hawaii.[34] When MacFarland continued to press Haan to provide actual names of individuals and concrete documentary evidence, Haan replied with vague and evasive answers.

Through the course of his month-long investigation, MacFarland came to believe that the ideas contained in the survey were not the work of Haan. "An oriental without an educational background could not write with the fluency and power of language as is evidenced by the grammar and expression in the said Survey," MacFarland wrote. He was convinced that "some one thoroughly versed in the English language edited the said Survey."[35] MacFarland believed that Haan had taken his ideas from a book entitled

The Great Pacific War: A History of the American-Japanese Campaign of 1931–33, published in London in 1925 and reprinted in the United States in 1932, written by a British naval expert, Hector C. Bywater.[36] In the preface to his hypothetical account of a war between the United States and Japan, Bywater explained that he did not believe "such a conflict is either close at hand or inevitable," but it "cannot be dismissed as wholly impossible."[37] During this interview with Haan, MacFarland brought forth a copy of *The Great Pacific War* and pointedly asked Haan if the ideas contained in his survey were based on the contents of Bywater's book. Haan acknowledged familiarity with the book and admitted to MacFarland that he had been influenced by it, but was adamant that he and his agents had personally gathered the data for the survey based on the "considerable war talk in Japanese circles."[38]

MacFarland remained unconvinced and turned instead to investigating Haan's personal background to determine his motives for writing the survey.[39] MacFarland interviewed a number of his acquaintances in Hawaii, including officials of the KNA. According to MacFarland, all those interviewed characterized Haan as "unreliable" and "untrustworthy."[40] KNA officials Henry Kim and Warren Kim were particularly critical of Haan. They confirmed that Haan had formerly been an officer in the KNA, and claimed that since his departure, Haan and his colleagues had attempted to secure positions of influence and leadership within the overall body of Korean organizations in Hawaii. KNA officials stated that Haan and his men sought to "display their power and authority" by constantly quoting statements allegedly made to them by U.S. Army Intelligence officers, who, according to Haan, granted him the power to unify all Korean organizations in Hawaii under his direct authority. In the process, MacFarland's interviewees claimed that Haan went about "creating and circulating falsehood about the officers of the Korean National Association."[41]

Despite this information, MacFarland decided to pursue further information on any possible involvement of the KNA. He sought out Korean National Association of Hawaii President Lee Chung Kum, who had signed off on Haan's survey. When questioned about his role in the writing of the survey, Lee informed MacFarland that Haan had approached him for his signature, claiming that "[Haan] would hold himself responsible for the information embodied in the report and the report would bring the Korean National Association and the Korean nationals into closer connection with the United States Government Agencies here." Haan also assured him that the survey "was only a matter of opinion" and so he agreed to sign the survey "without careful examination or due deliberation which my little knowledge of English language renders difficult."[42] Lee further denied knowing anything about the existence of Japanese espionage groups in Hawaii or anyone who did.

MacFarland's final report concluded that the facts and statements in Haan's survey were false, inaccurate, and plagiarized from *The Great Pacific War*. MacFarland matched each paragraph of the survey with what he believed to be the corresponding quote or passage from *The Great Pacific War*. A few paragraphs closely resembled several in Bywater's book, but for the most part, MacFarland seemed to overstate Haan's reliance on the book. Regardless, MacFarland advised that further investigation was unnecessary and recommended closing the case. His superiors in the Department of Justice and U.S. Army accepted his recommendation.[43] However, various branches of the U.S. government would monitor Haan's activities and compile extensive files on him for the next decade.[44]

Though state authorities determined Haan's survey to be fraudulent, Haan cannot be categorically dismissed. During his interview, he revealed some important insights into his thinking and strategies. MacFarland wrote in his final report that Haan had confided the survey "was prepared as a matter of protection to Koreans residing in the Territory of Hawaii" in the event of a war between the United States and Japan. By submitting the survey to military officials in Hawaii, Haan hoped that "the Koreans in the Territory would not be molested by the authorities" since the survey "would tend to establish the hostility of the Koreans towards the Japanese."[45] "Haan also mentioned that there is a general impression in oriental circles that in the event of war between the United States and Japan, the United States would take action to deprieve [sic] all orientals, that is the alien born, and those born in the United States, of their citizenship." Haan explained to MacFarland that the survey was intended to demonstrate that Koreans were "intensely loyal to the United States."[46]

Haan understood that the relationship of Koreans to the American government was closely tied to the national security interests of the United States. In the event of war between the United States and Japan, American state agencies would likely look on Koreans and Japanese with equal suspicion. With his survey, Haan hoped to convince military officials that Koreans were intensely anti-Japanese and would overwhelmingly support the American cause.

In his comments to MacFarland, Haan showed that he was well aware of a racial nationalism, a common bond of blood and skin color, that would seek to abrogate the legal rights of not only Koreans but also all Asians in the United States in the event of a war between the United States and

Japan. At the same time, Haan recognized the strains of civic nationalism in American society, positing political and social equality for all, that could ameliorate the deleterious effects of racial nationalism.[47] In presenting his survey, Haan aimed to promote a form of civic nationalism that demonstrated Korean loyalty and commitment to the core political values of American society.

Haan's strategy was similar to that of previous Korean nationalists who sought to highlight the congruent interests between the United States and a free, democratic Korea. However, his lobbying tactics represented a departure in that he sought to link the status of Koreans in the United States with events abroad. Instead of seeking the recognition of the KPG, he sought the political recognition of group rights for Koreans in the United States, representing a distinctly "American" perspective for Koreans in America.

Without citizenship rights, Koreans in the United States lacked real legal recognition in the eyes of the U.S. state. Considered "unfit" for inclusion in the American polity, their social and political identities remained firmly rooted in their connections to their homeland. Enduring allegiances to the homeland among immigrant groups in the United States were typically associated with disloyalty, giving rise to perceptions of divided or dual loyalties. In his widely influential *Exit, Voice and Loyalty*, Albert O. Hirschman notes that *exit* within the political arena has "often been branded as criminal, for it has been labeled desertion, defection, and treason."[48]

Paradoxically, for Koreans in the United States, who already stood at the social, economic, and political peripheries of American society, exit through mobilization around homeland-related causes represented the only means to exercise a meaningful voice within the U.S. polity.[49] Through their involvement in the Korean nationalist movement, Korean immigrants came to demand the recognition and fair treatment of their interests and status abroad as well as in the United States. In this way, they sought political membership as ethnic Americans in the public sphere that involved recognition of their national status as Koreans, separate and distinct from the Japanese. Haan tried to demonstrate that for many Korean immigrants, "foreign" interests and "domestic" interests were inextricably linked in a way that did not contradict their loyalty and allegiances to the United States. However, for a racialized group like Koreans in the United States, the emphasis on their foreignness could easily arouse the fears of an ever-present racial nationalism in American society that would seek to exclude Koreans from any participation in the domestic sphere.

On March 27, 1935, Kilsoo Haan, representing the Sino-Korean Peoples League, submitted a petition to the Senate and House of Representatives of the Territorial Legislature of Hawaii. Requesting that it investigate the pernicious and rampant influence of Japanization activities in Hawaii, Haan wrote that "the tenacious and persistent resisting of Americanism by the Japanese leaders" had become "detrimental to Hawaii's present political status." In particular, Haan called for an official inquiry into organizations and activities "that emphasize racial consciousness and Japanese loyalty and culture in such a manner that the second generation Japanese are hampered in their preparation for American citizenship."[50]

Based on a report from an agent of the Sino-Korean Peoples League in Tokyo, Haan claimed to have uncovered a recent decision by the Japanese government to sponsor a plan for the free distribution of textbooks about Japan to high school students in Hawaii. According to Haan, the textbooks were to be distributed through the Society of International Cultural Relations, an organization based in Japan dedicated to disseminating information about Japan in order to promote cultural ties with other nations. Quoting from a Japanese press report, Haan wrote that the "materials on instructions on Japan will cover almost every phase of modern Japan, embracing topics on the government, economic and social, art, etc., which will be presented in a way that will appeal to the average high school students in America." He warned that this was not simply a benign gesture toward increased cultural understanding and that the Japanese government had ulterior motives for using the "so-called international cultural movement and the various peace movements as a weapon for the purpose of maneuvering the United States into a position of inferiority and hope to degenerate the national spirit."[51]

Haan asserted that Japan's claims over its territorial acquisitions under the banner of "Asia for Asiatics" exposed "an intense nationalistic as well as racial solidification" that fiercely opposed Western policies and presence in East Asia. "Such insidious foreign influences, dangerous to Americanism are being carried out indirectly," he believed, through various Japanization activities, including the textbook plan, in Hawaii. With the overwhelming number of Japanese residents living in Hawaii, he continued, "Unless the lawmakers of Hawaii find ways and means to harness and avert such activities, Hawaii's situation will be perilous."[52]

Pointing out that an overwhelming portion of American-born Japanese in Hawaii were dual citizens of the United States and Japan, Haan asked rhetorically if they were to be considered "technically 100 percent American citizens or half-American or half-Japanese?"[53] These children, who accounted for nearly 60 percent of the public school children in Hawaii, would in the near future become voting citizens of the United States, which had significant implications for Hawaii's political status. It was uncertain if they would act as U.S. citizens or as subjects of Japan. In seeking "to develop a political interest and loyalty centering around their Emperor," Haan asserted that all Japanization activities ultimately served to undermine the Americanization of second-generation Japanese and imperiled Hawaii's future political status and overall security.[54]

Haan's petition to government authorities, as in his previous efforts, served to demonstrate his loyalty and the loyalty of the Korean people to American political and social ideals. In his petition to state legislators, Haan stated, "We believe in Americanism and in the preservation of its ideal." Quoting from George Washington and Thomas Jefferson, he warned "against the insidious viles of foreign influence" inherent in all Japanization activities in Hawaii.[55]

Despite his efforts, Haan's petition failed to elicit a positive response from state officials. On May 18, 1935, he received a letter from the Education Committee of the Hawaiian Senate informing him that his petition to the state legislature had been referred to the Education Committee, but that the committee decided to take no action.[56] Frustrated by his failures to generate any response from officials in Hawaii, Haan increasingly set his sights on Washington, D.C. On March 6, 1936, he wrote to Secretary of State Cordell Hull explaining his disappointment that his repeated efforts to alert leaders in Hawaii of insidious Japanization activities had yielded "very little success." Because Hawaii stood as "America's first line of defense," Haan expressed his concern that the current situation posed an "impending danger." He requested that the State Department initiate an investigation.[57]

In May, Haan sent Hull another letter informing him that he had "succeeded in getting into the inner circle of the Japanese Consulate" in Hawaii. He wrote that he was infiltrating the consulate as a spy in order to obtain classified information to aid the United States. "One cannot be too confident of our own strength until we are fully aware of the other's ideas and scheme of expansion, commercially as well as politically."[58]

Haan was admitted to the "inner circle" of the Japanese consulate on a "90 days trial," after which he would be included in higher-level activities within the organization. During his trial period, consulate officials, according to Haan, ordered him to not engage in any anti-Japanese propaganda in Hawaii and to submit a plan for containing Korean political activities. If the consulate decided to use his plan, he would be financially compensated. Haan claimed that his purpose for notifying Hull of his involvement with the Japanese consulate was to ensure that U.S. government officials would not "misunderstand my motive and brand me a pro-Japanese and therefore anti-American." Assuring Hull that he was loyal to the United States, he described his four-year record in working with U.S. Army G-2 and Navy intelligence officials in Hawaii, when he claimed he was first approached by army intelligence to assist them in their activities.[59] Haan concluded by saying that he was at a crossroads in his activities. "I am forced through circumstances and events that I must choose my future action. If I am of any value to America, I mean to your department, I hope you would kindly help me financially as well as morally. If I am of no value to you than [sic] I must drop my contact with the Japanese consulate and mind my own livelihood."[60] Neither Hull nor the State Department responded to Haan.

As his ability to carry on his activities in Hawaii continued to diminish, Kilsoo Haan apparently decided to leave the Japanese consulate in 1937 and depart for the U.S. mainland.[61] Before leaving Hawaii, he was involved in one last major episode. In 1937, the U.S. House and Senate in Washington, D.C., appointed a joint committee of twelve senators, twelve representatives, and Hawaii State Representative Samuel King to conduct an investigation into a congressional proposal to grant statehood to Hawaii. In October 1937, the committee held hearings on all five islands in Hawaii and collected a voluminous record of testimony from both proponents and opponents of statehood. An overwhelming portion of the population expressed a desire for statehood on the grounds that Hawaii had met all the typical requirements for admission into the union, such as population size, geographical area, and economic resources. Proponents also stressed the willingness and ability of the residents to maintain a stable, orderly government.[62]

Opponents also presented forceful arguments, most of which focused on anti-Japanese sentiments. In his testimony, Kilsoo Haan stated his opposition to statehood based on his view that the strong presence of the Japanese government throughout the islands presented a threat not only to the well-being and security of Hawaii but also to the American nation at large.[63] He criticized the Japanese government's strong control over the social and political allegiances of the numerically dominant inhabitants of Japanese descent on the islands. Since their loyalty to the United States was uncertain, Haan claimed that the Japanese, if mobilized into a single voting bloc, posed a great threat to the political future of Hawaii. Although his testimony overlapped with that of other opponents to statehood, Haan understood well that the great majority of Hawaiians, including his Korean compatriots, had voiced strong support.[64] He concluded his testimony on a somber note:

> I have taken this issue very sincerely and seriously, and I have been very much upset during the last few days, deciding whether I should appear or not. . . . I do this with perfect understanding that my life career here in Hawaii will be very much in jeopardy, and furthermore I have taken this step knowing the welfare of my family itself would be in a somewhat dangerous position therefore I do not appeal to you or ask you gentlemen to protect me in any manner. I do ask that you gentlemen will give the facts I have presented to you very serious consideration, and if it works out for the betterment of the people of Hawaii, and the future Pacific peace, I will be more than satisfied.[65]

Despite the strong swell of support for statehood from the local residents, the arguments of the opponents, including Haan, greatly influenced the congressional committee, which recommended denying statehood to Hawaii. Recent developments on the international front in 1937 also figured prominently in the committee's decision. In July, Japanese and Chinese troops engaged in a skirmish at the Marco Polo Bridge, 9 miles southwest of Peking, which quickly escalated into an undeclared, full-scale war. U.S. relations with Japan deteriorated rapidly after the outbreak of war, as Secretary of State Cordell Hull and President Franklin Roosevelt sharply criticized Japan's actions. The committee believed that Congress would immediately reject Hawaiian statehood given the international crisis involving Japan, largely beyond the control of the residents of Hawaii.[66]

The war in China provided Haan and the Korean nationalist movement with new opportunities for action. The Chinese government immediately sought to strengthen its alliances with the Koreans, convening a joint conference with major Korean leaders from both the right and left. Chinese officials stressed the urgent need to form a united front against the Japanese and offered substantial financial resources to the Korean nationalists. It particularly requested that Korean leaders mobilize and train Koreans for intelligence operations.[67]

Both leftist and rightist groups within the Korean independence movement scrambled to consolidate their respective forces. Supporters of the KPG, who represented the more conservative side, made significant progress in uniting their forces. Kim Won-bong's National Revolutionary Party created alliances with other left-wing groups in China and formed the Korean National Front Federation. The left, under the direction of Kim Won-bong, also created an armed military unit called the Korean Volunteer Corps, composed of two companies, to assist Chinese forces. One company was dispatched to the north into Manchuria, while the other remained in China proper. Nonetheless, they continued to operate largely in isolation. Near the end of 1938, the Chinese Nationalist government, which had united forces with the Chinese Communists to fight the Japanese, urged the Koreans to form a similar united front of their own.[68]

The war between China and Japan presented opportunities to bring greater attention to the Korean cause by the U.S. government. Under these circumstances, Haan aimed to expand the activities of the Sino-Korean Peoples League. In September 1938, Kilsoo Haan permanently left Hawaii. He first went to San Francisco to begin a nationwide speaking tour to publicize his views on Korean independence. He planned to conclude his tour in Washington, D.C., where he hoped to meet with top government officials in the Roosevelt administration, including the president himself.[69] When he reached Washington in the spring of 1939, Haan requested in writing to meet with Secretary of State Cordell Hull. Senator Guy Gillette of Iowa, whom Haan had befriended in Hawaii during the congressional statehood hearings, wrote Hull an introductory letter on Haan's behalf.[70] Gillette spoke of Haan being in "possession of information and in control of certain channels of information that not only aided the Committee but would be of interest to the State Department." Representatives for Cordell Hull, however, replied to both Haan and Gillette that the secretary's busy schedule meant he would be unable to meet with Haan.[71]

Pressing further, Haan explained that he had a series of urgent requests and pleas for the State Department to consider. On April 12, 1939, he sent Hull a lengthy memorandum that stressed diplomacy.[72] Declaring the reestablishment of the Sino-Korean Peoples League, he officially announced the objectives of the League:

1. To create and foster a Chinese-Korean relationship and promote both nations' culture and welfare.
2. To unite Korean efforts in combating Japanese aggression and regain independence for Korea.
3. To inform America of the inimical designs of the Japanese and secure American aid for the Chinese war effort.[73]

Haan asked the State Department to issue a public statement or letter expressing "sympathy to the Chinese, the Koreans and the liberal-minded

Japanese peasants, thus uplifting their morale in resisting Japanized Fascism in Asia."[74] Haan explained that the United States could extend its public sympathy under the auspices of the "good offices" clause of the 1882 Treaty of Amity and Commerce and, by extending its moral influence, could ensure that the conflict in East Asia would remain "localized." Haan asserted, "Sympathy will go a long way—in reality, its effect will be greater than supplying quantities of arms, munitions, or other aid."[75]

The new diplomatic emphasis in Haan's proposal to Hull partly reflected his optimism arising from increased military cooperation between Chinese and Korean forces against the Japanese after 1937. It also indicated his keen awareness of the unwillingness of the U.S. government to enter a foreign war, reflected in the passage of various neutrality laws throughout the 1930s.[76] The Neutrality Act of 1935 prohibited the sale of arms to all belligerent nations once the president had determined the existence of a state of war, making no distinction between aggressor and victim. The 1935 law did not include an embargo on the trade of supplies such as oil, steel, and copper, which could be easily converted into war materials. Two years later, Congress enacted the Neutrality Law of 1937, which defined belligerents not only in terms of nations at war but also included civil wars, empowered the president to add strategic materials other than munitions to the embargo list, and prohibited all U.S. citizens from traveling on belligerent ships. The difficulties of maintaining neutrality became evident after war broke out between China and Japan. President Roosevelt decided not to proclaim the existence of a state of war in China because he believed invoking the Neutrality Act would prevent China from purchasing strategic goods from the United States. Roosevelt's decision ended up benefiting Japan more than China since the former's volume of trade with the United States was far greater than the latter's.[77]

Well aware of these problems with the Neutrality Acts, Haan pointed out that American sales of strategic materials, including oil, steel, and copper, to Japan provided the Japanese military with a significant percentage of the necessary war-related materials to carry out its military campaigns against China. Haan proposed that Congress enact a measure prohibiting the sale of these strategic materials to Japan for a two-year period, during which time the U.S. government would appropriate 300 to 400 million dollars to purchase these same materials from the American firms who had been selling them to Japan. The United States then would hand over these materials to the U.S. Army and Navy, thereby significantly strengthening America's national defense. The government would still be promoting economic recovery at home by ensuring that the businesses involved did not experience any monetary or employment losses.[78]

The U.S. refusal to sell war-related materials to Japan, Haan believed, would serve to "break the morale of the mass of Japanese who are cooperating with the militarists under the misapprehension" that the United States was supporting the policies of the Japanese military. The plan would ultimately lead to the breakdown of Japan's military program in and out of Japan. It would ensure that the United States would not be drawn into war, while simultaneously stimulating the American economy. If the United States did not take the necessary steps to stop Japanese aggressions in China at the present moment, he cautioned that the Japanese would mount further aggressions into the Philippines, Hawaii, Guam, Midway, and Alaska, all of which threatened U.S. interests.[79]

Haan continued to link the "domestic" interests of Koreans in the United States with activities and events abroad involving the Korean nationalist movement. He saw wartime opportunities to expand his intelligence work to include activities on the U.S. mainland. In the third and final part of his memorandum, he outlined a plan to utilize a coterie of some 250 to 300 Koreans residing in the United States, who had emigrated after 1924 for educational purposes. Haan argued that these highly educated Koreans, graduates of American universities or currently matriculated in a degree program at a university, were particularly well suited to conduct intelligence operations for the United States. All were fluent in spoken Japanese and written Chinese and had a strong command of the English language. They would "gladly serve America if such opportunities are granted them," he pledged.[80]

These students were legally permitted to stay in the United States only temporarily due to their student status, and after completing their educational requirements, they were required to return to Korea.[81] Many dreaded going back to Korea for fear of persecution by Japanese colonial officials. According to Haan, the Japanese colonial government had accused nearly all student returnees after 1924 of conducting anti-Japanese activities while abroad. They were subsequently imprisoned under harsh conditions and forced publicly to pledge support and allegiance to the Japanese empire, leaving many "mentally and physically unfit for society" after their release from prison. Under these circumstances, he asked the State Department to grant these students "political refugee" status, allowing them to remain in the United States until the liberation of Korea. In turn, these students could prove valuable assistance in protecting the national security of the United States.[82]

Haan saw opportunities to expand the activities of the Sino-Korean Peoples League on the U.S. mainland by working in concert with such Korean students. He proposed a cooperative plan between the League and intelligence units in the U.S. Army and Navy for developing "self-defense measures" for the United States.[83] Based on his experiences during his three months of speaking engagements in California, he claimed to have "interviewed hundreds of men and women" who had expressed widespread support for an organization like the Sino-Korean Peoples League on the mainland.[84]

Haan implored the American government to adhere to its principles of democracy and freedom in considering his requests and pleas. He stated, "We believe America is the beacon light of democracy and the Government the pillar upholding this light. . . . That is why we believe that the present war between Japan and China is more than a war for territories or for raw materials. This is a war between two political philosophies—Democracy vs. Japanized Fascism." Koreans and Americans shared "the principle [that] all democratic people must forget the racial and nationalistic line and stand by together to save democracy from being trampled by the militarists of Japan in Asia."[85] While Haan's rhetorical appeals once again invoked the egalitarian civic traditions in American society, his statements could also equally arouse the racist and intolerant sentiments of a racial nationalism that would make little or no distinction between the Japanese and Koreans.

Seemingly aware of this duality, Haan made further appeals to the State Department. On April 28, 1939, he managed to personally meet with Maxwell M. Hamilton, who headed the Division of Far Eastern Affairs. Haan gave Hamilton a copy of his lengthy letter to Hull, as well as a copy of his testimony before the House of Representatives Committee on Foreign Affairs on April 26. Haan once again asserted that the status of Koreans in the United States as ethnic Americans guided their motivation to aid the United States. "Primarily we are interested in America, and the Koreans in Hawaii are particularly concerned with the safety of Hawaii, due to the present political situation in Korea, as well as in China." At the same time, Haan expressed his frustrations and anxieties over the constraints placed on Koreans due to their racial and alien status in the United States:

> Frankly speaking, an American who lives in Hawaii can pack up his trunk and come to America whenever he finds the conditions or situation is intolerable, whereas a Korean, whether the conditions are livable or not, is forced to stay in Hawaii. None of us desire to go back to Korea and a greater

number of aliens are not allowed to come to America. Hence, our position is a forced one. Therefore, under this situation, we would like to do everything within our power and within our means to have Hawaii remain under the Stars and Stripes.[86]

Hamilton told Haan that the State Department's official policies had already been set forth by the secretary of state and the president, and that he lacked any authority to make changes in foreign policy. He also did not have the authority to change Korean students' immigration status and suggested that Haan discuss the matter with the Visa Division.[87]

The overwhelming territorial advances made by the Axis powers in Europe and Asia soon after the outbreak of World War II in 1939 greatly heightened anxieties on the American home front. In 1940, the American government, particularly fearful of fifth column threats, took greater measures to safeguard the nation's internal security. As part of these protective efforts, Congress enacted the Alien Registration Act (also known as the Smith Act), which fortified existing laws regarding the admission and deportation of aliens and required the fingerprinting of all aliens in the United States. Its primary purpose was to check subversive activities, making it unlawful for any person to advocate or teach the overthrow or destruction of the U.S. government by force or violence.

With the passage of the Alien Registration Act, Kilsoo Haan saw an opportunity to advance the status and rights of Koreans living on the U.S. mainland and Hawaii. He contacted Earl Harrison, Director of Alien Registration, and requested that Koreans in the United States and Hawaii have the right to register as Koreans and not as Japanese subjects as they were defined by international law. Harrison granted Haan's request, which Haan widely publicized as a significant victory in the legal recognition of Korean rights in the United States.[88]

Haan's concern about the predicament of Koreans in the United States increased as Japan mounted its aggressive military assault in the Pacific. In a letter to U.S. Secretary of the Treasury Henry Morgenthau, Jr., Haan, representing the Sino-Korean Peoples League, expressed his desire "to clarify some of the apprehensions which exist among the Korean people in the Hawaiian Islands and in America." Mentioning growing reports that the U.S. government would likely freeze all the financial assets of the Axis powers held in the United States, Haan explained his particular concern that "if and when America freezes all the Japanese financial holdings or confiscates the Japanese financial holdings in the event of war, all such properties and financial holdings belonging to the Koreans too may be frozen or confiscated." Referring to the ruling of Earl Harrison at the Department of Justice the previous year, Haan petitioned the Treasury Department to exempt Koreans in America from having their financial holdings seized.[89]

In June, Haan wrote to John W. Pehle, Controller for Foreign Funds in the Treasury Department, which had frozen the U.S. financial holdings of Germany and Italy and most of the subjugated nations under Axis control in Europe. The freezing of Japanese financial assets in the United States had not yet occurred but seemed imminent as relations between the United States and Japan became increasing strained.[90] Haan wrote that "Koreans are truly an unwilling subjected people under the Jap-militarist government—we 3,150 alien Koreans are in reality political refugees, living under the protection and good grace of the American government. . . . We are loyal to America and will be always ready to serve the best interest of the United States in this time of grave National Emergency." As such, Haan once again urged the Treasury Department to provide an "early understanding" of the situation of Korean immigrants by exempting them from any order to freeze Japanese financial assets in America.[91]

In a letter to J. Edgar Hoover, Director of the FBI, in July, Haan requested that the Sino-Korean Peoples League be permitted to issue identification cards to Korean aliens in the United States to distinguish them from the Japanese. Hoover referred the letter to the Immigration and Naturalization Service at the Department of Justice, which granted his request.[92] Haan publicly announced the ruling as yet another step toward the national recognition of Korean status in the United States.

Despite the optimism generated by Haan's efforts, the Japanese attack on Pearl Harbor on December 7, 1941, brought devastating consequences for the status of Koreans living throughout the United States and Hawaii. In the attack's immediate aftermath, the United States declared war on Japan, and all Japanese aliens in the United States became "enemy aliens," subject to certain restrictions. The Treasury Department ordered the freezing of the financial holdings of all Japanese nationals. In Hawaii, the U.S. military declared martial law and assumed full authority over civilian affairs, whereby the Japanese in Hawaii were subjected to additional stringent restrictions. Regarded as subjects of Japan due to Korea's subjugation under Japanese rule, Koreans in the United States found themselves classified as enemy aliens and subject to many of the same restrictions imposed on alien Japanese.[93]

Despite all of Haan's efforts to position Koreans as distinct from the Japanese, the U.S. government failed to do so. Undeterred, Haan promptly took action to rectify the situation. Days after Pearl Harbor, Haan petitioned several government and military officials to aid Koreans in the United States. On December 9, Haan once again wrote to John W. Pehle at the Treasury Department, asking Pehle to exempt Korean financial holdings from being frozen or confiscated as enemy property, and notifying him that the funds of Koreans in Hawaii, California, and Chicago had already been frozen by the banks, pending further orders from the Treasury Department. Haan emphasized the need for Koreans to carry on their regular business transactions to maintain their livelihoods, but also for the continuation of their activities in assisting the United States' war effort against Japan. Pehle sent a short, noncommittal response stating that the release of blocked funds would be considered on an individual basis determined by facts and circumstances for each case. He recommended that Haan direct any affected individuals to meet with their local banking officials to explain their situation.[94]

On December 9, Haan wrote to Brigadier General Sherman Miles, Chief of U.S. Army intelligence at the U.S. War Department, to ask Miles if his office could issue identification badges to Korean residents with their photograph and alien registration number so they might be properly identified as Koreans and not as Japanese. He explained to Miles that "Koreans throughout Hawaii and America are very much in distress due to the fact that they fear misunderstanding which may come about as to the identity of Koreans as from the Japanese." He, however, emphasized that the identification cards could only be effective if they indicated some official proof of approval from the Army or Justice Department.[95]

A few days later, Haan wrote to officials at the State Department requesting that Koreans no longer be classified as Japanese subjects and be permitted to travel as friendly aliens, such as the Chinese. Pointing to his indefatigable record of exposing anti-American activities among the Japanese, Haan praised Koreans for proving themselves loyal and valuable allies of the United States. He emphasized that the recognition of Koreans as Koreans by the State Department or Justice Department was a "purely domestic policy, which has no bearing on foreign policy." Maxwell Hamilton informed him that the situation regarding Korean status in the United States was currently under consideration by his department and that he had brought the matter to the attention of the Department of Justice.[96]

Meanwhile, other Korean leaders came forward to petition the U.S. government to change the status of Koreans. Most notably, Syngman Rhee reemerged following the attack on Pearl Harbor. Rhee had spent much of the 1930s in Hawaii, involved in various educational and religious activities within the Korean community of Honolulu, but after the outbreak of war in Europe, he moved to Washington, D.C., to oversee the Korean Commission. Rhee approached Harold B. Hoskins in the Division of Far Eastern Affairs of the State Department, pointing out that all Korean aliens in the United States and Hawaii had registered as "a distinct Korean group" under the Alien Registration Act of 1940. He expressed his dismay upon learning from compatriots in Los Angeles and Chicago that local authorities had closed their bank accounts. Asserting that there was "every reason for the United States to treat the Koreans as a friendly people," Rhee asked the State Department to ensure the release of the frozen financial holdings of all Koreans in the United States and Hawaii.[97] Hoskins quickly informed Rhee that he had referred the matter to L. M. C. Smith at the Special Defense Unit at the Department of Justice.[98] Soon thereafter, the Justice Department announced that the financial holdings of Koreans would be unfrozen.[99] At a press conference, Korean leaders in Washington, D.C., took credit for the successful outcome, adding that the federal banks had erroneously "misinterpreted" an order to freeze Japanese assets by mistakenly including Koreans.[100]

Despite the favorable ruling, many Koreans were still uncertain of their status. In January 1942, the Department of Justice announced that all enemy aliens would be required to reregister under the Alien Registration Act. On January 14, Kilsoo Haan wrote Earl Harrison at the Department of Justice, requesting a clarification of Korean status. Given that the department had permitted Koreans to earlier register as Koreans, in 1940, he inquired whether Koreans were exempt from the reregistration program. If they did so, they would be officially classified as enemy aliens, which would be "contrary to all the good intention proclamations proclaimed by the State Department." Haan demanded that the U.S. government live up to its democratic ideals and principles, writing what when "the United States of America attempts forcefully to change our God-given rights to live and breathe as Koreans into Japs—what difference is there between Japan's inhuman treatment of subject people and of the United States?"[101] On January 23, Harrison officially confirmed "that Koreans who, under the Alien Registration Act of 1940, registered as Koreans, are not required to apply for Certificates of Identification, providing that such persons have not at any time voluntarily become German, Italian or Japanese citizens or subjects."[102] Attorney General Francis Biddle officially announced that Austrians, Austrian-Hungarians, and Koreans were exempt from the order requiring all German, Italian, and Japanese nationals 14 years old and older to apply for certificates of identification beginning February 2,

1942.[103] On February 9, Attorney General Biddle issued a statement lifting all enemy-alien restrictions from "the many thousand loyal aliens of Austrian, Austro-Hungarian, and Korean nationality who have never been sympathetic to the government imposed upon their homelands by military conquests."[104]

The situation was markedly different in Hawaii, where Koreans remained classified as enemy aliens until the end of martial law in late 1944. In the immediate aftermath of the Pearl Harbor attack, Lieutenant General Walker C. Short, commander of the Army's Hawaiian Department, established martial law and assumed full control over the islands. The Office of the Military Governor issued a series of "directives" that imposed special restrictive measures on Japanese nationals living in Hawaii. Although none of these directives specifically listed Koreans, military officials had categorized Koreans as subjects of Japan and lumped them together as enemy aliens. Under martial law, the military governor had assumed full authority over all civilian affairs, and federal offices such as the State and Justice Departments had little or no influence on the governance of Hawaii, so their exemptions from enemy-alien restrictions did not apply to Koreans in Hawaii.[105]

Koreans in Hawaii initiated an extensive campaign to overturn their legal status as enemy aliens. While some of the restriction measures were erased, their overall situation did not change substantially until the end of 1943.[106] Although their enemy-alien classification remained intact until the lifting of martial law, Military Governor Lieutenant General Robert C. Richardson exempted Koreans from enemy-alien curfew restrictions on December 4, 1943, which many Koreans in Hawaii had considered to be the most restrictive and unjust measure.[107]

These changes came in the wake of the announcement of the Cairo Declaration, in which the heads of state for the United States, Great Britain, and China pledged their determination to restore the independence of Korea "in due course." For Koreans throughout the diaspora, the Cairo Declaration represented the long-awaited recognition of Korean independence by the international community. Nationalist organizations in the United States and abroad once again began to lobby extensively for the official recognition of the exiled Korean Provisional Government. Koreans in the United States and Hawaii began to see the United States as a liberator that could guarantee the restoration of Korea's freedom and sovereignty.

Although this discursive shift marked a change in the content of the lobbying efforts of Korean immigrants, strategic reliance on U.S. sovereignty became further entrenched during and following the 1940s. Kilsoo Haan's activities during the 1930s are key to understanding the trajectory of the Korean nationalist movement. Just as the legal and racialized status of Koreans in the United States was often a tenuous one, so too was the status of the Korean independence and the Korean Provisional Government tenuous in relationship to the priorities of the U.S. government during World War II.

CHAPTER 7

"In Due Course"

Diasporic Nationalism, the United Korean Committee in America, and U.S. Sovereignty

The aforesaid three powers [United States, Great Britain, and China], mindful of the enslavement of the people of Korea, are determined that in due course Korea shall become free and independent.
　　　　　　—The Cairo Declaration, December 1943

Soon after the U.S. entry into World War II, Korean nationalist organizations once again took to lobbying intensively for the official recognition of the exiled Korean Provisional Government (KPG) in China. Seeing themselves as part of a common international struggle against Japan, Korean nationalist leaders expected the Allied powers, particularly the United States, to play a more active role in the liberation of their homeland. For many Koreans, recognition from the U.S. state rather than immediate independence became a focal point of nationalist activities. By the mid-1940s, this reliance on the U.S. government as the guarantor of Korean national interests became firmly ensconced in the strategic visions of many nationalist leaders, including the activities of the United Korean Committee in America (UKC).

Korean organizations in the United States created the UKC in early 1941 to consolidate their resources. The UKC did not make any claims to state power or claim to represent the Korean nation as a state entity. Rather, it positioned itself as a "pressure group" within the U.S. polity, seeking to win support for the diplomatic recognition of the KPG from U.S. policy makers and the American public. The UKC did not directly seek the independence of Korea but instead sought to establish liaisons with different administrative agencies in the United States and to impact legislation and foreign policy, which might lead to diplomatic recognition.[1]

Korean nationalist organizations operated as interest groups seeking recognition for Koreans as a distinct ethnic group within the U.S. polity, looking to advance the status of Koreans in America while also trying to influence U.S. foreign policy with regard to the Korean cause for independence. These types of organizational activities enabled Koreans to participate in American public life. During the twentieth century, such local voluntary activity became a defining characteristic of American pluralist democracy. In this light, the transnational communal activities of Koreans in the United States became increasingly synonymous with the development of an ethnic community.

In the spring of 1941, leaders from the two largest Korean immigrant political organizations, the Korean National Association (KNA) and the Tongjihoe, called a conference to bring about the unification of all Korean groups in the United States and Hawaii in light of the growing political and military crisis in the Pacific. Between April 10 and April 29, fourteen representatives from nine Korean nationalist organizations convened in Honolulu. The war between China and Japan continued to develop, and World War II had spread to the Pacific area.[2]

The new federation, called the United Korean Committee in America (UKC), brought together the Korean National Association of North America, Korean National Association of Hawaii, Central Headquarters of Tongjihoe of Hawaii, Sino-Korean Peoples League of Hawaii, Korean Independence Party, the Korean National Revolutionary Party of Los Angeles, Korean Women's Patriotic Society of Los Angeles, Korean Women's Relief Society of Hawaii, and Korean Independence League of Hawaii. Under the UKC consolidation, all organizations were to remain intact in name and body and were expected to continue attending to their own internal affairs. However, all diplomatic and political activities of the Korean independence movement were to be administered solely by the UKC.[3]

To coordinate these activities, two separate UKC headquarters were established, one in Honolulu and the other one in Los Angeles, home to the largest Korean population in Hawaii and the U.S. mainland, respectively. Organizers designated the Honolulu office (HONUKC) as the legislative branch, while the Los Angeles headquarters (LAUKC) would function as the executive branch. The conference participants also passed a resolution that called for the reestablishment of the Korean Commission in Washington, D.C., led once again by Syngman Rhee, to serve as the diplomatic arm of the KPG. The UKC ordered that all existing fundraising programs for the Korean independence movement be discontinued and replaced with a new single program called the Korean Independence Funds (*tongjipkum*). Each member organization of the UKC was responsible for collecting funds and contributions from its own members in the form of the Korean Independence Fund. The collected monies were then to be sent directly to UKC headquarters in Los Angeles, which would remit two-thirds of the total collections to the KPG and use the remaining one-third to cover administrative expenses of the UKC headquarters in Los Angeles and Honolulu, as well as the Korean Commission in Washington, D.C.[4]

UKC officials were to be elected from a pool of candidates drawn from the participating organizations and appointed in proportion to the total membership of each organization. As a result, individuals from the two largest organizations—the Tongjihoe and the KNA of Hawaii—held most of the leadership positions. At the founding convention, the UKC also appointed Kilsoo Haan as its representative for the American National Defense Program in Washington, D.C., where he would work with U.S. government agencies to mobilize Korean participation in American war efforts. His duties, however, were to remain separate from the diplomatic activities of Syngman Rhee and the Korean Commission.[5]

The creation of the UKC marked the first concerted efforts toward unifying Korean nationalist organizations in the United States since 1919. Unlike the KPG, the UKC did not seek to unify the entire Korean diaspora but rather to organize only those groups active in the United States and Hawaii, reflecting the localization of diasporic politics and the increasing reliance on U.S. sovereignty to achieve the national goals of the Korean independence movement.

The primary purpose of the UKC was to mobilize moral and financial support for the KPG in China, an objective that took on greater purpose and focus following the announcement of the Atlantic Charter. In August 1941, Franklin Roosevelt and Winston Churchill issued the Atlantic Charter as a joint statement of principles regarding the postwar aims of the United States and Great Britain. Korean nationalist leaders enthusiastically praised the Charter's broad declaration of support for the national self-determination of all peoples. Echoing parts of Woodrow

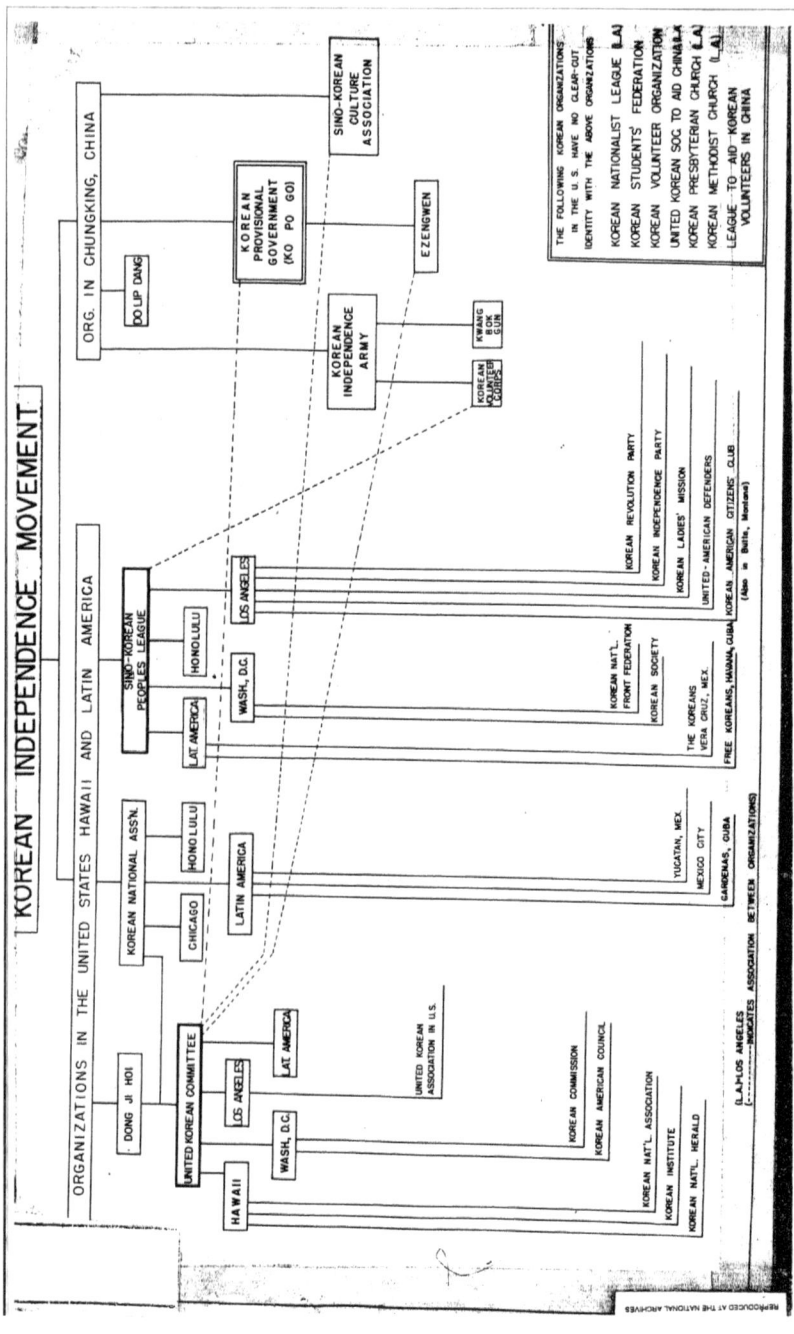

Figure 7.1.
Korean nationalist organizations in the Korean independence movement in the 1940s.
Source: National Archives.

Wilson's Fourteen Points, the Atlantic Charter proclaimed opposition to any imposed or undemocratic territorial changes and support for sovereign rights and self-government for all peoples, including those forcibly deprived of them. UKC leaders believed that the Atlantic Charter was "obviously an extension and confirmation of the fixed and fundamental policy of the [U.S.] State Department to refuse to acknowledge the suzerainty of any nation over the territory acquired by aggression."[6] Accordingly, they sought to acquire immediate diplomatic recognition of the KPG as the de facto government of the Korean people.

Korean nationalist organizations in search of international patronage were also motivated by the signing of the Declaration of the United Nations on January 1, 1942, in which twenty-six anti-Axis signatory nations affirmed the principles of the Atlantic Charter and pledged full wartime cooperation against the Axis powers.[7] Seeing themselves as part of a common international struggle against Japan, Korean nationalist leaders expected the Allied powers, particularly the United States, to play a more instrumental role in the freedom of their homeland. Buoyed by these diplomatic events, UKC President Charles Ho Kim appointed Jacob Kyuang Dunn Secretary of Public Relations for the UKC on January 7, 1942, as part of a concerted program of mobilization and publicity for diplomatic recognition of the KPG.[8] Fluent in English, college-educated in the United States, and extremely articulate, Dunn would come to play an active role in the internal affairs of the UKC and its dealings with U.S. government officials.

To capitalize on the recent turn of events, the UKC organized a conference in Washington, D.C., between February 27 and March 1, 1942, to publicize the cause of U.S. recognition of the KPG. Named the Korean Liberty Conference, the event symbolically coincided with the commemorative date of March 1, 1919, and bore close resemblance to the Korean Congress held in Philadelphia. Prominent Korean leaders such as Syngman Rhee and Philip Jaisohn spoke about the significance of the KPG, and a number of American dignitaries were also invited to speak on behalf of the KPG and Korean independence. Like the 1919 Congress, the Korean Liberty Conference extolled the values of American democracy and liberty and the Korean people's commitment to them.[9]

Syngman Rhee ceremoniously presided over the passage of five resolutions in the campaign to win diplomatic recognition for the KPG, all of which were unanimously adopted by the conference participants. The resolutions included:

1. Reaffirmation of the 1919 Korean Declaration of Independence and a pledge to continue the fight for the freedom and liberty of Korea
2. Reaffirmation of unconditional support and maintenance of the Korean Provisional Government in Chungking, China
3. Support and approval of the KPG's formal application to the U.S. State Department requesting that it become a signatory of the Declaration of United Nations
4. Authorization to petition the president of the United States for the official recognition of the KPG and its status as an active member in the Declaration of the United Nations
5. Authorization to petition the U.S. Congress for the recognition of the KPG[10]

Nearly one year after the formation of the UKC, these resolutions provided a basic working strategy for the newly unified Korean political groups in the United States and Hawaii. After years of factional disputes, the Korean Liberty Conference played a highly symbolic role in renewing the stature and authority of the KPG and securing support for it among its constituents. The Korean Liberty Conference also represented the official launching of a mass campaign for diplomatic recognition of the KPG. With a basic strategy in place, implementation would entail coordinated action among the United Korean Committee of Honolulu and Los Angeles, the Korean Commission, the Korean-American Council, and to a lesser extent Koreans in Korea, Japan, China, Manchuria, and Siberia.

Soon after the Korean Liberty Conference, James H. R. Cromwell, who headed the Korean-American Council in Washington, D.C., initiated a series of correspondence with U.S. Secretary of State Cordell Hull. The Korean-American Council was an organization of prominent American citizens, consisting of several Washington "insiders" who supported the cause of Korean independence. John Staggers, a well-known attorney in Washington, D.C., provided counsel on legal matters, journalist Jay Jerome Williams served as a public relations advisor, and James Cromwell, former U.S. Ambassador to Canada, was president. All three men were close associates of Syngman Rhee and worked closely with the Korean Commission, but exercised "prerogatives not permissible to the Korean Commission."[11]

On May 5, 1942, Cromwell petitioned the U.S. State Department to extend official recognition to the KPG, arguing that such recognition was entirely consistent with existing State Department policies of refusing "to acknowledge the suzerainty of any nation over any territory acquired by aggression." He added that the Atlantic Charter affirmed the U.S. government's commitment to these policies. The letter quickly turned antagonistic. The lack of action by the United States showed Koreans and the rest of the world only that "the Atlantic Charter was, in August of 1941, a thing of words rather than of deeds," but the Korean situation presented a unique opportunity to disprove this. Cromwell contended that Korean recognition also carried "practical and material aspects of vital importance to the United States." The 23 million Koreans in Korea represented an invaluable military asset for the United States in its war with Japan, which could be fully activated by the immediate recognition of the de facto government of Korea.[12]

Cordell Hull sent a blistering response. He pointed out that Koreans were one of several different national groups speaking for their countries of origin currently under military occupation by the Axis powers. Given this situation, Hull stated that the general policy of the U.S. government was "to avoid taking action which might, when the victory of the United Nations is achieved, tend to deprive peoples now under Axis yoke of full freedom to choose and establish their own governments." Hull continued that the question of recognition was further complicated by the presence of a "lack of unity, if not rivalry" within individual national groups seeking the independence of their countries. Given that several different Korean groups in the United States and other countries had sought to represent their compatriots in Korea, the U.S. government could not commit itself to a position that would require the "preferment" and maintenance of one alien group at the expense of another.[13]

Hull then accused Cromwell of trying to bargain for Korean recognition, implying that he was trying to politically blackmail the State Department by threatening to withhold Korean participation in the war effort as a means of forcing diplomatic recognition from the United States:

> It is difficult to believe that, as you imply, the group for whom you speak does not intend that the nation which they represent shall act on behalf of its freedom until this Government shall first have recognized your group as the de facto government of the nation for which they undertake to speak. Would this not imply—erroneously—that the service of which you speak is "for sale"; that the price is recognition of a certain group by the United States Government, this price to be paid in advance of any action by that nation? I find it indeed difficult to believe that such statements and implications contained in your letter represent the spirit of the people of Korea.[14]

Hull reiterated that the State Department was committed to the struggles of all subjugated peoples and that the U.S. government sought to provide "appropriate and practicable aid" for freedom from the "tyranny of aggressor nations." But U.S. support for the Atlantic Charter did not necessitate diplomatic recognition of a particular group that claimed to represent its nation. Hull concluded that the U.S. government welcomed contributions from any group in the common struggle against the Axis powers.[15]

Despite Hull's harsh admonitions, Cromwell responded to his letter. He maintained that the U.S. government had not taken concrete steps to provide Koreans with any type of "practicable aid" and accused the State Department of repeatedly failing to respond to the multiple requests for support from Korean representatives. Asking Hull to name the "other groups" who opposed recognition for the KPG, Cromwell countered that the Korean-American Council and its affiliated organizations represented the wishes of 90 percent of all Koreans in the United States. If 100 percent unity were required for practical aid and diplomatic recognition from the U.S. government, then "only totalitarian political organizations would ever be eligible."[16]

He continued that the KPG was best qualified "to undertake the grave responsibility of organizing revolutionary activities in Korea" and attached two lengthy documents as evidence of the KPG's legitimacy in representing Koreans back in Korea.[17] The first document contained numerous testimonials from former American residents in Korea attesting to the Korean people's trust and faith in Syngman Rhee and the KPG as their legitimate representatives. The second document, entitled "History of the Korean Provisional Government," consisted of a chronological narrative of its 23 years. The document also detailed the "long experience of its personnel in the arts of sabotage, guerilla warfare and secret organizations" that made the KPG uniquely qualified for organizing a mass revolution in Korea.[18] Cromwell concluded that his requests for aid to Korea were intended ultimately to help the United States win the war.

June 23 brought the final exchange between Cordell Hull and James Cromwell. Hull curtly told him that he was operating under incomplete information and that it appeared to the State Department that the Korean-American Council only "desires to engage in controversial argument."[19] He reaffirmed his Department's commitment to supporting the aspirations of all peoples, including Koreans, subjugated by the Axis powers. He referred any further discussions on the Korean question to Adolph Berle, Assistant Secretary of State.

In a memo most likely addressed to Syngman Rhee, Cromwell summarized his negotiations with the State Department. He concluded that the State Department was refusing to recognize the KPG on the basis that the existence of "various Korean groups" hindered the ability of the State Department to determine which group to recognize, though it refused to name those other groups. Cromwell concluded that further correspondence with the State Department would "obviously be a waste of time."[20]

Based on Cromwell's assessment, Syngman Rhee notified UKC headquarters in Los Angeles and Honolulu of tactical changes in the campaign for diplomatic recognition. He explained that the Korean-American Council had "exhausted every means in negotiating with the State Department.... Step by step a perfect record has been built up.... So the next step in our program is a nation wide publicity campaign." By distributing the history of the KPG and its negotiations with the U.S. government to obtain diplomatic recognition, Rhee and his associates at the Korean-American Council hoped to generate mass public support by exposing the State Department's myopic and flawed policy, given the current wartime exigencies. Rhee asked the UKC for $5,000 so that he could start the campaign without delay.[21]

A press release issued on August 14, 1942, by the Korean-American Council provided some indications of the new tactical direction. Released on the first anniversary of the Atlantic Charter, it critiqued "the callous disregard of the State Department to the Government of a country dedicated to democratic principles, and to the military potential of 23 million Koreans who hate their enslavers, the Japanese." The statement asserted that the Korean people, who were "ripe for revolt," could provide invaluable military aid to help the United States win the war.[22] However, that aid could only be mobilized through the State Department's implementation of the Atlantic Charter's pledge to restore the sovereign rights and self-government of those unjustly subjugated.

UKC officials, however, were reluctant to commit fully to such a plan. Honolulu UKC Chairman Lee Won Soon urged Rhee to hold off on the national publicity campaign. Referring to the acrimonious exchanges between Hull and Cromwell, Lee believed the independence movement could not risk further antagonizing potential supporters and that such "offending tactics" would only hurt their cause and delay recognition.[23]

Though the HONUKC was critical of Rhee and his plan, they remained sympathetic and supportive. In contrast, the Los Angeles headquarters, led by Executive Chairman Charles Ho Kim, was much less accommodating.

They saw the diplomatic blunder with the State Department as evidence of ineffective leadership and adamantly refused to grant the money on the grounds that they had no budgetary allotments for such contingent expenses. They further accused Rhee of squandering the financial support already provided.[24]

Rhee instead asked the Honolulu headquarters to send him a reduced amount of $2,500, for which it would not have to consult with Los Angeles headquarters.[25] The Honolulu UKC agreed to this, but emphasized that "unity and oneness in our purpose" were absolutely necessary and urged Rhee to negotiate an agreement with the Los Angeles office for the support of his publicity campaign. The Honolulu officials begged Rhee to stop trying to divide the two UKC offices:

> Supposing that we follow your request in sending cable remittance to you without consultation with L.A. Committee, where do you think we will stand in the future? We must stand together in our support in and for KOPOGO and the Korean Commission. We cannot afford to split again on this issue. Through the united effort of the United Korean Committee, KOPOGO and the Korean Commission receive undivided support financially and morally, and in case if we and L.A. Committee disagree on any issue, the united organization will be unfortunately wrecked and the subsequent result would be chaos and arguments back and forth among the Korean organizations. Repeated we can not afford to split again on this issue.[26]

Gravely concerned, UKC leaders in both Honolulu and Los Angeles took concrete steps to prevent further damage. In late September 1942, they agreed to send a representative from each branch to Washington, D.C., to consult with Rhee on developing a more efficient coordinated system of decision making and action. In preparation for the meeting, Jacob Dunn, Secretary of Public Relations, representing the Honolulu branch, and Charles Ho Kim, Executive Chairman of the LAUKC, wrote a four-point proposal entitled "United Korean Committee in America—A Memorandum." The conflicts regarding the national publicity campaign had exposed the need for more clearly defined coordination among the various groups involved in the struggle for national independence. The UKC pledged continued support for the Korean Commission and its mission of obtaining diplomatic recognition of the KPG, but criticized Rhee's recent attempts to make unilateral decisions without consulting the UKC and its members. The memo recommended that Rhee regularly inform the UKC headquarters of the "diplomatic and official business" of the Korean

Commission to ensure that the Commission could garner "the last ounce of public morale and financial support of the Korean people's full and limited capacity."[27]

To create some measure of accountability on Rhee's part, particularly on financial issues, and to curb his overall control over the daily operations of the Korean Commission, the memo called for the Korean Commission's reorganization to include the offices of a chairman, spokesperson, treasurer, and secretary. Rhee would continue to act as chairman, fully devoting his time to "planning and negotiating diplomatic subjects," while other administrative duties were to be delegated. The treasurer would maintain "close communication" in matters of finance with the UKC headquarters.[28]

Cognizant of the failed negotiations between the Korean-American Council and the U.S. Department of State earlier in the year, the UKC memo demanded that the Korean-American Council maintain a "separate identity and function" from the Korean Commission and the UKC.[29] Though affirming its support for the Korean-American Council, the UKC expressed its displeasure with the fallout from the antagonistic discussions. UKC officials hoped to avoid the Korean Commission's future involvement in "any possible American public or private political controversy . . . that might lead to embarrassment of the Korean Provisional Government as persona non grata."[30]

Though the memo pledged continued support for the Korean Commission, the last recommendation revealed a strong distrust of Rhee. The UKC planned to send two or three UKC representatives to China to work with KPG officials, explaining, "There has been a want of close and necessary information on vital questions between the Korean Provisional Government and the Korean Commission, between the Korean people in China and in the United States."[31] Besides serving as a liaison, the mission was also purported to be a fact-finding endeavor:

> For more convincing presentation of the case for Korean recognition or for obtaining American military aid there must be presented a truly Korean survey of facts and conditions relative to Korean groups, unity, personalities, plans, and potentialities. These facts may be best obtained through a mission as mentioned whose personnel must be made from responsible officials of the United Korean Committee in America.[32]

Rhee naturally saw the four-point memo as an attempt by the UKC to limit his power and authority over affairs in Washington. During his meetings with Jacob Dunn and Charles Ho Kim, he agreed, "There must be a line drawn between the Korean Commission and the two United Korean Committees so as to establish a basis of coordination among them." However, he asserted that implementing the recommendations contained in the UKC memo would only create additional "friction and misunderstanding" that resulted "when two or three organizations try to do the same thing in the same territory." Rhee offered a counterproposal. He claimed that the UKC was a "private" organization, representing the interests of the Korean populace residing in Hawaii and the mainland United States. In contrast, Rhee asserted that his office as chairman of the Korean Commission assumed the function of an "Envoy Extraordinary and Minister Plenipotentiary" to the KPG in China. As such, the Korean Commission possessed the status of a legation or embassy for the KPG, so "no private organization nor individual can encroach upon its authority." Rhee continued to see the primary responsibility of the UKC and its membership as fundraising to support the KPG and its Washington office, the Korean Commission. In turn, the Korean Commission would provide any necessary assistance to facilitate the UKC's fundraising activities, while avoiding "any interference in matters strictly concerning their own associations."[33]

Both Kim and Dunn left the meetings sorely disappointed. Shortly afterward, the LAUKC sent the HONUKC a telegram declaring that it could no longer support Rhee. Stating that the organization had "wasted enough time and public money" on Rhee, the LAUKC informed the Honolulu headquarters that it planned to petition the KPG for Rhee's recall from the post of chairman and a complete reorganization of the Korean Commission. The HONUKC urged the Los Angeles office to avoid taking any drastic measures, for fear that the KPG would look on the petition as an attempt to wrest control from Rhee based on personal rivalries. Denying personal motivations, the LAUKC saw the moment too important to take any further risks on Rhee, who had shown "no ability to carry out our diplomacy" and consistently put himself above his country.[34]

At the end of December 1942, James Cromwell of the Korean-American Council sent a series of letters to each UKC headquarters, defending the actions of Syngman Rhee and the Korean-American Council during the past year. He explained that Kilsoo Haan had surreptitiously obtained a copy of the letter in which Hull intimated that Cromwell was inappropriately bargaining for the recognition of the KPG during a time of national crisis. According to Cromwell, Haan widely publicized the confidential letter in his attempts to discredit the work of Syngman Rhee and the

Korean-American Council since Haan had been forced to resign from the UKC in February 1942 due to his rivalry with Rhee.[35] The letter was printed in the Korean immigrant press in the United States, causing the false "impression that [Korean-American Council] had been rebuked by the Secretary for seeking to sell revolutionary activities against the Japanese in exchange for recognition of the Korean Provisional Government." However, subsequent correspondences with the State Department clearly refuted the faulty impression caused by Haan's actions. Assistant Secretary of State Adolph Berle and Cromwell had come to agree "that the matter of Korea was strategic and military in nature and did not directly concern the State Department." Consequently, Cromwell determined that diplomatic recognition was no longer a prerequisite for obtaining "practicable aid" from the United States. Seeking to set the record straight by showing the "real attitude of Dr. Rhee and the Council," Cromwell demanded that UKC officials publish his letter in the UKC-affiliated newspapers: the *New Korea* and the *Korean National Herald-Pacific Weekly*.[36]

In providing this information, Cromwell also used the letters to neutralize Dunn and Kim's four-point memorandum. The proposal for additional officers in the Korean Commission was unnecessary and would only cause confusion: "Dr. Rhee is, in reality, the Ambassador of the Korean Provisional Government and we think one Ambassador in Washington is enough for the government." Cromwell also rejected the need for the UKC trip to Chungking, asserting that Rhee and KPG President Kim Ku had a long and distinguished record of successfully collaborating with each other for the cause of Korean independence. As a result, any sort of liaisons between the two officials was completely unnecessary and would only hinder their existing working relationship. Editors of both newspapers mutually agreed not to publish the letters for fear that they would foment hostilities.[37]

After arriving from Washington, D.C., LAUKC Chairman Charles Ho Kim set out on a lecture tour of Korean settlements throughout California. He vehemently denounced Syngman Rhee as an incompetent steward of the Korean Commission. Kim further criticized Rhee for refusing to consider the UKC recommendations for making the Commission more effective in its activities. According to Kim, Rhee's intransigence betrayed his intention to use the Commission for his own personal aggrandizement at the expense of the Korean people and his failure to represent the interests of his constituency. Kim ultimately hoped to have Rhee recalled from his post in Washington on the grounds that he was detrimental to the overall progress of the independence movement.[38]

Charles Ho Kim's lectures, however, had the opposite effect. His public charges against Rhee incensed important segments of the UKC constituency, including the pro-Syngman Rhee Tongjihoe. Tongjihoe members in California perceived Charles Ho Kim, a KNA member, to be engaged in a personal smear campaign against Rhee. Rhee supporters formed their own splinter group, calling themselves the Min Joong Dai Hoi (Great People's Assembly), within the UKC and convened two separate conventions in Los Angeles and Central California. The Min Joong Dai Hoi passed a number of resolutions in which they pledged their complete support and loyalty to Rhee and the Korean Commission, while denouncing the LAUKC as unpatriotic:

> [A] few unscrupulous and selfish persons in the Los Angeles Office of the United Korean Committee in America, usurping the good name of that organization and misusing the privileges of their official positions, [have] launched themselves into acts of individual self-aggrandizement at an incalculable expense to the public good, and thus at this most critical moment have deliberately caused a division among our people in America....[39]

The Min Joong Dai Hoi voted to no longer send its funds to the LAUKC and to instead remit them directly to the KPG and KORIC. Ironically, the attempt to create greater unity through the creation of the UKC in 1941 only led to more internecine conflicts within the Korean nationalist movement in the United States by 1943.

The search for prompt resolution of the impasse became the focal point of the Second Annual UKC Conference held in Los Angeles during the spring of 1943. The stabilization of relations between the Commission, headed by Syngman Rhee, in Washington and the leadership of the LAUKC headquarters was the top priority. UKC leadership hoped to define a clear and single channel of representation in Washington, D.C., which could effectively coordinate activities with Honolulu, Los Angeles, and Chungking.[40]

The efforts to broker a working compromise were led by the HONUKC, which had managed to steer clear of the acrimonious conflict between the LAUKC and the Commission. To avoid the appearance of any partisanship, negotiations for a compromise were directed by Warren Kim, a high-ranking member of the KNA of Hawaii and executive treasurer of the HONUKC, and Lee Won Soon, who served as chairman of both the HONUKC and the Hawaii chapter of the Tongjihoe. Warren Kim, to whom the LAUKC had entrusted its support, handled the primary negotiations with

Syngman Rhee. Under the terms of the compromise, the UKC as a whole would continue to support Syngman Rhee in his official capacity as chair of the Korean Commission. In turn, Rhee agreed to broaden representation in the Washington office, which involved an expansion of its personnel and increased involvement of the UKC in the formulation of its policies. To ensure the proper implementation of these changes, Kim and Rhee agreed on the creation of a coordinating commission, headed by Lee Won Soon and composed of representatives from both the KNA and Tongjihoe. If Rhee failed to observe the terms of this compromise, Kim told him in no uncertain terms that the UKC would initiate a mass campaign to mobilize Korean support in Hawaii and the continental United States against Rhee and establish a new Korean representative body in Washington as a direct rival to him.[41]

In seeking to restore and maintain unity, conference delegates also agreed that the LAUKC should not resume its monthly remittances to the Commission until the Min Joong Dai Hoi ceased sending money directly to Rhee and returned to the official practice of remitting funds through the LAUKC. The UKC conference also ordered the dissolution of the Min Joong Dai Hoi and advised its members to join either the Tongjihoe or KNA.[42]

Despite the compromise, the fiercely partisan makeup of the UKC remained intact. By the fall of 1943, the HONUKC also found itself in conflict with Syngman Rhee over his administration of the Korean Commission. Increasingly frustrated with Rhee's leadership in Washington, the HONUKC board of directors convened a special meeting in Honolulu on October 9, 1943, where they voted for the removal of Rhee from his post in Washington, D.C. After extensive deliberations, the board of directors decided to ask the KPG in Chungking to reorganize the Korean Commission in Washington, D.C., and in the process to dismiss Syngman Rhee from his position as chairman of the Korean Commission and reassign him to a new post as counselor to the Foreign Ministry of the Korean government. In his place, the UKC, under the sanction of the KPG, would assume the activities of the Korean Commission.[43]

Under the HONUKC proposals, Rhee would play an advisory role as an "elder statesman," but cease his day-to-day control over the affairs of the Korean Commission. The HONUKC announced their decision in its newspaper, *The Korean National Herald-Pacific Weekly*, in which the organization expressed its dissatisfaction with the ineffective and divisive leadership of Syngman Rhee as chair of the Korean Commission, his repeated failure to advance the Korean cause in government circles in

Washington, D.C., and his recurrent tactics of fomenting factionalism among Koreans in the United States.[44] At a regular session on November 9, 1943, UKC officials unanimously passed a resolution officially severing ties between the UKC at large and Syngman Rhee. On December 20, the UKC cancelled all support for the Korean Commission.[45] Days later, the Tongjihoe of Hawaii announced that its members had voted to withdraw all Tongjihoe participation from the UKC.[46] The united front was officially over.

The UKC's break with Rhee represented the emergence of a new generation of leaders among Koreans in the United States. By 1943, the Korean independence movement in America had been active for some 25 years, and longtime leader Syngman Rhee was nearly 70 years old. Younger men, such as Jacob Dunn, Warren Kim, Henry C. Kim, Ilhan New, Yongjeung Kim, and Kilsoo Haan, were emerging as prominent voices in the movement. This new cadre of leaders consisted of men in their forties and fifties, who had come to Hawaii as children or young students and had spent a great portion of their lives residing in the United States. This middle generation planned to pursue careers in their chosen fields and professions after obtaining their college and postgraduate degrees from U.S. institutions, but during World War II, many instead channeled all their time and energy into American defense and war activities.[47] As emergent political leaders, they often came into conflict with the senior generation of leaders whom they believed were stubbornly clinging to outdated, impractical modes of leadership. They called for a more active, vibrant, and practical leadership to mobilize war and independence activities among Koreans in Hawaii and the U.S. mainland.

For these younger leaders, effective Korean representation and leadership in Washington, D.C., during wartime were particularly crucial to the success of the Korean independence movement. Jacob Dunn was one of the most vocal critics of Syngman Rhee's leadership in Washington. In a series of editorials published in the *Korean National Herald-Pacific Weekly*, he emphasized that the war had provided unprecedented opportunities for advancing the Korean cause in Washington, D.C., suggesting that "when war has ended, the Korean people had better have done something more tangible than elocution and in some fashion be prepared to make their case extraordinarily strong or the question of an independent Korea will prove an autopsy."[48] Dunn proposed a new program of action for the UKC. Since the KPG had denied HONUKC's request for the reorganization of the Korean Commission, Dunn and the UKC called for the creation of a new UKC office in Washington, D.C., which would operate

Figure 7.2.
"Middle-generation" leaders: the Korean Revolutionary Party in Los Angeles, which worked in conjunction with the Sino-Korean People's League. Front row (*left to right*): Kyung Sun Lee, Sang Ryup Park, Choon Ho Pyon, Haeran Kim, and Kilsoo Haan. Back row (*left to right*): Key Hyung Chang, Doo Sik Shinn, and Nung Ik Choi.
Source: Korean American Digital Archive, University of Southern California.

separately from the Korean Commission and undertake a program of "research, publicity, and public relations." Dunn and other UKC leaders believed that the lack of a clear, well-informed policy on the Korean Question in Washington, D.C., presented the largest obstacle to the efficacy of Korean nationalist activities in the United States. "Information of Korean research as compiled by Koreans has been practically nil in the United States and none of significance is on any available file. Calls have been known to be made of certain Korean organizations in Washington and elsewhere for Korean data and have been regretfully unfilled."[49] As the war in the Pacific continued, the UKC Washington office needed to be able to provide "accurate and up-to-date information on Korean matters" as part of Korean contributions to the U.S. war effort. Dunn also stressed that such information "will be of inestimable need at the postwar conferences in the adjudication and settlement of questions dealing with the Far East and of Korea."[50]

Dunn's plans clearly positioned Korean immigrant political activities and aspirations within the context of the U.S. war effort and made Korean independence completely contingent on a U.S. victory over Japan. In the process, the transnational linkages between Korean nationalists in the United States and the KPG in China were relegated to a secondary concern. Dunn also entrusted the United States with guiding and assisting in the postwar planning of a liberated Korea, making Korean reliance on U.S. sovereignty a permanent condition.

The announcement of the Cairo Declaration on December 1, 1943, heightened UKC calls for the need to establish an office in Washington, D.C. As part of the three-power pledge to prosecute the war until Japan's unconditional surrender, the declaration announced that the signatories "were determined that in due course Korea shall become free and independent." Koreans in the United States celebrated this as the long-awaited commitment to their cause from the Allied powers and believed it represented an official statement assuring full Korean participation in the United Nations (UN) war efforts and in the postwar planning of Korea.[51]

However, the diplomatic communiqué contained several troubling elements. The phrase "in due course" indicated no specific timetable for Korean independence, suggesting that independence would come after the consideration of more pressing concerns. Moreover, the Cairo Declaration established that Korea would be liberated from the Japanese through the actions of the three powers, rather than directly through the hands of the Korean people themselves, which seemed to suggest that a liberated Korea would likely be ruled by some type of trusteeship or mandate under the United States and other powers until the Korean people were capable of self-governance.

Though some sectors of the Korean nationalist movement, particularly the KPG, were wary of these implications in the Cairo Declaration, UKC leaders like Jacob Dunn did not find the ambiguities inconsistent with their goals and activities for national independence. In an editorial in the *Korean National Herald-Pacific Weekly*, Dunn urged the Korean community to see the Cairo Declaration as encouraging Korean independence. He explained that the assurance of Korean independence "in due course" was justified on a practical level given the debilitating effects of 33 years of Japanese colonialism in Korea and "until such a time as Korean strength and organizational permanency is seen."[52] For UKC leaders, the intentions expressed in the Cairo Declaration were in keeping with their proposed program. UKC leaders recognized that the KPG did not have the authority or resources as a sovereign state to defeat the Japanese with its own military force and could only gain independence by becoming a part of the UN war campaign against the Japanese. UKC leaders argued that the current situation provided ample opportunities for Koreans throughout the diaspora to demonstrate "commendable and dependable statesmanship" by cooperating with the Allied powers in the common struggle against Japan, which would demonstrate their ability for self-administration.[53] Dunn confidently asserted: "We accept 'in due course' and are determined to prove our legitimacy to 'at once.' And in this stand we look to the United States in particular for counsel and guidance."[54]

Jacob Dunn and Warren Kim attended the Third Annual UKC Conference in Los Angeles held in April 1944. There, they presented their views and plans to the entire UKC delegate body, stressing the need to immediately establish a UKC office in Washington, D.C., to effectively centralize and direct Korean war participation.[55] By the end of the conference, the UKC delegates voted to accept the proposal and approved of its personnel, which included Warren Kim, Jacob Dunn, Chinho Tough, and Yongjeung Kim, all whom were among the newly emergent leaders of the middle generation.[56] Just two months later, Dunn and the others announced the opening of their Washington office to American government agencies and the KPG in Chungking.[57] UKC officials in Los Angeles and Washington declared without equivocation that the UKC's relationship with Syngman Rhee had been permanently severed and it would no longer support Rhee's activities as chairman of the Korean Commission. Stating that recognition from the U.S. State Department was "beyond practicable realization" for the foreseeable future due to Rhee's failures, the UKC suggested that the KPG engage in negotiations with the Chinese government for Chinese recognition, which they believed was more within the "realm of practical politics." At the same time, UKC leaders in Washington believed that the United States, of the three powers committed to Korean independence, was the most able to aid the Koreans during and after the war.[58] The UKC office in Washington thus indirectly positioned itself at the center of the nationalist movement due to its accessibility to American government agencies, reflecting its unconditional acceptance of U.S. sovereignty as a requisite to Korean independence.

As the diplomatic recognition of the KPG became a less pressing priority for the UKC, it strove to achieve other forms of U.S. recognition for the status of Koreans. On May 6, 1944, Lieutenant General Robert C. Richardson, Jr., Military Governor of Hawaii, issued General Order No. 59 that officially lifted the "enemy-alien" status held by all Koreans in Hawaii since December 1941. Koreans in Hawaii enthusiastically viewed this as the official recognition of Koreans as "friendly aliens," allied with the United States in the common war against Japan. No longer burdened with the stigma of enemy-alien status, they publicly expressed their gratitude and trust in the United States. A Korean writer boldly pronounced in the *Honolulu Advertiser* that "Koreans in Hawaii not only feel free but are inspired to redouble their work and sacrifices for complete Allied Victory and the Independence of Korea."[59]

A few weeks later, Hawaii delegate Joseph R. Farrington introduced a bill in the House of Representatives proposing to "authorize the admission into the United States, under a quota for Koreans, persons of the Korean race, to make them racially eligible for naturalization, and for other purposes."[60] Though Farrington publicly acknowledged that the bill would meet powerful opposition in Congress, he believed that it would illustrate for Americans the considerable contributions made by Koreans in the present war efforts, thus making them deserving of "the same rights and privileges as citizens of Caucasian stock."[61] Soon after the announcement of the bill, a UKC official in Hawaii told the *Honolulu Star Bulletin* that "leaders of the Korean community are unanimous in their feeling that the Koreans have at last been given some recognition in their forty years of fight for freedom."[62]

Other Korean statements of support focused on the more "domestic" implications of the bill. While acknowledging that the passage of the bill would benefit the large number of older-generation Koreans, an editorial in the *Korean National Herald* asserted that the right to naturalization for those of the middle generation held even greater significance for the Korean community as a whole:

> Well-educated and well-cultured in American ways of life, it seems a pity that this middle generation should be branded as alien. With the armour of American citizenship protecting their names and position, they should be able to contribute much to the civic and political welfare of the community. No doubt some of them are qualified to become territorial representatives and even senators as well as the municipal officers if only they were classed as citizens.[63]

For this writer, the Farrington bill provided Koreans, "who had abandoned the hope ever of becoming American citizens," a cherished opportunity to become a part of the daily fabric of American life. Through their involvement in the Korean nationalist movement, Korean immigrants came to demand the recognition and fair treatment of their interests and status abroad, as well as in the United States. In seeking to acquire a legitimate foreign policy voice in the United States, Koreans sought inclusion in the American polity and developed a collective identity as ethnic Americans.

Despite these seemingly promising developments, unexpected news from the KPG disrupted Korean nationalist activities in the United States. On August 12, 1944, the KPG, without any advance notice, issued a plan outlining the reorganization of Korean representation in Washington, D.C., which shut down both the Korean Commission and the UKC office. Instead, a new representative group was to be created under the name of the Korean Diplomatic Mission, which would take direct orders from the KPG and handle all diplomatic affairs with the U.S. government. Seeking to unify the nationalist activities among Koreans in the United States, the KPG ordered that the Mission be composed of representatives from all factions in the United States, namely Rhee's Tongjihoe and the KNA. It ordered Korean leaders in the United States to convene a nominating convention to recommend a list of possible candidates to hold officer posts, from which it would appoint seven to fifteen individuals.[64]

Though surprised by the sudden announcement, Korean leaders in the United States readily complied with the KPG's plan. In accordance with orders from the KPG, nationalist organizations in Hawaii and Los Angeles held separate nominating conventions, but the Tongjihoe refused to participate in either. As a result, the list of nominations submitted to the KPG did not contain any Tongjihoe members, including Syngman Rhee. In late November 1944, the KPG announced the officers for the reorganized diplomatic office in Washington, D.C. To the surprise of all, it appointed Syngman Rhee chairman, with representatives from the other organizations in supporting positions. Jacob Dunn and other younger leaders were not included. The KPG claimed that it rejected the submitted lists of nominees on the grounds that the Tongjihoe had not been represented and it had used its own discretion to select nine names from all the major organizations. The decision angered Koreans in the United States, who believed the KPG had completely disregarded their input and once again favored Syngman Rhee at the expense of the wishes of the Korean majority in the United States and Hawaii.[65] Efforts at the unification of Korean nationalist organizations had again failed miserably, leaving the movement even more fractured than before. In the aftermath of the KPG's decision, only the Tongjihoe would continue to support the KPG and KORIC. By the summer of 1945, four different Korean offices were operating in Washington, D.C., largely separate from each other.

Though the Koreans in the United States wholeheartedly trusted the United States to serve their interests in the cause for Korean independence, the U.S. government's confidence in the Korean people was hardly mutual. In fact, the formulation of U.S. policies for postwar Korea had had very little to do with the actual desires of the Korean people. Throughout World War II, the issue of Korean independence held a secondary position in the minds of most American policy makers. The suggestion in the Cairo Declaration that Korea should become independent "in due course" was due to the intervention of President Franklin D. Roosevelt.[66] Roosevelt's personal involvement in the writing of the Korean section of the Cairo communiqué—his inclusion of such a phrase—reflected a general attitude of disdain toward the Koreans by most U.S. policy makers, who believed the Korean people were unfit for self-government. The disunity among Korean exile nationalists in the United States no doubt contributed to these attitudes. By the time of the Cairo conference, the U.S. government had already committed itself to a policy of trusteeship for Korea after the war and, while there, Roosevelt hoped to reach a "mutual understanding" with China on the future of a postwar Korea.[67] At the Tehran Conference, two days later, he met with Josef Stalin and secured his tentative agreement on a trusteeship. When the Pacific War Council met on January 12, 1944, Roosevelt stated that Stalin had concurred "that Koreans are not yet capable of exercising and maintaining independent government and that they should be placed under a 40-year tutelage."[68]

Soon thereafter, the U.S. State Department began preparations for formulating specific plans for the nature of the trusteeship. In March 1944, the Inter-Divisional Area Committee on the Far East prepared three reports on the postwar occupation and military government of Korea. Warning against the serious political repercussions of a military occupation by one single power, the reports recommended a four-power trusteeship involving the United States, Great Britain, China, and the Soviet Union. When the Allied powers gathered at the Yalta Conference in February 1945, the United States proposed a four-power occupation based on a single centralized administration, rather than one organized around separate zonal divisions. In seeking to neutralize the traditional geopolitical rivalries between the Soviet Union and China over the mutually contiguous Korean peninsula, the United States pressed its case to direct the occupation, citing "the trust which Koreans will place in the United States not to harbor imperialistic designs."[69]

By the spring of 1945, the United States had managed to secure a multilateral agreement for a postwar trusteeship in Korea, but FDR's death created unexpected setbacks for the implementation of the original trusteeship plan as his successor, Harry S. Truman, had far less experience and skill in diplomatic matters. Moreover, Chinese warnings about Soviet domination of the Korean peninsula even under a four-power trusteeship greatly alarmed U.S. officials. With growing fears of Soviet motives, the United States began to retreat from its earlier proposals. By July 1945, the United States had successfully exploded an atomic bomb and secretly began to plan for an early end to the war with Japan. At the Potsdam Conference the same month, President Truman avoided any substantive discussions on the trusteeship for Korea, in the hopes that U.S. military forces could unilaterally occupy Korea while Soviet forces remained mired in battle with Japanese troops in Manchuria. However, the Japanese military folded rapidly after the atomic bombs dropped in Nagasaki and Hiroshima in early August, and Soviet forces advanced through Manchuria more quickly than anticipated by the United States. Aware that unilateral occupation of Korea was now highly unlikely, the U.S. military took immediate action to ensure partial occupation of the peninsula. Drawing a line at the 38th parallel, the Korean peninsula was divided into two separate zones: one under the Soviet Union and the other controlled by the United States. Ironically, the hasty actions of the United States to contain the Soviets ensured that at least half of the Korean peninsula would be firmly under Communist control.[70]

Conclusion

The postliberation division of the Korean peninsula at the 38th parallel and the joint Soviet and U.S. occupation polarized political forces in Korea, resulting in the establishment of two separate states in the north and south in 1948. Once again, foreign powers occupied the Korean peninsula, preventing its national self-determination. The postwar occupation and division soon led to the catastrophe of the Korean War, which left millions of Koreans dead, devastated the landscape and infrastructures throughout the entire peninsula, leaving the partition in place as a jagged border fewer than 40 miles north or south of the 38th parallel, and hardening the separation between North and South Korea all—of which resulted in decades of repressive authoritarian regimes in both Koreas.

The postwar conditions that contributed to the Korean War and its aftermath are often framed within a Cold War narrative that emphasizes the struggle between two superpowers for global dominance. Such perspectives, however, elide the significance of the Korean War as a civil war fought to unify the nation and to determine its political character and vision. As such, the ideological conflicts between the two Koreas after liberation were more the product of the anticolonial struggle against Japan than the result of U.S.-Soviet machinations.[1] The national liberation movement had not only sought to free Korea from Japanese colonial rule, but also to establish a sovereign political state that represented a "new Korea." Japanese repression in Korea necessitated that nationalist activities be conducted in the diaspora. However, the local contexts of the Korean diaspora, particularly the very different political worlds in which Korean émigrés operated, produced a variety of differing and conflicting visions of a new Korean nation-state. The ideological antagonism between rightist and leftist visions, in particular, became the primary source of conflict that divided the nationalist movement, preventing the formation of a unified national state.

The ideological conflicts that beset the nationalist movement became even sharper when Korea was liberated. Japan's surrender to Allied forces in August 1945 created a vacuum of leadership in Korea. The occupying forces found no acceptable government in place as no broad political coalition existed in and out of Korea that could assume leadership. Moreover, no individual or organization could make legitimate claims to have liberated Korea since liberation came as result of the Allied powers' victory over Japan. Chaos consequently ensued as Koreans from the entire political spectrum vied for national leadership.[2] The aspirants to power included prominent political leaders and their supporters from the diaspora who returned to Korea following liberation. These leaders emerged from the left-right divide in the nationalist movement abroad. On the right, Kim Ku and Syngman Rhee arrived from China and the United States, respectively. Among the most notable left-oriented returnees were Yo Un-hyong from China and Kim Il Sung from Manchuria. During their years abroad, both Yo and Kim had forged strong nationalist credentials through their active involvement in anti-Japanese activities.

One of the first to arrive in Korea, Yo Un-hyong, a moderate leftist, immediately initiated efforts to establish a broad left-right coalition of nationalist groups. These efforts to create a middle ground, however, failed to mount an effective challenge to extreme left and right elements who sought to maintain the inner division of Korea for their own political gain. Aligning themselves with the occupying forces and ruthlessly eliminating their political rivals, Kim Il Sung in the north and Syngman Rhee in the south emerged as the dominant political figures. With the backing of the Soviet Union and the United States, the two leaders established two separate states in 1948: the Democratic People's Republic of Korea in the north and the Republic of Korea in the south. Kim and Rhee each claimed the sole right to govern over the entire peninsula. These tensions soon escalated into a civil war between the two Koreas that developed into an international conflict.

The two Koreas formed after liberation clearly emerged from the two major strands of the independence movement: the American group and Siberian-Manchurian group. The political ideologies and rivalries formed during the anticolonial struggles provided the foundation for the leadership cadre, the governing structures, and policies of the two Korean states.

Kim Il Sung and his fellow Manchurian veterans who emerged to power in North Korea were profoundly influenced by their experiences with the anti-Japanese guerilla struggle in Manchuria that sought complete and unconditional independence for Korea. Kim drew heavily on the tradition of armed resistance and Korean autonomy in the frontier region of Manchuria in his efforts to create a revolutionary socialist system in the Democratic People's Republic of Korea that emphasized an ideology of self-reliance.[3]

In a similar manner, the origins of the South Korean state, headed by Syngman Rhee, were directly linked to the nationalist activities of the American group, which emphasized U.S. diplomatic recognition of the KPG. Dominating these efforts, Rhee's name became virtually synonymous with the KPG during much of its 26-year history. The KPG provided a blueprint for the new South Korean state. It not only adopted the name, the Republic of Korea, from the KPG, but also used the KPG's U.S.-inspired constitution in creating its own constitution in 1948. The strategic reliance on the U.S. nation-state as a guarantor of the national goals of Koreans that emerged from the nationalist movement also profoundly shaped the domestic and foreign policies of South Korea, which came to be manifested in a neocolonial relationship with the United States.

The unconditional acceptance of U.S. state power developed from the internal contradictions of state-making in the diaspora. The globalization of American power after World War I enabled the U.S. component of the diaspora to play an instrumental role in charting the vision of a new Korean nation-state that was reflected in the formation of the KPG and its ancillaries in 1919. Woodrow Wilson's wartime proclamations about national self-determination firmly established the sovereign nation-state as the standard form of political organization acknowledged around the world after World War I.[4] The efforts to create the KPG reflected Korean nationalists' understanding of the workings of the international system in which external recognition from other sovereign states was instrumental in a nation-state's authority and legitimacy. The creation of the Provisional Government in Shanghai therefore was a significant step in institutionalizing a sovereign political entity that could be considered a legitimate actor within the global community of nation-states. However, formed entirely in the diaspora, the Korean nation-state, as represented by the KPG, was a deterritorialized entity that was simultaneously founded on a nationalist discourse intrinsically grounded in territorialized constructions of the modern nation-state. In effect, the Korean nation-state had paradoxically transcended itself on its creation.⁵ As a consequence, the KPG lacked the basic defining feature of a sovereign state—the administrative control of a defined territory based on the legitimate monopoly over the means of violence to exact obedience from all persons within its territorial boundaries.⁶ Though the KPG exhibited the institutional framework of a sovereign state, it had neither a clearly defined territory to govern nor the coercive authority to control and direct its national constituency in the diaspora. As a result, the KPG was unable to develop a working consensus that could implement effective policies that addressed the multiple and diverse ideological and strategic perspectives on the liberation of Korea arising from the diaspora. Bitter contests developed over political strategies and preferred modes of governance. These difficulties of defining and achieving coherent political action under diasporic conditions posed a perpetual dilemma for the Korean nationalist movement throughout its existence. The nationalist movement failed to establish a unified national state that could act with sovereign authority to respond to the needs and well-being of its national constituents in the diaspora.

Given these constraints, U.S.-based Koreans increasingly came to rely on the United States to act as a sovereign state to pursue the national interests of Koreans throughout the diaspora. While American global power and influence enabled the U.S. component of the Korean diaspora to achieve a certain degree of political agency in and out of the United States, this political empowerment was ultimately subordinated to a hegemonic American worldview that envisioned a new postwar international order modeled in its own image. Korean diasporic political activities unintentionally served to affirm and reinforce U.S. global hegemony and power. Though direct colonialism in Korea had come to an end with the conclusion of World War II, the new Korean nation became entangled in a new set of neocolonial relations and dynamics in the postwar period. This neocolonial dependency would have tragic consequences for the Korean people: American military intervention in a civil war, repressive U.S.-backed military dictatorships in the south, the deepening of the gulf separating North and South Korea, and the continual presence of American military troops stationed on the Korean peninsula that persists to the early 21st century. In the end, Korean diasporic nationalism could never fully liberate itself from the power structures of imperialism from which it had so fervently struggled to be free.

Diasporic political mobilization also had unintended consequences for the status of Korean immigrants in the United States. Transnational participation in the diasporic nationalism of the independence movement exerted a nationalizing effect on Korean migrants in the United States as they were deeply invested in claiming and sustaining a national Korean identity outside of Korea as part of the nationalist quest for sovereign statehood. This national identity, as an expression of Korean nationalist politics, was firmly grounded in a sense of belonging and loyalty to a Korean nation and its state. However, as the result of the failure of the diaspora to create a national state that could act with sovereign authority, U.S.-based Koreans increasingly relied on the sovereignty of the U.S. state to advance their collective interests and status in both America and abroad. In pursuit of these interests, Korean immigrant organizations lobbied institutions of the U.S. state apparatus in the executive, legislative, judiciary, and military branches. In the process, Korean immigrants emerged as a distinct political interest group in the United States, whereby ethnicity served as an organizational resource for making nationalist claims and demands in the U.S. political arena. This claims-making on the American state reflected the articulation of an ethnic consciousness among Korean immigrants as they came to define their political interests in relation to U.S. state structures and society. In short, Korean nationalism played a key role in the Americanization of Korean immigrants.

The political assimilation of Korean immigrants, however, did not ensure free and equal access to American political processes. Racially biased citizenship laws in the United States prevented them from participating in electoral politics in a manner like European immigrant groups until after World War II with the passage of the 1952 McCarran-Walter Act.[7] With no choice but to engage in noncitizen-based politics, Korean immigrants were constantly in search of patronage from sponsors in the military, political, legal, and religious sectors of the U.S. polity. In endorsing the United States as a global power and leader, these activities helped Korean immigrants establish themselves as an American ethnic group with political interests in Korea, but their racialized status left them essentially pleading their cause as stateless supplicants. This political position, determined by racially biased laws, directly limited their participation in mainstream American life, ensuring that Korean American ethnicization was one of subordination to U.S. hegemony rather than participation in the benefits of that hegemony.

Given their experiences as racial minorities, the development of an ethnic consciousness among Koreans in America could have created new loyalties and alliances that diverged from the goals and allegiances associated with Korean independence. However, the historical evidence shows that no such coalitions coalesced in the years prior to 1945. So how did Korean immigrants in the United States reconcile the apparent contradictions between their seemingly indefatigable support for American political values and ideals of democracy, freedom, and self-determination and the daily realities of an exclusionary United States that denied them rights to become full and equal members of American society?

As reflected in the experiences of Korean immigrants in the United States, diasporic identifications with the homeland ironically facilitated assimilation into the American political system. Operating within the structures of U.S. global hegemony, the processes of Korean diasporic mobilization emphasized the positive pluralist, inclusionary aspects of American society, co-opting the possibilities of making more radical claims on the U.S. state.[8] In becoming ethnicized within the context of American pluralism, the politics of Korean immigrant nationalism did not seek to challenge or undermine the legitimacy of American political culture, structures, and institutions. In the years after 1945, the development of a collective identity in tune with U.S. global hegemony would position the U.S. component of the Korean diaspora to serve as a carrier of postwar American order. It allowed them to situate themselves in an anti-Communist U.S. national narrative in which America played the role of protector and guarantor of freedom for South Korea against the threat of North Korea and Communism, which continues to shape the politically conservative makeup of contemporary Korean American communities that have developed from renewed immigration since the Korean War. While the global Cold War has ended, it obstinately persists in the Korean diaspora and a peninsula still divided into two separate rival states, likely ensuring that the quest for sovereign statehood will remain unfulfilled for another generation.

NOTES

INTRODUCTION
1. *Hemet News*, June 20, 1913, 1; *Los Angeles Times*, June 27, 1913, I1; *Hemet News*, June 27, 1913, 1.
2. *Hemet News*, June 27, 1913, 1; *Los Angeles Times*, June 27, 1913, I1; *San Francisco Chronicle*, June 27, 1913, 8; *New York Times*, June 27, 1913, 9; *Sinhan Minbo*, July 4, 1913, 3.
3. *Hemet News*, June 27, 1913, 1; *Los Angeles Times*, June 27, 1913, I1; *Sinhan Minbo*, July 4, 1913, 3; *New York Times*, June 27, 1913, 9.
4. *San Francisco Chronicle*, June 27, 1913, 8; *New York Times*, June 27, 1913, 9; *Los Angeles Times*, June 28, 1913, I1.
5. *San Francisco Chronicle*, June 27, 1913, 8.
6. *Los Angeles Times*, June 27, 1913, I1; *Los Angeles Times*, June 28, 1913, 11; *New York Times*, June 28, 1913, 7.
7. *New York Times*, April 5, 1913, 3.
8. *Los Angeles Times*, June 28, 1913, I1; *New York Times*, June 29, 1913, C4.
9. *Sinhan Minbo*, July 4, 1913.
10. *Sinhan Minbo*, July 4, 1913, 2; and Melendy, *Asians in America*, 135.
11. *Sinhan Minbo*, July 4, 1913.
12. *Los Angeles Times*, July 2, 1913, I4; *Hemet News*, July 4, 1913, 1.
13. Moon, "Korean Immigrants in America," 389–91; Warren Y. Kim, *Koreans in America*, 56; Houchins and Houchins, "The Korean Experience in America," 561.
14. *Hemet News*, July 4, 1913, 1; *Sinhan Minbo*, July 4, 1913, 3.
15. *Los Angeles Times*, July 6, 1913, II-8; *Hemet News*, July 11, 1913, 1.
16. *Los Angeles Times*, July 6, 1913, II-8; *Hemet News*, July 11, 1913, 1.
17. Trewartha and Zelinsky, "Population Distribution and Change in Korea," 14.
18. The principle of the territorially sovereign state is derived from the Westphalian system of states, which has served as the basis for modern political identity and organization in the form of the modern Western nation-state system. See Biersteker and Weber, eds., *State Sovereignty as Social Construct*; Held, *Democracy and the Global Order*; and Guibernau, *Nations Without States*.
19. I derive my use of nationalism as fundamentally rooted in concerns for state-building from the works of John Breuilly, *Nationalism and the State*, and Matthew Frye Jacobsen, *Special Sorrows: The Diasporic Imagination of Irish,*

Polish, and Jewish Immigrants in the United States. Other useful formulations of nationalism that inform this study include Anderson, *Imagined Communities*; Chatterjee, *Nationalist Thought*; Dirks, Eley, and Ortner, eds., *Culture/Power/History*; Greenfeld, *Nationalism: Five Roads to Modernity*; Guibernau, *Nations Without States*; Schiller and Fouron, *Georges Woke Up Laughing*; Gerstle, *American Crucible*; Iriye, *The Globalizing of America 1913–1945*; and Rosenberg, *Spreading the American Dream*.

20. For further discussion on the concept of diaspora, see Butler, "Defining Diaspora"; Siu, *Memories of a Future Home*; Safran, "Diasporas in Modern Societies"; Clifford, "Diasporas"; Robin Cohen, *Global Diasporas*; McKeown, "Conceptualizing Chinese Diasporas"; Gabaccia, *Italy's Many Diasporas*; and Braziel and Mannur, eds., *Theorizing Diaspora*.

21. San Kim with Nym Wales, *Song of Ariran*, 113–14.

22. Chong-sik Lee, *The Politics of Korean Nationalism*; Scalapino and Lee, *Communism in Korea*, Part I; Suh, *The Korean Communist Movement*.

23. Rogers, *Afro-Caribbean Immigrants*; Janelle S. Wong, *Democracy's Promise*.

24. The literature is too voluminous to cite here. Representative works include Vecoli, "The Contadini in Chicago"; Greene, *Slavic Community on Strike*; Gutman, "Work, Culture, and Society in Industrializing America"; Yans-McLaughlin, *Italian Immigrants in Buffalo*; Camarillo, *Chicanos in a Changing Society*; Miller, *Emigrants and Exiles*; Cinel, *From Italy to San Francisco*; Gabaccia, *From Sicily to Elizabeth Street*; and Morawska, *For Bread and Butter*. John Bodnar, in *The Transplanted: A History of Immigrants in Urban America*, ably synthesizes the major findings from this large body of literature.

25. Nagel, "The Political Construction of Ethnicity," 79.

26. Ibid., and Brass, "Ethnic Groups and the State," 8; Glazer and Moynihan, "Introduction," *Ethnicity: Theory and Experience*.

27. The literature on political participation among American ethnic groups engaged in homeland politics is vast. Works most useful for this study include Jacobsen, *Special Sorrows*; Shain, *Marketing the American Creed Abroad*; Tony Smith, *Foreign Attachments*; Yans-McLaughlin, ed., *Immigration Reconsidered*; O'Grady, ed., *The Immigrants' Influence on Wilson's Peace Policies*; Gerson, *The Hyphenate in Recent American Politics*; Jaroszynska-Kirchmann, *The Exile Mission*; Von Eschen, *Race Against Empire*; Guglielmo, *White on Arrival*; Gabaccia, *Militants and Migrants*; Gerstle, *Working-Class Americanism*; Miller, *Emigrants and Exiles*; Poyo, "With All, and for the Good of All"; Ichioka, *The Issei*; Azuma, *Between Two Empires*; Ma, *Revolutionaries, Monarchists, and Chinatowns*; Yu, *To Save China, To Save Ourselves*; Chan, ed., *Chinese American Transnationalism*; K. Scott Wong and Sucheng Chan, eds., *Claiming America*; Tsai, *China and the Overseas Chinese*; Puri, *Ghadar Movement*; Juergensmeyer, "The Ghadar Syndrome"; and Jensen, *Passage from India*.

28. Vecoli, "Ethnicity and Immigration."

29. Hattam, "Ethnicity: An American Genealogy"; Gerstle, "Liberty, Coercion, and the Making of Americans."

30. Roediger and Barrett, "Making New Immigrants 'Inbetween'".

31. Sucheng Chan, "European and Asian Immigration," 61–62.

32. Hattam, "Ethnicity: An American Genealogy"; Brass, "Ethnic Groups and the State"; Gerstle, "Liberty, Coercion, and the Making of Americans"; Omi and Winant, *Racial Formation*; Iris Young, *Justice and the Politics of Difference*.
33. The prominent role played by leadership in the processes of ethnic and national group formation is well known. For instance, see Higham, *Ethnic Leadership in America*, and "Leadership"; Greene, *American Immigrant Leaders*; Duara, "Historicizing National Identity"; Eley and Suny, "Introduction," *Becoming National*; Hobsbawm, *The Age of Revolution*; Breuilly, *Nationalism and the State*; Gellner, *Nations and Nationalism*; Anthony D. Smith, *Theories of Nationalism*; Marr, *Vietnamese Tradition on Trial*; and Chatterjee, *Nationalist Thought*.

CHAPTER 1

1. Robinson, *Korea's Twentieth-Century Odyssey*, 20–23.
2. Trewartha and Zelinsky, "Population Distribution and Change in Korea," 14.
3. See Peter Duus, *The Abacus and the Sword*, for an excellent analysis of Japanese imperialist motives in Korea.
4. This relationship was articulated in the concept of *sadae kyorin*. *Sadae* (literally translated as "serving the big") referred to Korea's relations with China, whereas *kyorin* (literally translated as "friendly dealings with the neighbor") related to its relations with Japan. Under this Confucian-based East Asian world order, Korea perceived China as its elder brother and Japan as its equal. See Kim and Kim, *Korea and the Politics of Imperialism*, 12.
5. Cumings, *Korea's Place in the Sun*, 101–2; Kim and Kim, *Korea and the Politics of Imperialism*, 17–18.
6. Robinson, *Korea's Twentieth-Century Odyssey*, 27.
7. Kim and Kim, *Korea and the Politics of Imperialism*, 18–29; Cumings, *Korea's Place in the Sun*, 102–7.
8. Cumings, *Korea's Place in the Sun*, 115.
9. Eckert, et al. *Korea Old and New*, 222.
10. Ki-baik Lee, *A New History of Korea*, 288–90.
11. Duus, *The Abacus and the Sword*, 188–89.
12. Moon, "Korean Immigrants in America," 59.
13. Pomerantz, "The Background of Korean Emigration," 294–95.
14. Ibid., 299; Moon, "Korean Immigrants in America," 58; Bernice Kim, "The Koreans in Hawaii," 85.
15. Moon, "Korean Immigrants in America," 60–61.
16. Patterson, *The Korean Frontier in America*, 109.
17. Moon, "Korean Immigrants in America," 56–57.
18. The Organic Act of 1900 made all U.S. laws applicable in Hawaii, thus banning contract labor on the islands. However, many Koreans could not afford the passage to Hawaii from Korea. Plantation owners paid for the passage on the condition that the laborers had to work to repay the passage fare, although all types of contract labor were banned.
19. Bernice Kim, "The Koreans in Hawaii," 104.
20. Patterson, *The Korean Frontier in America*, 122; Moon, "The Koreans in Hawaii," 169.

21. Patterson, *The Korean Frontier in America*, 121–22; Choy, *Koreans in America*, 77.
22. Patterson, *The Korean Frontier in America*, 127–28; Pomerantz, "The Background of Korean Emigration," 302–4.
23. Patterson, *The Korean Frontier in America*, 128–35.
24. Ibid.
25. Ibid., 81–82.
26. Responding to nativist pressures, the 1924 Immigration Act established the permanent exclusion of any "alien ineligible for citizenship." Since Asians were denied the right of naturalization under an 1870 statute, further Asian immigration to the United States came to a decisive halt in 1924. Asian immigration would not resume again until after the end of World War II.
27. Patterson, *The Korean Frontier in America*, 188–89.
28. Yim, "Social Structure of Korean Communities in California," 520.
29. Ibid., 519.
30. Chan, *Asian Americans: An Interpretative History*, 37.
31. Yim, "Social Structure of Korean Communities in California," 519.
32. Chan, *Asian Americans: An Interpretative History*, 37.
33.. Moon, "The Koreans in Hawaii," 178.
34. Richard S. Kim, "Korean Tenant Rice Farming."
35. Moon, "The Koreans in Hawaii," 93, 97.
36. For more on Asian immigrant experiences in agriculture, see Sucheng Chan, *This Bittersweet Soil*, and Yuji Ichioka, *The Issei*.
37. Yim, "Social Structure of Korean Communities in California," 520; U.S. Bureau of Census, *Fifteenth Census of the United States: 1930*, Vol. II, *Population-General Report*, 27.
38. Yim, "Social Structure of Korean Communities in California," 520–21; Givens, "The Korean Community in Los Angeles County," 22; U.S. Bureau of Census, *Fifteenth Census of the United States: 1930*, Vol. II, *Population-General Report*, 81.
39. Korean migrations to Manchuria and Siberia began much earlier than the organized mass immigration of laborers to Hawaii. Large-scale migration of Koreans to Manchuria commenced in the 1860s. From 1866 to 1869, significant portions of northern Korea experienced consistently poor harvests, which caused severe famines at unprecedented levels. Massive administrative breakdowns resulting from rampant corruption and factionalism within the rapidly deteriorating Yi dynasty only exacerbated the dire situation for many Korean peasants residing in the northern regions of the Korean peninsula. As a result, large numbers of Korean families crossed the border into the Chientao region of Manchuria during this time.

    After the Japanese protectorate in 1905, migrations into Manchuria increased dramatically in the years between 1907 and 1910. After the protectorate agreement, Japan systematically confiscated agricultural lands from Koreans throughout the peninsula. Japan's economic encroachment displaced large numbers of peasants, many of whom immigrated to the fertile fields of Chientao. The post-1905 migrations also included increasing numbers of anti-Japanese political activists and intellectuals who sought refuge from persecution by the Japanese. Immigration to Manchuria increased steadily for decades after 1905. By the 1920s, the Korean population in Manchuria numbered more than half a million.

Like the mass migrations to Manchuria, Korean immigration to Soviet Far Eastern territories, particularly Siberia, commenced in the 1860s. Scores of peasants suffering from the economic hardships in northeastern Korea migrated to Siberia. After 1905, another series of mass migrations to Siberia occurred as a result of Japan's tightening of control over Korea. As in the case of immigration to Manchuria during this time, migrants to Siberia included both peasants and political refugees. By the 1920s, the Korean population in Siberia numbered well over 100,000.

40. Not unlike the U.S. component of the Korean diaspora, the experiences of Koreans in Manchuria and Siberia were entangled in the web of Sino-Japanese and Russo-Japanese geopolitical struggles, which often centered on competing claims of legal jurisdiction over the Korean émigré communities in Manchuria and Siberia, respectively. These conditions of statelessness and exile produced a common sense of marginality and lack of full belonging to any one nation-state experienced by Koreans across the diaspora.

A detailed examination of the political experiences of Korean émigrés in Manchuria and Siberia is beyond the scope of this study. However, there is a large body of scholarly materials on these experiences written in numerous languages including Korean, Chinese, Japanese, Russian, and English. A sampling of English-language materials used in this study include C. Walter Young, "Korean Problems in Manchuria," 249–80; Hyun Ok Park, "Korean Manchuria: The Racial Politics of Territorial Osmosis"; Brooks, "Peopling the Japanese Empire"; Piao, "The History of Koreans in China"; Armstrong, "Centering the Periphery"; Chong-Sik Lee, *Revolutionary Struggle in Manchuria*; Chong-sik Lee, *The Politics of Korean Nationalism*; Scalapino and Lee, *Communism in Korea*; Suh, *The Korean Communist Movement*; Hara, "The Korean Movement in the Russian Maritime Province"; Wada, "Koreans in the Soviet Far East"; Pak, "The Anti-Japanese Korean Independence Movement in Russian Territories"; Saveliev, "Militant Diaspora"; and Kolarz, *Peoples of the Soviet Far East*.

CHAPTER 2

1. *San Francisco Chronicle*, March 24, 1908; *Sinhan Minbo*, January 12, 1910.
2. *National Cyclopedia of American Biography*, Vol. 13, 577; "Mr. Durham White Stevens," *Prominent Americans Interested in Japan*, 13.
3. Nahm, "Durham White Stevens," 127–28.
4. Kim and Kim, *Korea and the Politics of Imperialism*, 121–25; *National Cyclopedia of American Biography*, Vol. 13, 577; *San Francisco Call*, March 24, 1908; Patterson, *The Korean Frontier in America*, 151; Nordmann, "Idealism, Immigration and Imperialism," 151; Nahm, "Durham White Stevens," 118–19.
5. Nahm, "Durham White Stevens," 120–21; Nordmann, "Idealism, Immigration and Imperialism," 152.
6. Duus, *The Abacus and the Sword*, 193; Nordmann, "Idealism, Immigration and Imperialism," 229–30.

7. Nordmann, "Idealism, Immigration and Imperialism," 232; Nahm, "Durham White Stevens," 125–26.
8. Nahm, "Durham White Stevens," 126.
9. *San Francisco Chronicle*, March 21, 1908.
10. *San Francisco Chronicle*, March 21, 1908; *San Francisco Call*, March 21, 1908; *San Francisco Examiner*, March 22, 1908.
11. Ibid., March 27, 1908.
12. Ibid., March 23, 1908.
13. *San Francisco Chronicle*, March 23, 1908; *San Francisco Call*, March 23, 1908; *Los Angeles Times*, March 23, 1908.
14. *San Francisco Call*, March 23, 1908.
15. *San Francisco Chronicle*, March 24, 1908; *San Francisco Chronicle*, March 23, 1908; *Los Angeles Times*, March 23, 1908; *San Francisco Call*, March 23, 1908.
16. *San Francisco Chronicle*, March 24, 1908; Moon, "Korean Immigrants in America," 337.
17. *San Francisco Examiner*, March 24, 1908; *San Francisco Call*, March 24, 1908; *Konglip Sinbo*, March 25, 1908.
18. *San Francisco Examiner*, March 24, 1908; *San Francisco Chronicle*, March 24, 1908; *Los Angeles Times*, March 24, 1908; *San Francisco Call*, March 24, 1908.
19. Ibid.
20. *San Francisco Call*, March 24, 1908; *San Francisco Examiner*, March 24, 1908.
21. *Los Angeles Times*, March 24, 1908; *San Francisco Call*, March 24, 1908.
22. *San Francisco Call*, March 24, 1908; *San Francisco Examiner*, March 25, 1908.
23. Moon, "Korean Immigrants in America," 338–39.
24. *San Francisco Call*, March 25, 1908; *Los Angeles Times*, March 24, 1908.
25. *San Francisco Chronicle*, March 25, 1908.
26. *San Francisco Examiner*, March 26, 1908; *San Francisco Chronicle*, March 26, 1908, March 27, 1908.
27. *San Francisco Chronicle*, March 27, 1908, April 1, 1908.
28. *San Francisco Call*, April 11, 1908; *Konglip Sinbo*, April 15, 1908.
29. *Konglip Sinbo*, April 15, 1908, May 20, 1908, June 10, 1908.
30. *Konglip Sinbo*, March 25, 1908.
31. *Los Angeles Times*, March 25, 1908; *Konglip Sinbo*, March 25, 1908.
32. *San Francisco Chronicle*, December 22, 1908.
33. Warren Y. Kim, *Koreans in America*, 50–53; Moon, "Korean Immigrants in America," 295–300.
34. Moon, "Korean Immigrants in America," 355.
35. Ibid.
36. *Konglip Sinbo*, April 1, 1908.
37. *San Francisco Chronicle*, March 28, 1908; *San Francisco Call*, April 9, 1908; *San Francisco Examiner*, April 9, 1908; *Los Angeles Times*, July 28, 1908, September 22, 1908.
38. *Konglip Sinbo*, March 25, 1908.
39. *Konglip Sinbo*, April 29, 1908.
40. *Konglip Sinbo*, March 25, 1908. Also quoted in *San Francisco Chronicle*, March 27, 1908.

41. *Konglip Sinbo*, March 25, 1908; *San Francisco Chronicle*, March 27, 1908.
42. *San Francisco Examiner*, March 26, 1908.
43. *San Francisco Chronicle*, March 24, 1908; *San Francisco Examiner*, March 25, 1908, March 26, 1908, March 27, 1908; *Los Angeles Times*, March 25, 1908.
44. *San Francisco Chronicle*, March 25, 1908; *San Francisco Examiner*, March 24, 1908, March 25, 1908.
45. *San Francisco Chronicle*, March 24, 1908; *San Francisco Call*, March 24, 1908.
46. For instance, in the March 24, 1908, edition of the *San Francisco Chronicle*, numerous lengthy articles sympathetic to Korean grievances against Stevens and Japan included: "Coreans Regard Him as Agent of Japan," "Koreans Tell How They Planned to Kill Him," "Corean Youths Tell Why They Wanted Stevens' Life," "Corean Youths Attempt the Assassination of D.W. Stevens— Regard Him as Betrayer of Country," and "Says Japanese Rule Is Cruel."
47. Moon, "Korean Immigrants in America," 351; Warren Y. Kim, *Koreans in America*, 83.
48. *San Francisco Call*, April 9, 1908.
49. Moon, "Korean Immigrants in America," 351.
50. *Konglip Sinbo*, June 17, 1908, July 28, 1908.
51. *Los Angeles Times*, December 9, 1908.
52. *San Francisco Chronicle*, December 17, 1908, December 18, 1908; *San Francisco Examiner*, December 18, 1908, December 23, 1908; *San Francisco Call*, December 17, 1908, December 19, 1908; *Los Angeles Times*, December 15, 1908.
53. *San Francisco Chronicle*, December 22, 1908; *Los Angeles Times*, December 21, 1908, December 23, 1908.
54. *San Francisco Examiner*, December 23, 1908; *San Francisco Chronicle*, December 24, 1908, December 28, 1908.
55. *San Francisco Call*, December 24, 1908; *Los Angeles Times*, December 23, 1908; *San Francisco Chronicle*, December 23, 1908.
56. *Los Angeles Times*, December 23, 1908; *San Francisco Call*, December 17, 1908, December 23, 1908; *San Francisco Chronicle*, December 24, 1908.
57. *San Francisco Chronicle*, December 24, 1908; *San Francisco Examiner*, December 27, 1908; Moon, "Korean Immigrants in America," 360; Warren Y. Kim, *Koreans in America*, 84.
58. *San Francisco Examiner*, December 27, 1908; *San Francisco Call*, December 27, 1908.
59. *San Francisco Chronicle*, January 3, 1909. After serving ten years of his sentence in San Quentin, Chang was released on parole for good behavior on January 10, 1919. However, he suffered from severe depression in the years after his release and committed suicide at the age of 55 in 1930.
60. *San Francisco Chronicle*, January 3, 1909; *Los Angeles Times*, January 3, 1909.
61. *Sinhan Minbo*, February 26, 1914.
62. Moon, "Korean Immigrants in America," 303.
63. Warren Y. Kim, *Koreans in America*, 55–57.
64. *Sinhan Minbo*, March 24, 1909.
65. Won-yong Kim, *Chaemi Hanin 50-yonsa*, 86; Moon, "Korean Immigrants in America," 303–5.

66. *Sinhan Minbo*, February 10, 1909.
67. Gardner, "An Ch'Ang-Ho, Advocate of Gradualism," 151–52; Moon, "Korean Immigrants in America," 275–76; Warren Y. Kim, *Koreans in America*, 55–57.
68. *Sinhan Minbo*, December 1, 1909.
69. *Sinhan Minbo*, November 30, 1909.
70. These Koreans in Merida were among the 1,000 Koreans who first migrated to Mexico in 1905. A contingent of these immigrants eventually migrated to Cuba, where a Korean National Association chapter was also established.
71. *Sinhan Minbo*, February 26, 1914; Won-yong Kim, *Chaemi Hanin 50-yonsa*, 86–96; Warren Y. Kim, *Koreans in America*, 54.
72. Despite the change in name from the Kukminhoe (Korean National Association) to Daehanin Kukminhoe (All Korea Korean National Association), the organization continued to be referred to generally as Kukminhoe or Korean National Association (KNA).
73. Given the great distance between them, proxies from the San Francisco office served as representatives for the Mexico, Manchuria, and Siberia branches.
74. Won-yong Kim, *Chaemi Hanin 50-yonsa*, 92; *Sinhan Minbo*, February 26, 1914; Lyu, "Korean Nationalist Activities, Part I (1900–1919)", 58.
75. Won-yong Kim, *Chaemi Hanin 50-yonsa*, 91–93.
76. Gardner, "An Ch'Ang-Ho, Advocate of Gradualism," 156.

CHAPTER 3

1. Eckert, et al., *Korea Old and New*, 279–80; Ki-baik Lee, *A New History of Korea*, 344.
2. Iriye, *The Globalizing of America, 1913–1945*; Rosenberg, *Spreading the American Dream*; Eckes and Zeiller, *Globalization and the American Century*; Ninkovich, *The Wilsonian Century*; McMahon, "The Republic as Empire."
3. Man-gil Kang, *A History of Contemporary Korea*, 23–34.
4. Yossi Shain, ed. *Governments-in-Exile in Contemporary World Politics*.
5. Man-gil Kang, *A History of Contemporary Korea*, 32.
6. Man-gil Kang, "Nature and Process of the Korean National Liberation Movement," 7.
7. Chong-sik Lee, *The Korean Workers' Party*, 3–6; Scalapino and Lee, *Communism in Korea*, 22; Armstrong, *The North Korean Revolution*, 20–21.
8. Scalapino and Lee, 9; Man-gil Kang, *History of Contemporary Korea*, 53.
9. Scalapino and Lee, *Communism in Korea*, 5; Man-gil Kang, *A History of Contemporary Korea*, 34; Pak, "Anti-Japanese Korean Independence Movement in Russian Territories," 38; Chong-sik Lee, *The Korean Workers' Party*, 105; Chong-sik Lee, *The Politics of Korean Nationalism*, 139–40, 157; Armstrong, *The North Korean Revolution*, 20–21.
10. Man-gil Kang, *A History of Contemporary Korea*, 24, 29, 34–37; Ki-baik Lee, *New History of Korea*, 364.
11. Man-gil Kang, *A History of Contemporary Korea*, 36; Chong-sik Lee, *The Politics of Korean Nationalism*, 140.
12. Ki-baik Lee, *New History of Korea*, 365–66; Chong-sik Lee, *The Korean Workers' Party*, 105; Ch'oe, et al., *Sources of Korean Tradition*, Vol. II, 341.

13. Soon-ok Hong, "Legitimating of the Shanghai Provisional Government"; Man-gil Kang, *A History of Contemporary Korea*, 30–32.
14. Kimura, "Korean Minorities in Soviet Central Asia," 86–87; Piao, "History of Koreans in China," 49.
15. Soon-ok Hong, "Legitimating of the Shanghai Provisional Government," 58–63; Man-gil Kang, *A History of Contemporary Korea*, 31.
16. Scalapino and Lee, *Communism in Korea*, 10, 12.
17. Man-gil Kang, *A History of Contemporary Korea*, 23–24.
18. San Kim with Nym Wales, *Song of Ariran*, 113–14.
19. Manela, *The Wilsonian Moment*.
20. Manela, *The Wilsonian Moment*; Iriye, *The Globalizing of America, 1913–1945*, 46–48; DeConde, *Ethnicity, Race, and American Foreign Policy*, 88–89; Schulzinger, *Time for War*, 9.
21. Chong-sik Lee, *The Politics of Korean Nationalism*; Scalapino and Lee, *Communism in Korea*; Suh, *The Korean Communist Movement*.
22. *Proceedings of the First Korean Congress*, 27.
23. Ibid., 26.
24. Ibid., 29.
25. The details of Jaisohn's naturalization case are somewhat obscure. At the time, Koreans were barred from U.S. citizenship. However, Jaisohn apparently received assistance from socially prominent individuals in Philadelphia who sponsored his naturalization through a private bill submitted to the U.S. Congress. Jaisohn's marriage to Muriel Armstrong, a niece of former U.S. President James Buchanan, in 1896 seems to corroborate his close association with prominent social circles. I am indebted to K.W. Lee for this information about Jaisohn's naturalization case.
26. *Proceedings of the First Korean Congress*, 8.
27. Ibid., 79–82.
28. *Korea Review* 1, no. 3 (May 1919): 90.
29. *Proceedings of the First Korean Congress*, 29–30.
30. Patterson, *The Korean Frontier in America*.
31. In his insightful study of the dynamics of exile politics, political scientist Yossi Shain explains that exile groups often seek to attract international support for their struggles by "latching onto issues that the global international community finds symbolically resonant." See Shain, *The Frontier of Loyalty*, 127.
32. Timothy S. Lee, "Protestantism and the 1919 March First Movement," 139; U. S. National Archives, *Records of the Department of State Relating to Internal Affairs of Korea (Chosen), 1910–1929*, reel 3, Decimal File 895.00/639, 22.
33. *Proceedings of the First Korean Congress*, 30.
34. Ibid., 26–27.
35. Cynn, *The Rebirth of Korea*.
36. *Proceedings of the First Korean Congress*, 80–82.
37. Ki-baik Lee, *A New History of Korea*, 344–45.
38. *Proceedings of the First Korean Congress*, 36.
39. Ibid., 35.
40. Zihn Choi, "Early Korean Immigrants to America," 66.

41. *Proceedings of the First Korean Congress*, 14–17.
42. Ibid., 30–31.
43. Ibid., 70–71.
44. U.S. National Archives, *Records of the War Department General and Special Staffs*, Record Group 165, Military Intelligence Division (hereafter cited as U.S. National Archives, Record Group 165), Decimal File 1766-1391/2b-2c.
45. *Korea Review* 1, no. 4 (June 1919): 13.
46. Ibid., 12–13.
47. *Korea Review* 2, no. 4 (June 1920): 18.
48. Henry Chung expanded on these points in his two scholarly books on the significance of the "Korean Question" for international stability and peace: *The Oriental Policy of the United States* and *The Case of Korea*.
49. U.S. National Archives, *Records of the Department of State Relating to Internal Affairs of Korea (Chosen), 1910–29*, reel 3, Decimal File 895.00/639, 47.
50. Commission on Relations with the Orient, *The Korean Situation*, 6.
51. Reed, *The Missionary Mind*.
52. Thomson, Stanley, and Perry, *Sentimental Imperialists*.
53. Baldwin, "The March First Movement," 150.
54. Choy, *Koreans in America*, 160; Warren Y. Kim, *Koreans in America*, 132–33.
55. U.S. Congress, *Congressional Record: 1st Session of the 66th Congress*, Vol. 58, Part 3, 2594–97.
56. Unbeknown to Hulbert, as well as most members of the U.S. Congress at the time, the United States in 1905, under the initiative of President Theodore Roosevelt, had actually accommodated Japan's colonial ambitions in Korea. Prior to the beginning of the peace negotiations at Portsmouth, the United States and Japan had secretly signed the Taft-Katsura agreement, in which the United States agreed to Japanese control in Korea in return for Japanese acceptance of American dominance in Hawaii and the Philippines. American acquiescence to, and complicity with, Japan's control over Korea removed all remaining obstacles for Japan to assume full control over the Korean peninsula, precipitating Japan's declaration of Korea as a protectorate in November 1905, and formal annexation as a colony in 1910.
57. *Congressional Record, 1st Session of the 66th Congress*, Vol. 58, Part 4, 3924–26.
58. *Congressional Record, 1st Session of the 66th Congress*, Vol. 58, Part 6, 6172.
59. Ibid., 7476.

CHAPTER 4

1. Definitions of the concept of civil society have been subject to widely differing interpretations. Such variance in defining civil society owes to the fact that its meanings and usages have changed over time. My use of the term "civil society" here is derived from more contemporary formulations that conceptualize civil society as local intermediate associations of voluntary activity, operating in a sphere of autonomy from the state and the market, such as social movement groups, political lobbying groups, labor unions, religious groups, and business and other professional associations. For instance, see Robert Putnam, *Making Democracy Work: Civic Traditions in Modern Italy*. In the context of U.S. political

discourse, this conceptualization of civil society is often associated with the political culture of pluralism and interest groups. For other useful discussions, see Cohen and Arato, *Civil Society and Political Theory*; Edwards, *Civil Society*; Ehrenberg, *Civil Society: The Critical History of an Idea*; Diamond, "Rethinking Civil Society: Toward Democratic Consolidation"; and Edwards, Foley, and Diani, eds., *Beyond Tocqueville: Civil Society and the Social Capital Debate in Comparative Perspective*.
2. Myers, *Korea in the Cross Currents*, 26–27.
3. Soon-ok Hong, "Legitimating of the Shanghai Provisional Government," 41–64; Man-gil Kang, *A History of Contemporary Korea*, 30–32; Zihn Choi, "Early Korean Immigrants to America," 55.
4. Warren Y. Kim, *Koreans in America*, 142–47.
5. U.S. National Archives, Record Group 165, Military Intelligence Division (MID) 1766-1004, "Memoranda Concerning Korean Commission Policy and with Regards to Controversies with the Korean National Association."
6. Zihn Choi, "Early Korean Immigrants to America," 57.
7. Moon, "Korean Immigrants in America," 216. For more on Korean rice farming activities, see Richard S. Kim, "Korean Tenant Rice Farming in Glenn County, California, 1916–1925: An Economic Niche for an Immigrant Community in Transition."
8. Box 4: Folder 11. Hei Sop Chin Collection, Korean American Research Project, Department of Special Collections, University of California, Los Angeles (hereafter cited as Hei Sop Chin Collection).
9. U.S. National Archives, Record Group 165, MID 1766-1004; *Korea Review* 1, no. 4 (November 1919): 12; Warren Y. Kim, *Koreans in America*, 126; and *Sinhan Minbo*, March 20, 1919.
10. U.S. National Archives, Record Group 165, MID 1766-1391: 18B (9/4/19), 17B (9/5/19), 18B (9/10/19), 18B (9/11/19).
11. U.S. National Archives, Record Group 165, MID 1766-1391, 17S (9/12/19).
12. Ibid., 17B (9/17/19).
13. Ibid., 17B (9/17/19).
14. The telegrams were sent to local chapters under the jurisdiction of the KNA that included: California (San Francisco, Dinuba, Riverside, Santa Barbara, Sacramento, Manteca, Los Angeles, Upland, Maxwell, Stockton, and Marysville); Washington (Yakima, Seattle, and Wenatchee); Colorado (Denver, Pueblo, and Brighton); Utah (Ogden and Brigham); Nevada (Overton); Wyoming (Rock Springs and Superior); Akron, Ohio; Detroit; Chicago; and New York City.
15. U.S. National Archives, Record Group 165, MID 1766-1391, 17W-17CC (9/18/19).
16. U.S. National Archives, Record Group 165, MID 1766-1004, "Memoranda Concerning Korean Commission Policy and with Regards to Controversies with the Korean National Association."
17. The struggle between the KNA and KORIC did not involve control over Koreans residing in Hawaii. In contrast to the KNA headquarters on the mainland, the KNA of Hawaii firmly supported Syngman Rhee. Records indicated that it directly remitted approximately $7,000 to KORIC in Washington,

D.C., during KORIC's conflict with the KNA office in San Francisco. U.S. National Archives, Record Group 165, MID 1766-1391: 17P (9/24/19, 11/1/19); 17Q (12/3/19, 12/17/19); 17R (12/24/19, 12/27/19).
18. U.S. National Archives, Record Group 165, MID 1766-1391: 17C (9/19/19).
19. U.S. National Archives, Record Group 165, MID 1766-1004; U.S. National Archives, Record Group 165, MID 1766-1391: 18B (9/22/19) and 18C (9/22/19).
20. U.S. National Archives, Record Group 165, MID 1766-1391: 17C (9/22/19) and 17EE (9/22/19).
21. Ibid., 17D-17E (9/24/19).
22. Ibid., 18C (9/25/19).
23. Ibid., 18C (9/23/19).
24. Ibid., 17C (9/23/19) and 17D (9/24/19).
25. Ibid., 17S (9/24/19).
26. As in Hawaii, KNA chapters east of Chicago were loyal supporters of Syngman Rhee and did not contest his directives issued through the Korean Commission.
27. Ibid., 18D (9/28/19).
28. U.S. National Archives, Record Group 165, MID 1766-1391: 17C (9/29/19).
29. U.S. National Archives, Record Group 165, MID 1766-1004.
30. Rhee, *Syngman Rhee Telegrams*, Vol. II; September 14, 1919, 130.
31. Warren Y. Kim, *Koreans in America*, 120–21.
32. U.S. National Archives, Record Group 165, MID 1766-1391: 18N (10/9/19).
33. Ibid., 18E (10/9/19).
34. Ibid., 17T (10/10/19).
35. Ibid., 17T (10/10/19).
36. Ibid., 17F (10/11/19).
37. Warren Y. Kim, *Koreans in America*, 127.
38. Diamond, "Rethinking Civil Society," 7.
39. Warren Y. Kim, *Koreans in America*, 127.
40. Diamond, "Rethinking Civil Society," 7.
41. Warren Y. Kim, *Koreans in America*, 127.
42. Rhee, *Syngman Rhee Telegrams*, Vol. II; October 15, 1919, 207.
43. U.S. National Archives, Record Group 165, MID 1766-1391: 18E (10/17/19).
44. Ibid., 18F (10/23/19) and 18G-H (10/26/19).
45. Ibid., 17G (10/23/19).
46. Rhee, *Syngman Rhee Telegrams*, Vol. II; October 24, 1919, 230.
47. U.S. National Archives, Record Group 165, MID 1766-1391: 17H and 18O (10/24/19).
48. Rhee, *Syngman Rhee Telegrams*, Vol. II; October 25, 1919, 232.
49. U.S. National Archives, Record Group 165, MID 1766-1391: 18G-H (10/26/19); *Syngman Rhee Telegrams*, Vol. II; October 25 and 26, 1919, 243 and 252.
50. Rhee, *Syngman Rhee Telegrams*, Vol. II; October 26, 1919, 244.
51. U.S. National Archives, Record Group 165, MID 1766-1391: 17U (10/26/19); Rhee, *Syngman Rhee Telegrams*, Vol. II; October 26, 1919, 241.
52. U.S. National Archives, Record Group 165, MID 1766-1391: 18h (10/29/19) and 17j (10/29/19).

53. Rhee, *Syngman Rhee Telegrams*, Vol. II; October 29, 1919, 261–68.
54. U.S. National Archives, Record Group 165, MID 1766-1391: 17j (11/19/19).
55. Ibid., 17k (12/01/19).
56. Ibid., 18j (12/19/19).
57. Ibid., 17L (12/19/19).
58. Ibid., 18J (12/31/19).
59. Choy, *Koreans in America*, 158.
60. Ban, "Korean Nationalist Activities," 494.
61. Chong-sik Lee, *The Politics of Korean Nationalism*, 309. These estimates are likely to be grossly underestimated. According to the financial records of the Korean Commission, Koreans in Hawaii alone contributed over $65,000 to the Korean Commission between 1919 and 1921. "Financial Papers," Box 3: Folder 11, Hei Sop Chin Collection, Korean American Research Project, Department of Special Collections, University of California, Los Angeles.
62. Chong-sik Lee, *The Politics of Korean Nationalism*, 149.
63. Rhee, *Syngman Rhee Telegrams*, Vol. II; December 14, 1919, 357.
64. Chong-sik Lee, *The Politics of Korean Nationalism*, 135, 147–53; Dae-Sook Suh, *The Korean Communist Movement*, 11–13.
65. Chong-sik Lee, *The Politics of Korean Nationalism*, 147–48; Scalapino and Lee, *Communism in Korea*, Part I, 5; Suh, *The Korean Communist Movement*, 11–13.
66. Chong-sik Lee, *The Politics of Korean Nationalism*, 148; Scalapino and Lee, *Communism in Korea*, Part I, 18–19; Suh, *The Korean Communist Movement*, 14.
67. Chong-sik Lee, *The Politics of Korean Nationalism*, 148; Scalapino and Lee, *Communism in Korea*, Part I, 15–16; Man-gil Kang, *A History of Contemporary Korea*, 33.
68. Man-gil Kang, *A History of Contemporary Korea*, 36.
69. Ibid., 35–37; Chong-sik Lee, *The Politics of Korean Nationalism*, 159–60; Ki-baik Lee, *New History of Korea*, 364.
70. Following the March First uprising in Korea, Japanese authorities came to view Koreans in Manchuria and the Maritime Province as disloyal and a dangerous threat to the Japanese empire, often referring to them as "recalcitrant Koreans" (*futei senjin*). Consequently, Japanese officials adopted oppressive measures to suppress and subordinate Koreans in Manchuria to Japanese authority. For more, see C. Walter Young, "Korean Problems in Manchuria as Factors in the Sino-Japanese Dispute," 249–80; Barbara J. Brooks, "Peopling the Japanese Empire: The Koreans in Manchuria and the Rhetoric of Inclusion," 25–44; Hyun Ok Park, "Korean Manchuria: The Racial Politics of Territorial Osmosis," 193–217; and Changyu Piao, "The History of Koreans in China and the Yanbian Korean Autonomous Prefecture," 60–84.
71. Chong-sik Lee, *The Politics of Korean Nationalism*, 159; Ki-baik Lee, *New History of Korea*, 364–65; Man-gil Kang, *A History of Contemporary Korea*, 36–37; Hara, "The Korean Movement in the Russian Maritime Province," 16–18.
72. Ban, "Korean Nationalist Activities," 466–69; Man-gil Kang, *A History of Contemporary Korea*, 36; Scalapino and Lee, *Communism in Korea*, Part I, 32; San Kim with Nym Wales, *Song of Ariran*, 116; Hyung-chan Kim, *Tosan Ahn Ch'ang-ho: A Profile of a Prophetic Patriot*, 162–64.

73. Chong-sik Lee, *The Politics of Korean Nationalism*, 149–50.
74. At the end of 1920, Kiusic Kimm resigned from the Korean Commission in Washington, D.C., and departed for Shanghai.
75. Chong-sik Lee, *The Politics of Korean Nationalism*, 150.
76. Ibid., 151.
77. Scalapino and Lee, *Communism in Korea*, Part I, 24, 36; Suh, *The Korean Communist Movement*, 16–17, 23.
78. Scalapino and Lee, 9–10, 36; Suh, *The Korean Communist Movement*, 21–24; Scalapino and Lee, "The Origins of the Korean Communist Movement (I)," 10; Choe, et al., *Sources of Korean Tradition*, Vol. II, 353.
79. Scalapino and Lee, "The Origins of the Korean Communist Movement (I)," 10; Wada, "Koreans in the Soviet Far East," 28; Chey, "Soviet Koreans and Their Culture," 62–63; Saveliev, "Militant Diaspora," 153.
80. Chong-sik Lee, *The Politics of Korean Nationalism*, 161–62; Scalapino and Lee, *Communism in Korea*, Part I, 5, 11, 33–37.
81. Scalapino and Lee, *Communism in Korea*, Part I, 32–34; Chong-sik Lee, *The Politics of Korean Nationalism*, 160–63; Suh, *The Korean Communist Movement*, 29–34.
82. Chong-sik Lee, *The Politics of Korean Nationalism*, 161, 177; Scalapino and Lee, *Communism in Korea*, Part I, 34–35; Suh, *The Korean Communist Movement*, 32–44.
83. The experiences of Koreans in Siberia would come to an abrupt and tragic end in 1937 when Joseph Stalin directly ordered the forced relocation of the entire Korean population in the Russian Far East to Kazakhstan and Uzbekistan in Soviet Central Asia. In all, some 170,000 Koreans were deported to these interior territories within the span of two months. The experiences of Koreans in Soviet Central Asia are beyond the scope of this book. For more, see the edited collection of essays in Dae-Sook Suh, *Koreans in the Soviet Union*; Michael Gelb, "An Early Soviet Ethnic Deportation: The Far-Eastern Koreans"; Songmoo Koh, *Koreans in Soviet Central Asia*; Terry Martin, "The Origins of Soviet Ethnic Cleansing"; and J. Otto Pohl, *Ethnic Cleansing in the USSR, 1937–1949*.
84. *Korea Review*, "An Appeal from the Korean Mission to the Washington Conference," October 1921, 6–8; Chong-sik Lee, *The Politics of Korean Nationalism*, 171–73.
85. U.S. National Archives, Records of the Department of State Relating to the Internal Affairs of Korea, Record Group 59, 1910-1929, Box 7146, Decimal File 795.00, Fred Dolph, "Brief for Korea," April 11, 1921, 9, 18.
86. Ibid., 12.
87. Ibid., 22.
88. *Korea Review*, December 1921, 4–7.
89. Ibid., 6.
90. Ibid., December 1921, "Friends of Korea Appeal to American Delegates," 7–8.
91. Ibid., "A Petition from Korea," December 1921, 15.
92. Chung, *Korea and the United States through War and Peace*, 83.
93. *Korea Review*, February 1922, 1–2.

94. Won-yong Kim, *Chaemi Hanin 50-yonsa*, 483–85; Chong-sik Lee, *The Politics of Korean Nationalism*, 165–66.
95. Warren Y. Kim, *Koreans in America*, 108–09; Chong-sik Lee, *The Politics of Korean Nationalism*, 165–66.
96. Chong-sik Lee, *The Politics of Korean Nationalism*, 166–67.
97. Warren Y. Kim, *Koreans in America*, 109; Chong-sik Lee, *The Politics of Korean Nationalism*, 168–69.
98. According to historian Man-gil Kang, the mid-1920s marked the end of the first period of the national liberation movement, which spanned the first half of the 1920s commencing with the March First uprising. See "The Nature and Process of the Korean National Liberation Movement during the Japanese Colonial Period," *Korea Journal* 36, no. 1 (1996): 5–19; and *A History of Contemporary Korea*. These works by Kang provide useful syntheses of the large body of Korean-language materials on independence movement activities among Korean émigrés in Manchuria and Siberia.
99. Ibid.
100. See Man-gil Kang, "The Significance of the Shin'gan-Hoe Society Movement in the History of the Korean National Movements," (*Korea Journal* 27), and *A History of Contemporary Korea* (pp. 60–69). Also, Michael E. Robinson, *Korea's Twentieth-Century Odyssey: A Short History* (pp. 56–73), and *Cultural Nationalism in Colonial Korea, 1920–1925*.

CHAPTER 5

1. Won-yong Kim, *Chaemi Hanin 50-yonsa*, 99–126; Warren Y. Kim, *Koreans in America*, 60–65; Sun-Pyo Hong, "The Unification Movement of the Hawaii Korean Community in the 1930s (hereafter cited as "Unification Movement"),179–80; Lyu, "Korean Nationalist Activities in Hawaii, Part II (1919–1945)," 69–70.
2. When the Kungminhoe (KNA) of Hawaii changed its name to Kyomindan in 1922, the organization decided to continue to use its English-language designation of the Korean National Association (KNA). As a result, the court system of Hawaii recognized the Kyomindan as the KNA. Since this chapter is primarily based on court records from the 1931 trial, I will adhere to the court's use of the name "KNA" rather than the Kyomindan.
3. "Police Guard Korean Hall to Keep Peace," *Honolulu Advertiser*, January 15, 1931; "Korean Faction May Resort to Court Action," *Honolulu Advertiser*, January 16, 1931; "Outline from Their Own Record (Minutes) of the Irregulars' Convention of Delegate Assembly," Box 4, Folder 1, Hei Sop Chin Collection; and D.Y. Shon, et al., "The Case of the Korean National Association" (March 27, 1931), State Archives of Hawaii, History and Miscellaneous.
4. "Korean Faction May Resort to Court Action," *Honolulu Advertiser*, January 16, 1931.
5. The original primary source materials are inconsistent in recording the personal names of Korean individuals. Because it is nearly impossible to determine the McCune-Reischauer spelling based on the transliterations in the original documents, I here use the spelling of personal names as printed in the

documents. Also, in order to maintain consistency with the rest of the book, I place the family surnames of individuals before their given names.

6. "Outline from Their Own Record (Minutes) of the Irregulars' Convention of Delegate Assembly," Hei Sop Chin Collection; and D.Y. Shon, et al., "The Case of the Korean National Association," State Archives of Hawaii, History and Miscellaneous.
7. "Koreans Battle to Determine Official Staff," *Honolulu Advertiser*, January 14, 1931; "Police Guard Korean Hall to Keep Peace," *Honolulu Advertiser*, January 15, 1931.
8. "Korean Faction May Resort to Court Action," *Honolulu Advertiser*, January 16, 1931.
9. Ibid.
10. Ibid.
11. Ibid.
12. "Korean Row Coming Into Court Today," *Honolulu Advertiser*, January 24, 1931.
13. "Koreans' Private War No Concern of Judge Brooks," *Honolulu Advertiser*, January 26, 1931.
14. "Gun, Wrench Used as Rival Camps Battle," *Honolulu Advertiser*, January 28, 1931.
15. "Judge Scores Korean Feud Disorders," *Honolulu Advertiser*, January 28, 1931.
16. Ibid.
17. "Deportation of Rioters Threatened," *Honolulu Advertiser*, January 30, 1931.
18. Ibid.
19. Hawaii State Judiciary, First Judicial Circuit, Territory of Hawaii, Petition for Writ of Mandamus to the Circuit Court, *Pai Yil Chin, et al. v. D. Y. Shon, et al.*, S.P. 170-1-170 (1931).
20. Ibid., 2–3.
21. Ibid., 3.
22. Ibid., 4–7.
23. Alternative Writ of Mandamus, Ibid., 7–8.
24. Return to Alternative Writ of Mandamus, Ibid., 2.
25. Ibid., 2–3.
26. Peremptory Writ of Mandamus, Ibid.
27. Appeal and Notice of Appeal, Ibid.
28. Hawaii State Judiciary, First Judicial Circuit, Territory of Hawaii, Petition on Writ of Quo Warranto to Circuit Court, *Shon Duk Yin, et al. v. Kim Chung Hyun and Choy Baik Yurl*, S.P. 171-1-171 (1931).
29. Ibid., 2–3.
30. Ibid., 4.
31. Ibid.
32. Ibid., 5.
33. Ibid.
34. Ibid.
35. Answer, Ibid.
36. "Outline from Their Own Record (Minutes) of the Irregulars' Convention of Delegate Assembly," Box 4, Folder 1, Hei Sop Chin Collection.

37. Ibid.
38. Answer, *Shon Duk Yin, et al. v. Kim Chung Hyun and Choy Baik Yurl*.
39. Hawaii State Judiciary, First Judicial Circuit, Territory of Hawaii, Petition to Circuit Court, *Pai Yil Chin, et al. v. Shon Kuk Yin, et al.*, E3171 (1931), 1–2.
40. Ibid., 5–7.
41. Ibid., 2–3.
42. Ibid., 3–4.
43. Ibid., 4–5.
44. Restraining Order, Chambers Summons, Receipts, and Answer, Ibid.
45. Answer, 2–3.
46. Ibid., 3.
47. Ibid., 4.
48. Ibid.
49. Ibid., 5.
50. Ibid., 6–10.
51. Ibid., 215–18; Sun-Pyo Hong, "Unification Movement," 182–84; Choy, *Koreans in America*, 163–64.
52. Sun-Pyo Hong, "Unification Movement," 182–84; Warren Y. Kim, *Koreans in America*, 125.
53. Sun-Pyo Hong, "Unification Movement," 182–85.
54. Henry Cu Kim, *The Writings of Henry Cu Kim*, 223; D. Y. Shon, et al., "The Case of the Korean National Association.". (March 27, 1931), State Archives of Hawaii, History and Miscellaneous.
55. Ibid.; "Conflict of Theories," Box 4, Folder 1, Hei Sop Chin Collection.
56. D. Y. Shon, et al., "The Case of the Korean National Association," State Archives of Hawaii, History and Miscellaneous.
57. Ibid.; Henry Cu Kim, *The Writings of Henry Cu Kim*, 233–34.
58. "Koreans Tell Their Story of Disorders," *Honolulu Advertiser*, February 23, 1931.
59. Ibid.
60. Ibid.; D. Y. Shon, et al., "The Case of the Korean National Association," 1, State Archives of Hawaii, History and Miscellaneous.
61. Ibid.
62. Ibid.
63. Hawaii State Judiciary, First Judicial Circuit, Territory of Hawaii, Brief on Behalf of the Petitioners to Circuit Court, *Pai Yil Chin, et al. v. Shon Kuk Yin, et al.*, E3171 (1931), 1.
64. Ibid., 1–3.
65. Ibid., 2–3.
66. Ibid., 3–7.
67. Ibid., 7–8.
68. "Brief on Behalf of Respondents"; Ibid., 4–5.
69. Ibid., 7.
70. Ibid., 5–10.
71. Ibid., 29.
72. Ibid., 11.
73. Ibid., 11–12.

74. Ibid., 26–27.
75. Ibid., 19–22.
76. Ibid., 40–41.
77. Decision; Ibid., 1–9.
78. Ibid., 9.
79. Ibid.
80. Lyu, "Korean Nationalist Activities in Hawaii, Part II (1919–1945)," 70.

CHAPTER 6

1. U.S. National Archives, Records of the Department of State, Record Group 59, Decimal File 894 (1930–39), (hereafter cited as U.S. National Archives, Decimal File 894) LM58 Reel 12, 894.202 11a: Haan, Kilsoo, Sino-Korean Peoples League, "Petition to the State and House of Representatives: Regular Session of 1935—Territorial Legislature," March 27, 1935, 14.
2. Sánchez, *Becoming Mexican American*, 11; Schultz, *Ethnicity on Parade*, 11–12; Conzen, Gerber, Morawska, Pozzetta, and Vecoli, "Forum: The Invention of Ethnicity," 5.
3. Choy, *Koreans in America*; Hyun, *A Condensed History of the Kungminhoe*; Warren Y. Kim, *Koreans in America*; Melendy, *Asians in America*; Savage, "The American Response to the Korean Independence Movement."
4. U.S. National Archives, Record Group 165, Regional File, Box 2267, Folder 1: Korea—Government Reports Concerning Haan, "Federal Bureau of Investigation Memorandum on Kilsoo Haan," August 28, 1942, 1; Box 2265, Folder 13: Korea—Nationalist Groups, "Korean Independence Movement in the United States and Hawaii," December 2, 1942, 7; Box 2260—Korea, File 3020: Kilsoo K. Haan, "Memorandum on Kilsoo K. Haan Propaganda Activities," December 20, 1943, 9.
5. U.S. National Archives, Office of Naval Intelligence, Oriental Desk, 1936–46, Record Group 38 (hereafter cited as U.S. National Archives, Record Group 38), Box 15, Folder—Analysis of the Korean Situation, "Topical Study—Analysis of the Korean Situation," August 13, 1943, 16; U.S. National Archives, Record Group 165, Box 2265, Folder 13: Korea—Nationalist Groups, "Korean Independence Movement in the United States and Hawaii," December 2, 1942, 2; Box 2260—Korea, File 3020: Kilsoo K. Haan, "Memorandum on Kilsoo K. Haan Propaganda Activities," December 20, 1943, 9.
6. U.S. National Archives, Record Group 165, Military Intelligence Division (MID) 1766-S-146-2, "A Survey of Public Opinion among the Japanese in the Territory of Hawaii," 3.
7. Ibid., 5.
8. Ibid., 4–6.
9. Ibid., 6.
10. Ibid., 8.
11. Ibid.
12. Ibid., 6.
13. U.S. National Archives, Record Group 165, MID 2657-H-392-2, "Korea's Appeal: American-Korean Treaty 1882," April 20, 1933, 1.
14. Ibid., 1–13.

15. Ibid., 12.
16. U.S. National Archives, Record Group 165, MID 2657-H-392-2, "Petitions to the Republic Government of China by the Koreans in Hawaii," April 11, 1931, 2. Haan also included a letter sent to him from the Kuomintang of Hawaii. The letter, dated January 11, 1932, announced that the Kuomintang of Hawaii at their most recent delegates' convention had unanimously passed a resolution pledging their support for Korean independence. They continued that they would formally submit the resolution to the Central Executive Committee of the Chinese Nationalist government in China.
17. U.S. National Archives, Record Group 165, MID 2657-H-392-2, "Korea's Appeal," April 20, 1933, 8.
18. Ibid.
19. Ibid., 9.
20. Ibid.
21. Ibid., 10.
22. U.S. National Archives, Record Group 165, MID 2657-H-392-2, "Korea's Appeal: A-K-R-O-N," April 20, 1933, 1, 3.
23. Chong-sik Lee, *The Politics of Korean Nationalism*, 185–88.
24. Kim Won-bong was also known as Kim Yaksan, which he used as his pen name.
25. Man-Gil Kang, *A History of Contemporary Korea*, 70–72; Chong-sik Lee, *The Korean Workers' Party*, 189–90.
26. Scalapino and Lee, *Communism in Korea*, 174; Chong-sik Lee, *The Korean Workers' Party*, 190–91.
27. Ibid. Chong-sik Lee observed that the Chinese Nationalist government was likely unaware of Kim Won-bong's Communist activities.
28. Ibid., 191–92.
29. U.S. National Archives, Record Group 165, Box 2265, Folder 13: Korea—Nationalist Groups, "Korean Independence Movement in the United States and Hawaii," December 2, 1942, 2; Box 2260—Korea, File 3020: Kilsoo K. Haan, "Memorandum on Kilsoo K. Haan Propaganda Activities," December 20, 1943, 9.
30. Man-gil Kang, *A History of Contemporary Korea*, 70–72, and "The Nature and Process of the Korean National Liberation Movement," 583–84; Chong-sik Lee, *The Korean Workers' Party*, 193–95.
31. U.S. National Archives, Record Group 165, MID 1766-S-146-2, "Necessity for Agent of Bureau of Investigation in Hawaii," March 14, 1933.
32. Ibid.
33. U.S. National Archives, Record Group 165, MID 1766-S-146-5, J. P. MacFarland, "Report of Investigation in Hawaii—Survey of Public Opinion Among the Japanese in the Territory of Hawaii," May 6, 1933, 3–15.
34. Ibid., 19.
35. Ibid., 2.
36. Bywater, *The Great Pacific War*; U.S. National Archives, Record Group 165, MID 1766-S-146-5, J. P. MacFarland, "Report of Investigation in Hawaii—Survey of Public Opinion Among the Japanese in the Territory of Hawaii," May 6, 1933, 2.

37. Bywater, *The Great Pacific War*; v.
38. U.S. National Archives, Record Group 165, MID 1766-S-146-5, J. P. MacFarland, "Report of Investigation in Hawaii," May 6, 1933, 19.
39. U.S. National Archives, Record Group 165, MID 1766-S-146/2-3, April 12, 1933; April 24, 1933; May 6, 1933.
40. U.S. National Archives, Record Group 165, MID 1766-S-146-5, J. P. MacFarland, "Report of Investigation in Hawaii," May 6, 1933, 22.
41. Ibid., 25.
42. Ibid., 23–24.
43. Ibid., 26; U.S. National Archives, Record Group 165, MID 1766-S-146-2, May 10, 1933; 1766-S-146-3, May 24, 1933; 1766-S-146-4, June 30, 1933; 1766-S-146-5, June 21, 1933.
44. Historian Gary Gerstle notes that the rise of what he calls the U.S. "disciplinary state" brought about a rapid expansion in the state's surveillance of anti-American activities, particularly among foreign-born aliens and racial minorities. This surge in state surveillance was reflected in the dramatic growth of the Bureau of Investigation, and the army's Military Intelligence Division, both of which figured prominently in Haan's experiences. See Gerstle, *American Crucible*, 91–94. See also Capozzola, *Uncle Sam Wants You: World War I and the Making of the Modern American Citizen*.
45. U.S. National Archives, Record Group 165, MID 1766-S-146-5, J. P. MacFarland, "Report of Investigation in Hawaii," May 6, 1933, 20.
46. Ibid., 21.
47. In his synthesis of U.S. history, Gary Gerstle argues that two contradictory visions of citizenship have shaped the history of twentieth-century America: civic nationalism and racial nationalism. For Gerstle, the core elements of civic nationalism are inscribed in the founding principles of the American republic that promised the equality of all people and a democratic government based on the people's consent. At the same time, a racial nationalism constituted an equally powerful ideological tradition, which was also present on the birth of the American nation. Under the thinking of racial nationalism, those of Asian, African, and Latino descent were inherently unfit for full and equal participation in the nation and were thus to be excluded from the rights of citizenship. (Gerstle, *American Crucible*, 4–8.)
48. Hirschman, *Exit, Voice and Loyalty*, 17.
49. In *Exit, Voice and Loyalty*, Albert O. Hirschman posits that *exit* and *voice* represent two different alternatives for individuals responding to a decline in the quality of a product or service provided by an organization. The dissatisfied individual may *exit* by switching over to a product from a rival firm or by leaving the organization. On the other hand, the individual may instead resort to the *voice* option by seeking to change the product quality or policies of the organization. Hirschman defines *voice* "as any attempt at all to change, rather than to escape from, an objectionable state of affairs ... through appeal to a higher authority with the intention of forcing a change in management, or through various types of actions and protests, including those that are meant to mobilize public opinions" (p. 30).

50. U.S. National Archives, Decimal File 894 (1930–39), LM58 Reel 12, 894.202 11a: Haan, Kilsoo, Sino-Korean Peoples League, "Petition to the State and House of Representatives: Regular Session of 1935—Territorial Legislature," March 27, 1935, 2.
51. Ibid., 4–6.
52. Ibid., 2, 12.
53. Ibid., 10.
54. Ibid., 3–10.
55. Ibid., 3–14.
56. U.S. National Archives, Decimal File 894 (1930–39), LM58 Reel 12, 894.202 11a: Lyhan, W. K., "Letter from Education Committee of Hawaiian Senate," May 18, 1935.
57. U.S. National Archives, Decimal File 894 (1930–39), LM58 Reel 12, 894.202 11a: Lyhan, W. K., "Letter to Cordell Hull," March 6, 1936.
58. U.S. National Archives, Record Group 165, MID 2657-H-392-13, "Letter to Hull," May 22, 1936, 1–2.
59. Ibid., 3–5.
60. U.S. National Archives, Record Group 165, MID 2657-H-392-13, "Letter to Hull," May 22, 1936, 7.
61. Despite Haan's claims to have infiltrated the Japanese consulate to conduct counterintelligence work for the U.S. government, his involvement with the consulate remained a continuing source of concern and suspicion by U.S. intelligence officers. Intelligence reports indicate that Kilsoo Haan's involvement with the Japanese consulate in Hawaii had begun as early as 1930, noting that he had been sporadically employed by the Japanese consulate from 1930 to 1937. Although he claimed to have severed his connections with the Japanese consulate in 1937, U.S. intelligence officers believed that his connections to the Japanese consulate remained intact after 1937. As a result, Haan remained under close surveillance by the U.S. intelligence community, which believed that his activities could be the work of a Japanese fifth columnist. U.S. National Archives, Record Group 165, Records of the War Department, Box 2260—Korea, File 3020: Kilsoo K. Haan, "Memorandum on Kilsoo K. Haan Propaganda Activities," December 20, 1943; Record Group 165, Box 2265, Folder 13: Korea—Nationalist Groups, "Korean Independence Movement in the United States and Hawaii," December 2, 1942; Record Group 165, Regional File, Box 2267, File 1: Korea—Government Reports Concerning Haan, "Memorandum: Kilsoo K. Haan," April 28, 1942; Record Group 38, Box 15, Folder—Analysis of the Korean Situation, "Topical Study—Analysis of the Korean Situation," August 13, 1943.
62. Bell, *Last Among Equals*, 64; U.S. Congress, Joint Committee on Hawaii, Statehood for Hawaii: Hearings before the Joint Committee on Hawaii, Congress of the United States, 75th Congress, 2nd session pursuant S. Congress Resolution 18, October 6–22, 1937.
63. U.S. Congress, Joint Committee on Hawaii, Statehood for Hawaii: Hearings before the Joint Committee on Hawaii, Congress of the United States, 447.
64. Bell, *Last Among Equals*, 65.

65. U.S. Congress, Joint Committee on Hawaii, Statehood for Hawaii: Hearings before the Joint Committee on Hawaii, Congress of the United States, 468.
66. Bell, *Last Among Equals*, 66.
67. Chong-sik Lee, *The Politics of Korean Nationalism*, 202; Man-gil Kang, *A Contemporary History of Korea*, 71–72.
68. Chong-sik Lee, *The Politics of Korean Nationalism*, 203–12; Man-gil Kang, *A Contemporary History of Korea*, 71–73; Man-gil Kang, "Nature and Process of the Korean National Liberation Movement," 584.
69. U.S. National Archives, Decimal File 894 (1930-39), LM58 Reel 12, 894.20211a/36-38.
70. For Haan's participation in the congressional hearings for Hawaiian statehood, see Roger Bell, *Last Among Equals: Hawaiian Statehood and American Politics*; U.S. Congress, Joint Committee on Hawaii, Statehood for Hawaii: Hearings before the Joint Committee on Hawaii, Congress of the United States, 75th Congress, 2nd session pursuant S. Congress Resolution 18, October 6–22, 1937.
71. U.S. National Archives, Decimal File 894 (1930-39), LM58 Reel 12, 894.20211a/40-41.
72. U.S. National Archives, Decimal File 894 (1930-39), LM58 Reel 12, 894.20211a/42, "Memoranda to Hull," April 12, 1939, 1.
73. U.S. National Archives, Record Group 38, Box 15, Folder—Analysis of the Korean Situation, "Topical Study—Analysis of the Korean Situation," August 13, 1943, 16; Record Group 165, Box 2265, Folder 13: Korea—Nationalist Groups, "Korean Independence Movement in the United States and Hawaii," December 2, 1942, 3; Record Group 165, Box 2260—Korea, File 3020: Kilsoo K. Haan, "Memorandum on Kilsoo K. Haan Propaganda Activities," December 20, 1943, 10.
74. U.S. National Archives, Decimal File 894 (1930-39), LM58 Reel 12, 894.20211a/42, "Memoranda to Hull," April 12, 1939, 3.
75. Ibid., 3.
76. In all, four Neutrality Acts were passed: in 1935, 1936, 1937, and 1939.
77. In November 1939, Congress passed the Neutrality Act of 1939, which contained a cash-and-carry provision that allowed belligerents to purchase American arms and strategic materials, but required them to pay cash in advance and to transport goods on their own ships.
78. U.S. National Archives, Decimal File 894 (1930–39), LM58 Reel 12, 894.20211a/42, "Memoranda to Hull," April 12, 1939, 1–3.
79. Ibid., 1–4.
80. Ibid., 5–6.
81. The passage of the 1924 Immigration Act barred the entry of all Asians, including Koreans, as legal immigrants to the United States. Responding to nativist pressures, the 1924 Immigration Act established the permanent exclusion of any "alien ineligible for citizenship." Since Asians were denied the right of naturalization under an 1870 statute, further Asian immigration to the United States came to a decisive halt in 1924. Asian immigration would not resume again until after the end of World War II.

82. U.S. National Archives, Decimal File 894 (1930–39), LM58 Reel 12, 894.20211a/42, "Memoranda to Hull," April 12, 1939, 5–6.
83. Ibid.
84. Ibid.
85. Ibid., 6, 10.
86. U.S. National Archives, Decimal File 894 (1930–39), LM58 Reel 12, 894.20211a/44, "Letter to Hamilton," April 28, 1939.
87. U.S. National Archives, Decimal File 894 (1930–39), LM58 Reel 12, 894.20211a/44, "Hamilton Memorandum," April 28, 1939.
88. U.S. National Archives, RG 165, Regional File, Box 2266, Folder 5: Korea—Propaganda Releases (1939–41).
89. Ibid.
90. On July 26, 1941, a day after Japan's seizure of French Indo-China, the U.S. government ordered the complete cessation of trade with Japan and the freezing of her assets in the United States.
91. U.S. National Archives, Record Group 165, Regional File, Box 2266, Folder 4: Korea—Propaganda Releases (1939–41).
92. Ibid.
93. U.S. National Archives, Record Group 165, Regional File, Box 2266, Folder 4: Korea—Propaganda Releases (1939–41); Record Group 165, Regional File, Box 2266, Folder 5: Korea—Propaganda Releases (1939–41); Macmillan, "Unwanted Allies: Koreans as Enemy Aliens in World War II"; Eubank, "The Effects of the First Six Months of World War II on the Attitudes of Koreans and Filipinos Toward the Japanese in Hawaii."
94. U.S. National Archives, Record Group 165, Regional File, Box 2266, Folder 4: Korea—Propaganda Releases (1939–41).
95. Ibid.
96. Ibid.
97. U.S. National Archives, Record Group 59, 895.01/60-2/26, Rhee to Hoskins, December 9, 1941.
98. U.S. National Archives, Record Group 59, 895.01/60-1/26, Hoskins to Smith, December 10, 1941.
99. *Sinhan Minbo*, December 18, 1941.
100. U.S. National Archives, Record Group 59, 895.01/93; Record Group 165, Regional File, Box 2266, Folder 4: Korea—Propaganda Releases (1939–41).
101. U.S. National Archives, Record Group 59, 895.01/60-10/26, Haan to Harrison, January 14, 1942.
102. U.S. National Archives, Record Group 59, 895.01/60-10/26, Harrison to Haan, January 23, 1942.
103. *Los Angeles Times*, January 26, 1942.
104. Samuel W. King papers, State Archives of Hawaii, M-473-869, "The Legal Status of Koreans: A Muddle Caused by Our Indecisive Foreign Policy," undated.
105. U.S. National Archives, Record Group 165, Regional File, Box 2266, Folder 4 and Folder 5: Korea—Propaganda Releases (1939–41); Macmillan, "Unwanted Allies"; Eubank, "Effects of the First Six Months of World War II."

106. For more extended treatment of these experiences of Koreans in Hawaii, see Macmillan, "Unwanted Allies"; and Lili M. Kim, "The Pursuit of Imperfect Justice."
107. *Honolulu Star Bulletin*, December 4, 1943.

CHAPTER 7

1. Riggs, *A Study of the Repeal of Chinese Exclusion*.
2. The Korean Provisional Government, originally headquartered in Shanghai, moved to Chungking after Japan's occupation of North China.
3. Lyu, "Korean Nationalist Activities in Hawaii," 81.
4. Ibid.
5. U.S. National Archives, Record Group 38, Office of Naval Intelligence (ONI), Box 15, 12; Record Group 319, Army-Intelligence Decimal File, 1941–1948, Box 394, Folder 291.2 (Koreans).
6. "Documents Pertaining to the Friction between UKC and Korean Commission, 1942–1943," Box 4, Folder 17, Hei Sop Chin Collection, 1.
7. The signatory nations included the United States, United Kingdom, Soviet Union, China, Australia, Belgium, Canada, Costa Rica, Cuba, Czechoslovakia, Dominican Republic, El Salvador, Greece, Guatemala, Haiti, Honduras, India, Luxembourg, Netherlands, New Zealand, Nicaragua, Norway, Panama, Poland, South Africa, and Yugoslavia.
8. "Documents Pertaining to the Friction between UKC and Korean Commission, 1942–1943," Box 4, Folder 17, Hei Sop Chin Collection, 1.
9. United Korean Committee in America, *Korean Liberty Conference*.
10. Ibid., 37–39.
11. Ibid., 12.
12. "Documents Pertaining to the Friction between UKC and Korean Commission, 1942–1943," Box 7, Folder 17, Hei Sop Chin Collection, 2–6.
13. Ibid., 2–3.
14. Ibid., 3.
15. Ibid.
16. Ibid., 1, 4.
17. Ibid., 5.
18. Ibid., 5–6.
19. Ibid., 1.
20. Ibid.
21. Ibid., 3.
22. Ibid., 7.
23. Ibid., 1, 5.
24. Ibid.
25. Ibid., 8.
26. Ibid., 13.
27. Ibid., 18–20.
28. Ibid.
29. Ibid.
30. Ibid., 20.

31. Ibid.
32. Ibid.
33. Ibid., 27.
34. Ibid., 33–34.
35. U.S. National Archives, Record Group 319, Army-Intelligence Decimal File, 1941–1948, Box 394, Folder 291.2 (Koreans).
36. "Documents Pertaining to the Friction between UKC and Korean Commission, 1942–1943," Box 4, Folder 17, Hei Sop Chin Collection, 39–41.
37. Ibid., 37, 42–44, 47.
38. Ibid., 64–69.
39. "The Korean People's Convention of Central California: A Proclamation," Box 4, Folder 17, Hei Sop Chin Collection, 1.
40. U.S. National Archives, Record Group 165, Regional File 2267, Folder 5: Korea—"A Report on the Progress of the Free Korean Movement, Part I," March 24, 1943, 2.
41. U.S. National Archives, Record Group 165, Regional File 2267, Folder 5: Korea—"A Report on the Progress of the Free Korean Movement, Part II," June 18, 1943, 4–10.
42. Ibid., 9–10.
43. *The Korean National Herald-Pacific Weekly*, October 6, 1943.
44. Ibid., September 15, 1943.
45. Ibid., January 6, 1944.
46. Ibid., December 29, 1943.
47. United Korean Committee in America, *Condensed Reference—Korea and the Pacific War*, 23–25.
48. *The Korean National Herald-Pacific Weekly*, September 29, 1943; October 20, 1943; October 27, 1943; November 24, 1943; December 15, 1943; December 22, 1943.
49. Ibid., October 27, 1943.
50. Ibid.
51. Ibid., December 8, 1943.
52. Ibid., December 29, 1943.
53. Ibid., December 29, 1943 and January 12, 1944; *The Korean National Herald*, March 29, 1944.
54. *The Korean National Herald-Pacific Weekly*, December 19, 1943.
55. *The Korean National Herald*, March 8, 1944 and April 19, 1944; University of Hawaii, Hamilton Library, Korea Special Collections, (hereafter cited as Hamilton Library, Korea Special Collections) Folder 3, "Cairo and Korean Independence."
56. *The Korean National Herald*, April 19, 1944.
57. Hamilton Library, Korea Special Collections, Folder 5.
58. "Letters to Korean Provisional Government, 1944," Box 4, Folder 8, Hei Sop Chin Collection.
59. *Honolulu Advertiser*, May 25, 1944; *Honolulu Star Bulletin*, May 25, 1944; *Korean Independence*, June 28, 1944.
60. U.S. Congress, *Congressional Record: Proceedings and Debates of the 2nd session of the 78th Congress*, Vol. 90, Part 4, 5231.

61. *The Korean National Herald*, July 19, 1944; August 2, 1944. The bill was referred to the House Committee on Immigration and Naturalization, where it was subsequently shelved. Farrington reintroduced the bill in Congress in January 1945, but with the same results.
62. *The Korean National Herald*, June 7, 1944; *Honolulu Star Bulletin*, June 5, 1944.
63. *The Korean National Herald*, June 7, 1944.
64. Ibid., August 23, 1944; August 30, 1944; September 13, 1944; September 27, 1944; October 11, 1944; October 18, 1944; November 29, 1944; December 13, 1944.
65. Ibid., August 23, 1944; August 30, 1944; September 13, 1944; September 27, 1944; October 11, 1944; October 18, 1944; November 29, 1944; December 13, 1944.
66. According to Cumings, an earlier American draft of the Korean portion of the Cairo Declaration read that Korean independence would come "at the earliest possible moment." However, a later draft showed that FDR had changed the phrase to "at the proper moment." The phrase in the final draft read "in due course," which was likely Winston Churchill's rephrasing of Roosevelt's revision. See Cumings, *The Origins of the Korean War*, Vol. I, 107.
67. Savage, "The American Response to the Korean Independence Movement," 216; Matray, *The Reluctant Crusade*, 8–19; Hong-Kyu Park, "From Pearl Harbor to Cairo," 347–51; Cumings, *The Origins of the Korean War*, 106.
68. Savage, "The American Response to the Korean Independence Movement," 217; Cumings, *The Origins of the Korean War*, 107.
69. Savage, "The American Response to the Korean Independence Movement," 218–19; Matray, *The Reluctant Crusade*, 21–22; Cho, *Korea in World Politics*, 29.
70. Savage, "The American Response to the Korean Independence Movement," 219–21.

CONCLUSION

1. Robinson, *Korea's Twentieth-Century Odyssey*; Cumings, *Korea's Place in the Sun*.
2. For fuller discussions of this complex situation, see Robinson, *Korea's Twentieth-Century Odyssey*; Cumings, *Korea's Place in the Sun*; Man-gil Kang, *A History of Contemporary Korea*; Hart-Landsberg, *Korea: Division, Reunification, and U.S. Foreign Policy*; and Henderson, *Korea: The Politics of the Vortex*.
3. Armstrong, *The North Korean Revolution*.
4. Manela, *The Wilsonian Moment*.
5. Cooper, "What Is the Concept of Globalization Good For?", 199.
6. H. H. Gerth and C. Wright Mills, eds., *From Max Weber: Essays in Sociology*, 78.
7. Passed by U.S. Congress in 1952, one provision of the McCarran-Walter Act granted naturalization rights to Korean and Japanese immigrants.
8. Shain, *Marketing the American Creed Abroad*, 1999.

BIBLIOGRAPHY

PRIMARY SOURCES
Archival and Manuscript Collections
Hawaii State Judiciary

    First Judicial Circuit, Territory of Hawaii

Stanford University, Hoover Institute

    Korea Files.
    Serial Collection.
    Survey of Race Relations.

State Archives of Hawaii

    Romanzo Adams Collection.
    Joseph R. Farrington Collection.
    History and Miscellaneous.
    Victor S. K. Houston Collection.
    Samuel W. King Papers.

U.S. National Archives and Records Adminstration, Washington, D.C.

    Army-Intelligence Project, Record Group 319, Decimal File 1941–1948.
    Records of the Department of State, Record Group 59.
    Records of the Department of State Relating to the Internal Affairs of Korea (Chosen), 1910–1929, 1930–1939, 1940–1944.
    Records of the Office of the Chief Naval Operation, Record Group 38, Office of Naval Intelligence (ONI).
    Records of the Office of Strategic Services, Record Group 226, OSS Field Station Files.
    Records of the United States Army Command, Record Group 338, Records of the Military Government of the Territory of Hawaii.
    Records of the War, Department Record Group 165, Military Intelligence Division (MID).

University of California, Los Angeles, Department of Special Collections

    Korean American Research Project, Hei Sop Chin Collection.

University of Hawaiʻi, Hamilton Library

    Hawaiian Sugar Planters' Association (HSPA) Collection.
    Korea Collection.

University of Hawaiʻi, Sinclair Library, Special Collections

    Bernard Hormann Organized Student Papers.
    Hawaiian Social Research Laboratory (HSRL).
    Institute of Pacific Relations.

University of Southern California

    Korean Heritage Library.

Government Serials, Publications, and Reports

Reports of the Immigration Commission. "Immigrants in Industries, Part 25: Japanese and Other Immigrant Races in the Pacific Coast and Rocky Mountain States-Agriculture." Washington, DC: U.S. Government Printing Office, 1911.

Report of State Board of Control of California. "California and the Oriental: Japanese, Chinese, and Hindus." Sacramento: California State Printing Office, 1922.

U.S. Bureau of Census. *Fourteenth Census of the United States. 1920*. Washington, DC: U.S. Government Printing Office, 1922.

———. *Fifteenth Census of the United States. 1930*. Washington, DC: U.S. Government Printing Office, 1933.

U.S. Congress. *Congressional Record*, 66th Congress, 1st session. Washington, DC: U.S. Government Printing Office, 1919.

———. *Congressional Record*, 66th Congress, 2nd session. Washington, DC: U.S. Government Printing Office, 1920.

———. *Congressional Record*, 78th Congress, 1st session. Washington, DC: U.S. Government Printing Office, 1943.

———. *Congressional Record*, 78th Congress, 2nd session. Washington, DC: U.S. Government Printing Office, 1944.

———. *Congressional Record*, 79th Congress, 1st session. Washington, DC: U.S. Government Printing Office, 1945.

U.S. Congress. *Japanese Immigration and Colonization: Skeleton Brief*. Washington, DC: U.S. Government Printing Office, 1921.

U.S. Congress. *Joint Committee on Hawaii, Statehood for Hawaii: Hearings before the Joint Committee on Hawaii, Congress of the United States*, 75th Congress, 2nd session pursuant S. Congress Resolution 18. Washington, DC: U.S. Government Printing Office, 1938.

U.S. Department of State. *Foreign Relations of the United States (FRUS)*. Washington, DC: U.S. Government Printing Office.

U.S. Government Reports and Reports of California Bureau of Labor Statistics. "Japanese Immigration: Occupations, Wages, Etc." San Francisco: Japanese and Korean Exclusion League, 1907.

Other Primary Sources

Bywater, Hector C. *The Great Pacific War: A History of the American-Japanese Campaign of 1931–33*. London: Constable & Co. Ltd., 1925.

Burnett, Scott S. *Korean-American Relations: Documents Pertaining to the Far Eastern Diplomacy of the United States. Vol. III, The Period of Dimininishing Influence, 1896–1905*. Honolulu: University of Hawai'i Press, 1989.

Charr, Easurk Emsen. *The Golden Mountain: The Autobiography of a Korean Immigrant, 1895–1960*. Urbana: University of Illinois Press, 1996.

Chung, Henry. *The Case of Korea*. New York: Fleming H. Revell Company, 1919.

———. *Korea and the United States through War and Peace, 1943–1960*. IMKS Historical Materials series. Seoul: Yonsei University Press, 2000.

———. *The Oriental Policy of the United States*. New York: Fleming H. Revell Company, 1922.

Commission on Relations with the Orient. *The Korean Situation: Authentic Accounts of Recent Events by Eye Witnesses*. New York: Federal Council of the Churches of Christ in America, 1919.

Cynn, Hugh Heung-wo. *The Rebirth of Korea: The Reawakening of the People, Its Causes, and the Outlook*. New York: Abingdon Press, 1920.

Gulick, Sidney L. *American Democracy and Asiatic Citizenship*. New York: Charles Scribner's Sons, 1918.

Ireland, Alleyne. *The New Korea*. New York: E.P. Dutton and Company, 1926.

Japanese and Korean Exclusion League. *Japanese Immigration: Occupations, Wages, Etc*. San Francisco: Japanese and Korean Exclusion League, 1907.

Kang, Younghill. *East Goes West*. New York: Charles Scribner's Sons, 1937.

———. *The Grass Roof*. New York: Charles Scribner's Sons, 1931.

Kim, Henry Cu. *The Writings of Henry Cu Kim: Autobiography with Commentaries on Syngman Rhee, Pak Yong-man, and Chong Sun-man*. Dae-Sook Suh, ed. and trans. Honolulu: University of Hawaii Press, 1987.

Kim, San, with Nym Wales. *Song of Ariran: A Korean Communist in the Chinese Revolution*. San Francisco: Ramparts Press, 1973.

Korean Commission to America and Europe. *Korea Must Be Free*. New York: I-X-L Printing Co., 1930.

League of Nations. *Appeal by the Chinese Government—Report of the Commission on Enquiry*. Geneva, Switzerland: League of Nations, 1932.

———. *Appeal by the Chinese Government. Supplementary Documents to the Report of the Commission of Enquiry*. Geneva, Switzerland: League of Nations, 1932.

McCune, George M., and John A. Harrison. *Korean-American Relations: Documents Pertaining to the Far Eastern Diplomacy of the United States, Vol. I, The Initial Period, 1883–1886*. Berkeley: University of California Press, 1951.

McKenzie, F. A. *Korea's Fight for Freedom*. New York: Fleming H. Revell Company, 1920.

———. *The Tragedy of Korea*. London: Hodder and Stoughton, 1908.
McKenzie, R. D. *Oriental Exclusion: The Effect of American Immigration Laws, Regulations, and Judicial Decisions Upon the Chinese and Japanese on the American Pacific Coast*. Chicago: University of Chicago Press, 1928.
National Cyclopedia of American Biography. New York: James T. White and Co., 1906.
Palmer, Spencer J. *Korean-American Relations: Documents Pertaining to the Far Eastern Diplomacy of the United States*, Vol. II, *The Period of Growing Influence, 1887–1895*. Berkeley: University of California Press, 1963.
Proceedings of the First Korean Congress. Philadelphia: Korean Information Bureau, 1919.
Rhee, Syngman. *The Syngman Rhee Telegrams*. 4 vols. IMKS Historical Materials series. Seoul: Joong Ang Ilbo, Institute for Modern Korean Studies, Yonsei University, 2000.
Suh, Dae-Sook. *Documents of Korean Communism, 1918–1948*. Princeton, NJ: Princeton University Press, 1970.
United Korean Committee in America. *Korean Liberty Conference*. Los Angeles and Honolulu: United Korean Committee in America, 1942.
United Korean Committee in America, Planning and Research Board. *Condensed Reference: Korea and the Pacific War*. Los Angeles: Haynes Corporation, 1943.
We Who Fight the Common Enemy. Honolulu: Legislative Committee of the Korean Civic Association, 1945.
Young, C. Walter "Chinese Colonization and the Development of Manchuria." In J. B. Condliffe, ed. *Problems of the Pacific 1929*. Chicago: University of Chicago Press, 1930.
———. "Korean Problems in Manchuria as Factors in the Sino-Japanese Dispute." *Supplementary Documents to the Report of the Commission of Inquiry*. Study No. 9. Geneva, Switzerland: League of Nations, 1932.

Newspapers and Periodicals
Hemet News
Honolulu Advertiser
Honolulu Star Bulletin
Kongnip Sinmun
Korea Review
Korean Independence
Korean National Herald
Korean National Herald-Pacific Weekly
Korean Pacific Weekly
Kungminbo
Los Angeles Times
New York Times
Pacific Commercial Advertiser
San Francisco Call
San Francisco Chronicle

San Francisco Examiner
Sinhan Minbo
Sino-Korean Volunteer News

SECONDARY SOURCES
Dissertations, Theses, and Unpublished Papers

Ahn, Hyung-ju. "Korean Interpreters at Japanese Alien Detention Center During World War II: An Oral History Analysis." M.A. thesis, California State University, Fullerton, 1995.

Baldwin, Frank Prentiss Jr. "The March First Movement: Korean Challenge and Japanese Response." Ph.D. dissertation, Columbia University Press, 1969.

Ban, Byung Yool. "Korean Nationalist Activities in the Russian Far East and North Chientao, 1905–1921." Ph.D. dissertation, University of Hawai'i at Manoa, 1996.

Em, Henry H. "Nationalist Discourse in Modern Korea: Minjok as a Democratic Imaginary." Ph.D. dissertation, University of Chicago, 1995.

Eubank, Lauriel E. "The Effects of the First Six Months of World War II on the Attitudes of Koreans and Filipinos Toward the Japanese in Hawaii." M.A. thesis, University of Hawai'i, 1943.

Gardner, Arthur Leslie. "The Korean Nationalist Movement and An Ch'Ang-Ho, Advocate of Gradualism." Ph.D. dissertation, University of Hawai'i, 1979.

Givens, Helen L. "The Korean Community in Los Angeles County." M.A. thesis, University of Southern California, 1939.

Kim, Bernice Bong Hee. "The Koreans in Hawaii." M.A. thesis, University of Hawai'i, 1937.

Kim, Richard S. "Korean Tenant Rice Farming in Glenn County, California 1916–1925: An Economic Niche for an Immigrant Community in Transition." M.A. thesis, University of California, Los Angeles, 1993.

Lee, John K. "The Notion of 'Self' in Korean-American Literature: A Sociohistorical Perspective." Ph.D. dissertation, University of Connecticut, 1990.

Lyons, Yvonne Louise. "The Korean Independence Movement." M.A. thesis, University of California, Berkeley, 1949.

Moon, Hyung June. "The Korean Immigrants in America: The Quest for Identity in the Formative Years, 1903–1918." Ph.D. dissertation, University of Nevada, Reno, 1977.

Nordmann, David. "Idealism, Immigration and Imperialism: Durham Stevens and the Rise and Fall of United States Diplomacy with Japan and Korea, 1873–1908." Ph.D. dissertation, University of Indiana, 2001.

Savage, Timothy Lincoln. "The American Response to the Korean Independence Movement, 1910–1945." M.A. thesis, University of Hawai'i, 1994.

Shin, Paull Hobom. "The Korean Colony in Chientao: A Study of Japanese Imperialism and Militant Korean Nationalism, 1905–1932." Ph.D. dissertation, University of Washington, 1980.

Son, Young Ho. "From Plantation Laborers to Ardent Nationalists: Koreans' Experiences in America and Their Search for Ethnic Identity." Ph.D. dissertation, Lousiana State University, 1989.

Books and Articles

Abelman, Nancy Lie John. *Blue Dreams: Korean Americans and the Los Angeles Riots*. Cambridge, MA: Harvard University Press, 1995.

Allen, Richard C. *Korea's Syngman Rhee: An Unauthorized Portrait*. Rutland, VT: Charles E. Tuttle Co., 1960.

Ambrosius, Lloyd E. *Wilsonianism: Woodrow Wilson and His Legacy in American Foreign Relations*. New York: Palgrave McMillan, 2002.

Anderson, Benedict. *Imagined Communities: Reflections on the Origin and Spread of Nationalism*. London: Verso, 1983.

Anderson, Wanni W., and Robert C. Lee. *Displacements and Diasporas: Asians in the Americas*. New Brunswick, NJ: Rutgers University Press, 2005.

Armstrong, Charles K. "Centering the Periphery: Manchuria Exile(s) and the North Korean State." *Korean Studies* 19 (1995): 1–16.

———. *The North Korean Revolution, 1945–1950*. Ithaca, NY: Cornell University Press, 2003.

Arthur, Paul. "Diasporan Intervention in International Affairs: Irish America as a Case Study." *Diaspora* 1, no. 2 (1991): 143–62.

Azuma, Eiichiro. *Between Two Empires: Race, History, and Transnationalism in Japanese America*. New York: Oxford University Press, 2005.

Ban, Byung Yool. "Korean Emigration to the Russian Far East, 1860s–1910s." *Seoul Journal of Korean Studies* 9 (1996): 115–43.

Barkan, Elliott R., Hasia Diner, and Alan M. Kraut, eds. *From Arrival to Incorporation: Migrants to the U.S. in a Global Context*. New York: New York University Press, 2008.

Barnhart, Michael A. "Driven by Domestics: American Relations with Japan and Korea, 1900–1945." In Warren I. Cohen, ed. *Pacific Passage*, 190–212. New York: Columbia University Press, 1996.

Barrier, N. Gerald, and Verne A. Dusenbery, eds. *The Sikh Diaspora: Migration and the Experience Beyond Punjab*. Columbia, MO: South Asia Books, 1989.

Basch, Linda, Schiller Nina Glick, and Blanc-Szanton Cristina, eds. *Nations Unbound: Transnational Projects, Postcolonial Predicaments, and Deterritorialized Nation-States*. Amsterdam: Gordon and Breach, 1994.

Bell, Roger. *Last Among Equals: Hawaiian Statehood and American Politics*. Honolulu: University of Hawai'i Press, 1984.

Biersteker, Thomas J., and Cynthia Weber, eds. *State Sovereignty as Social Construct*. New York: Cambridge University Press, 1996.

Blaut, James M. *The National Question: Decolonising the Theory of Nationalism*. London: Zed Books, 1987.

Bodnar, John. *The Transplanted: A History of Immigrants in Urban America*. Bloomington: Indiana University Press, 1985.

Brass, Paul R. "Ethnic Groups and the State." In Paul R. Brass, ed. *Ethnic Groups and the State*, 1–56. London: Croom Helm Ltd., 1985.

———. *Ethnicity and Nationalism: Theory and Comparison*. New Delhi: SAGE, 1991.

Braziel, Jana Evans and Anita Mannur, eds. *Theorizing Diaspora: A Reader*. Malden, MA: Blackwell, 2003.

Breuilly, John. *Nationalism and the State*. Chicago: University of Chicago Press, 1993.

Brinkley, Alan. *Liberalism and Its Discontents*. Cambridge, MA: Harvard University Press, 1998.

———. "Writing the History of Contemporary America: Dilemmas and Challenges." *Daedalus* 113, no. 3 (1984): 121–41.

Brook, Timothy, and Andre Schmidt, eds. *Nation Work: Asian Elites and National Identities*. Ann Arbor: University of Michigan Press, 2000.

Brooks, Barbara J. "Peopling the Japanese Empire: The Koreans in Manchuria and the Rhetoric of Inclusion." In Sharon A. Minichiello, ed. *Japan's Competing Modernities: Issues in Culture and Democracy, 1900–1930*, 25–44. Honolulu: University of Hawai'i Press, 1998.

Brown, Thomas N. *Irish-American Nationalism, 1870–1890*. Philadelphia: J.B. Lippincott Company, 1966.

Butler, Kim D. "Defining Diaspora, Refining a Discourse." *Diaspora* 10, no. 2 (2001): 189–219.

Campbell, A. E. "The Paradox of Imperialism: The American Case." In Wolfgang J. Mommsen and Jürgen Osterhammel, eds. *Imperialism and After: Continuities and Discontinuities*, 34–50. London: Allen & Unwin, 1986.

Chakraborty, Dipesh. "Reconstructing Liberalism? Notes toward a Conversation Between Area Studies and Diaspora Studies." *Public Culture* 10, no. 3 (1998): 458–81.

Chambers, Simone, and Will Kymlicka, eds. *Alternative Conceptions of Civil Society*. Princeton, NJ: Princeton University Press, 2002.

Chan, Sucheng. "Asian American Historiography." *Pacific Historical Review* 65, no. 3 (1996): 363–99.

———. *Asian Americans: An Interpretative History*. New York: Twayne Publishers, 1991.

———. "European and Asian Immigration into the United States in Comparative Perspective, 1820s to 1920s." In Virginia Yans-McLaughlin, ed., *Immigration Reconsidered: History, Sociology, and Politics*, 37–75. New York: Oxford University Press, 1990.

———. *This Bitter-Sweet Soil: The Chinese in California Agriculture, 1860–1910*. Berkeley: University of California Press, 1986.

Chang, Gordon, "Asian Immigrants and American Foreign Relations." In Warren I. Cohen, ed., *Pacific Passages: The Study of American-East Asian Relations on the Eve of the Twenty-First Century*, 103–18. New York: Columbia University Press, 1996.

Chatterjee, Partha. *The Nation and Its Fragments: Colonial and Postcolonial Histories*. Princeton, NJ: Princeton University Press, 1993.

———. *Nationalist Thought and the Colonial World*. Minneapolis: University of Minnesota Press, 1986.

Chay, John. "The American Image of Korea to 1945." In Youngnok Koo and Dae-Sook Suh, eds. *Korea and the United States: A Century of Cooperation*, 53–76. Honolulu: University of Hawai'i Press, 1984.

Chay, Jongsuk. *Diplomacy of Asymmetry: Korean-American Relations to 1910*. Honolulu: University of Hawai'i Press, 1990.

Cheng, Lucie, and Edna Bonacich, eds. *Labor Immigration Under Capitalism: Asian Workers in the United States before World War II*. Berkeley: University of California Press, 1984.

Chey, Youn-Cha Shin. "Soviet Koreans and Their Culture in the USSR." In Dae-Sook Suh, ed. *Koreans in the Soviet Union*, 60–84. Honolulu: Center for Korean Studies, University of Hawai'i Press, 1987.

Cho, Soon Sung. *Korea in World Politics, 1940–1950: An Evaluation of American Responsibility*. Berkeley: University of California Press, 1967.

Ch'oe, Yŏng-ho, Peter H. Lee, and Wm. Theodre de Bary, eds. *Sources of Korean Tradition*, Vol. II, *From the Sixteenth to the Twentieth Centuries*. New York: Columbia University Press, 2000.

Choi, Zihn. "Early Korean Immigrants to America: Their Role in the Establishment of the Republic of Korea." *East Asian Review* 14, no. 4 (Winter 2002): 43–71.

Choy, Bong-Youn. *Koreans in America*. Chicago: Nelson-Hall, 1979.

Chuh, Kandice, and Karen Shimakawa, eds. *Orientations: Mapping Studies in the Asian Diaspora*. Durham, NC: Duke University Press, 2001.

Chung, Sung-hwa. *The Politics of Anti-Japanese Sentiment in Korea: Japanese-South Korean Relations Under American Occupation, 1945–1952*. Westport, CT: Greenwood Press, 1991.

Clark, Donald N. "'Surely God Will Work Out Their Salvation': Protestant Missionaries in the March First Movement." *Korean Studies* 13 (1989): 42–75.

Clifford, James. "Diasporas." *Cultural Anthropology* 9, no. 3 (1994): 302–38.

Cohen, Jean L., and Arato Andrew. *Civil Society and Political Theory*. Cambridge, MA: MIT Press, 1992.

Cohen, Robin. *Global Diasporas: An Introduction*. Seattle: University of Washington Press, 1997.

Conzen, Kathleen Neils. "Mainstreams and Side Channels: The Localization of Immigrant Cultures." *Journal of American Ethnic History* (1991): 5–20.

Conzen, Kathleen Neils, David Gerber, Ewa Morawska, George Pozzetta, and Rudolph Vecoli. "The Invention of Ethnicity: A Perspective from the U.S.A." *Journal of American Ethnic History* 12 (1992): 3–41.

Cooper, Frederick. "What Is the Concept of Globalization Good For? An African Historian's Perspective." *African Affairs* 100 (2001): 189–213.

Cumings, Bruce, "Bringing Korea Back In: Structured Absence, Glaring Presence, and Invisibility." In Warren I. Cohen, ed. *Pacific Passages: The Study of American-East Asian Relations on the Eve of the Twenty-First Century*, 337–74. New York: Columbia University Press, 1996.

———. "Korean-American Relations: A Century of Contact and Thirty-Five Years of Intimacy." In Warren I. Cohen, ed. *New Frontiers in American-East Asian Relations*, 237–82. New York: Columbia University Press, 1983.

———. *Korea's Place in the Sun: A Modern History*. New York: W.W. Norton and Company, 1997.

———. *The Origins of the Korean War: Liberation and the Emergence of Separate Regimes, 1945–47*. Princeton, NJ: Princeton University Press, 1981.

———. *Parallax Visions: Making Sense of American-East Asian Relations at the End of the Century*. Durham, NC: Duke University Press, 1999.

Curry, Roy Watson. *Woodrow Wilson and Far Eastern Policy, 1913–1921*. New York: Octagon Books, 1968.

Dahl, Robert A. *Dilemmas of Pluralist Democracy: Autonomy vs. Control*. New Haven, CT: Yale University Press, 1982.
———. *Pluralist Democracy in the United States: Conflict and Consent*. Chicago: Rand McNally and Company, 1967.
Dallin, David J. *Soviet Russia and the Far East*. New Haven, CT: Yale University Press, 1948.
Daniels, Roger. *The Politics of Prejudice: The Anti-Japanese Movement in California and the Struggle for Japanese Exclusion*. Berkeley: University of California Press, 1977.
Dawley, Alan. *Struggles for Justice: Social Responsibility and the Liberal State*. Cambridge, MA: Belknap Press of Harvard University Press, 1991.
DeConde, Alexander. *Ethnicity, Race, and American Foreign Policy*. Boston: Northeastern University Press, 1992.
Deuchler, Martina. *Confucian Gentlemen and Barbarian Envoys: The Opening of Korea, 1876–1885*. Seattle: University of Washington Press, 1977.
Diamond, Larry. "Rethinking Civil Society: Toward Democratic Consolidation." *Journal of Democracy* 5, no. 3 (1994): 4–17.
Dirlik, Arif. "Asians on the Rim: Transnational Capital and Local Community in the Making of Contemporary Asian America." *Amerasia Journal* 22, no. 3 (1997): 1–24.
———. *Postmodernity's Histories: The Past as Legacy and Project*. Lanham, MD: Rowman & Littlefield Publishers, 2000.
Duara, Prasenjit. "Historizing National Identity or Who Imagines What and When." In Geoff Eley and Ronald Grigor Suny, eds. *Becoming National*. Oxford: Blackwell, 1996.
———. *Rescuing History from the Nation: Questioning Narratives of Modern China*. Chicago: University of Chicago Press, 1995.
Duus, Peter. *The Abacus and the Sword: The Japanese Penetration of Korea, 1895–1910*. Berkeley: University of California Press, 1996.
Duus, Peter, H. Myers Ramon, and R. Peattie Mark, eds. *The Japanese Informal Empire in China, 1895–1937*. Princeton, NJ: Princeton University Press, 1989.
———, eds. *The Japanese Wartime Empire, 1931–1945*. Princeton, NJ: Princeton University Press, 1996.
Eberly, Don E., ed. *The Essential Civil Society Reader: Classic Essays in the American Civil Society Debate*. Lanham, MD: Rowman & Littlefield Publishers, 2000.
Eckert, Carter, et al. *Korea Old and New: A History*. Seoul: Ilchokak Publishers and Korea Institute, Harvard University Press, 1990.
Eckes, Alfred E. Jr., and Thomas W. Zeiller. *Globalization and the American Century*. Cambridge, UK: Cambridge University Press, 2003.
Edwards, Michael. *Civil Society*. 2nd ed. Cambridge, UK: Polity Press, 2009.
Eley, Geoff, and Ronald Grigor Suny, eds. "Introduction: From the Moment of Social History to the Work of Cultural Representation." In *Becoming National: A Reader*, 3–37. New York: Oxford University Press, 1996.
Enloe, Cynthia. "The Growth of the State and Ethnic Mobilization: The American Experience." *Ethnic and Racial Studies* 4, no. 2 (1981): 123–36.
Evans, Peter, Dietrich Rueschemeyer, and Theda Skocpol, eds. *Bringing the State Back In*. Cambridge, UK: Cambridge University Press, 1985.

Fairbank, John K., ed. *The Missionary Enterprise in China and America.* Cambridge, MA: Harvard University Press, 1974.

Foner, Nancy. "What's New about Transnationalism? New York Immigrants Today and at the Turn of the Century." *Diaspora* 6, no. 3 (1997): 355–75.

Fuchs, Lawrence H. *American Ethnic Politics.* New York: Harper Torchbooks, 1968.

———. *The American Kaleidoscope: Race, Ethnicity, and the Civic Culture.* Hanover, NH: Wesleyan University Press, 1990.

Gabaccia, Donna R. *Italy's Many Diasporas.* Seattle: University of Washington Press, 2000.

———. "Is Everywhere Nowhere? Nomads, Nations, and the Immigrant Paradigm of United States History."*Journal of American History* 86, no. 3 (1999): 1115–34.

Galloway, L. Thomas. *Recognizing Foreign Governments: The Practice of the United States.* Washington, DC: American Enterprise Institute for Public Policy Research, 1978.

Gardner, Lloyd C. *A Covenant with Power: American and World Order from Wilson to Reagan.* New York: Oxford University Press, 1984.

Gelb, Michael. "An Early Soviet Ethnic Deportation: The Far-Eastern Koreans." *Russian Review* 54, no. 3 (1995): 389–412.

Gerson, Louis L. *The Hyphenate in Recent American Politics and Diplomacy.* Lawrence: University of Kansas Press, 1964.

Gerstle, Gary. *American Crucible: Race and Nation in the Twentieth Century.* Princeton, NJ: Princeton University Press, 2001.

———. "Liberty, Coercion, and the Making of Americans." *Journal of American History* 84 (1997): 524–59.

———. "The Protean Character of American Liberalism." *American Historical Review* 99, no. 4 (1994): 1043–73.

———. *Working-Class Americanism: The Politics of Labor in a Textile City, 1914–1960.* New York: Cambridge University Press, 1989.

Gerth, H.H. and C. Wright Mills, eds. *From Max Weber: Essays in Sociology.* New York: Oxford University Press, 1946.

Gilroy, Paul. *The Black Atlantic: Modernity and Double Consciousness.* Cambridge, MA: Harvard University Press, 1993.

Gjerde, John. "The Burden of Their Song: Immigrant Encounters with the Republic." In Donna R. Gabaccia and Vicki L. Ruiz, eds. *American Dreaming, Global Realities: Rethinking U.S. Immigration History,* 9–34. Urbana: University of Illinois Press, 2006.

Glazer, Nathan, and Daniel P. Moynihan. "Introduction." In Nathan Glazer and Daniel P. Moynihan, eds. *Ethnicity: Theory and Experience,* 1–26. Cambridge, MA: Harvard University Press, 1975.

Gleason, Philip. *Speaking of Diversity: Language and Ethnicity in Twentieth-Century America.* Baltimore: Johns Hopkins University Press, 1992.

Glick Schiller, Nina. "Transmigrants and Nation-States: Something Old and Something New in the U.S. Immigrant Experience." In Charles Hirschman, Philip Kasinitz, and Josh DeWind, eds. *The Handbook of International Migration: The American Experience,* 94–119. New York: Russell Sage Foundation, 1999.

Glick Schiller, Nina Fouron, and Georges Eugene. *Georges Woke Up Laughing: Long-Distance Nationalism and the Search for Home*. Durham, NC: Duke University Press, 2001.

Glick Schiller, Nina, Linda Basch, and Cristina Szanton Blanc. "From Immigrant to Transmigrant: Theorizing Transnational Migration." *Anthropology Quarterly* 68, no. 1 (1995): 48–63.

Greene, Victor R. *American Immigrant Leaders, 1800–1910: Marginality and Identity*. Baltimore: Johns Hopkins University Press, 1987.

———. *For God and Country: The Rise of Polish and Lithuanian Ethnic Consciousness in America 1860–1910*. Madison, : State Historical Society of Wisconsin, 1975.

Greenfeld, Liah. *Nationalism: Five Roads to Modernity*. Cambridge, MA: Harvard University Press, 1992.

Grodzins, Morton. *The Loyal and Disloyal: Social Boundaries of Patriotism and Treason*. Chicago: University of Chicago Press, 1956.

Guaranizo, Luis Eduardo. "On the Political Participation of Transnational Migrants: Old Practices and New Trends." In Gary Gerstle and John Mollenkopf, eds. *E Pluribus Unum? Contemporary and Historical Perspectives on Immigrant Political Incorporation*, 213–63. New York: Russell Sage Foundation, 2001.

Guglielmo, Thomas A. *White on Arrival: Italians, Race, Color, and Power in Chicago, 1890–1945*. New York: Oxford University Press, 2003.

Guibernau, Montserrat. *Nationalisms: The Nation-State and Nationalism in the Twentieth Century*. Cambridge, UK: Polity Press, 1996.

———. *Nations Without States: Political Communities in a Global Age*. Cambridge, UK: Polity Press, 1999.

Hahm, Pyong-Choon. "The Korean Perception of the United States." In Youngnok Koo and Dae-Sook Suh, eds. *Korea and the United States: A Century of Cooperation*, 23–52. Honolulu: University of Hawai'i Press, 1984.

Hall, John A. *Civil Society: Theory, History, Comparison*. London: Polity Press, 1995.

Hall, Stuart. "Cultural Identity and Diaspora." In J. Rutherford, ed. *Identity: Community, Cultural, and Difference*, 222–37. London: Lawrence & Wishart, 1990.

Handlin, Oscar. *The Uprooted: The Epic Story of the Great Migration That Made the American People*. Boston: Little, Brown, and Company, 1951.

Hara, Teruyuki. "The Korean Movement in the Russian Maritime Province, 1905–1922." In Dae-Sook Suh, ed. *Koreans in the Soviet Union*, 1–23. Honolulu: Center for Korean Studies, University of Hawai'i Press, 1987.

Harrington, Fred Harvey. *God, Mammon, and the Japanese: Dr. Horace N. Allen and Korean-American Relations, 1884–1905*. Madison, WI: University of Wisconsin Press, 1944.

Harrington, Mona. "Loyalties: Dual and Divided." In Michael Walzer, et al., eds. *The Politics of Ethnicity*, 93–138. Cambridge, MA: Belknap Press of Harvard University Press, 1982.

Harrison, Robert. *State and Society in Twentieth-Century America*. London: Longman, 1997.

Hart-Landsberg, Martin. *Korea: Division, Reunification, and U.S. Foreign Policy*. New York: Monthly Review Press, 1998.

Hattam, Victoria. "Ethnicity: An American Genealogy." In Nancy Foner and George M. Frederickson, eds. *Not Just Black and White: Historical and Contemporary Perspectives on Immigration, Race, and Ethnicity in the United States*, 42–60. New York: Russell Sage Foundation, 2004.

Hayashi, Brian Masaru. *"For the Sake of Our Japanese Brethren": Assimilation, Nationalism, and Protestantism Among the Japanese of Los Angeles, 1895–1942*. Stanford, CA: Stanford University Press, 1995.

Hein, Cho. "The Historical Origin of Civil Society in Korea." *Korea Journal* 37, no. 2 (1997): 24–41.

Held, David. *Democracy and the Global Order: From the Modern State to Cosmopolitan Governance*. Cambridge, UK: Polity Press, 1995.

Hellman, Donald C., Youngnok Koo, and Dae-Sook Suh. "The American Perception of Korea: 1945–1982." In Youngnok Koo and Dae-Sook Suh, eds. *Korea and the United States: A Century of Cooperation*, 77–88. Honolulu: University of Hawai'i Press, 1984.

Henderson, Gregory. *Korea: The Politics of the Vortex*. Cambridge, MA: Harvard University Press, 1968.

Higham, John, ed. *Ethnic Leadership in America*. Baltimore: Johns Hopkins University Press, 1978.

———. "From Process to Structure: Formulations of American Immigration History." In Peter Kivisto, and Dag Blanck, eds. *American Immigrants and Their Generations: Studies and Commentaries on the Hansen Thesis after Fifty Years*, 11–41. Urbana: University of Illinois Press, 1990.

———. "Integrating America: The Problem of Assimilation in the Nineteenth Century." *Journal of American Ethnic History* 1, no. 1 (1981): 7–25.

———. "Leadership." In Michael Walzer, et al., eds. *The Politics of Ethnicity*, 69–92. Cambridge, MA: Belknap Press of Harvard University Press, 1982.

Hing, Bill Ong. *Making and Remaking Asian American through Immigration Policy, 1850–1990*. Stanford, CA: Stanford University Press, 1993.

Hirschman, Albert O. *Exit, Voice and Loyalty: Responses to Decline in Firms, Organizations, and States*. Cambridge, MA: Harvard University Press, 1970.

Hobsbawm, E. J. *Nations and Nationalism Since 1780*. Cambridge, UK: Cambridge University Press, 1990.

Hobsbawm, Eric, and Terence Ranger. "Introduction: Inventing Traditions." In Eric Hobsbawm and Terence Ranger, eds. *The Invention of Tradition*, 1–14. Cambridge, UK: Cambridge University Press, 1983.

Hoffman, Frank. "The Muo Declaration: History in the Making (Translation and Commentary)." *Korean Studies* 12 (1989): 22–41.

Hong, Kyong-man. "Formation of Korean Protestantism and Its Political Nature." *Korea Journal* 23, no. 12 (1983): 18–29.

Hong, Soon-ok. "The Legitimating of the Shanghai Provisional Government." *Observer Korea* 3, no. 3 (1971): 41–64.

Hong, Sun-Pyo. "The Unification Movement of the Hawaii Korean Community in the 1930s." In Yŏng-ho Ch'oe, ed. *From the Land of Hibiscus: Koreans in Hawaii, 1903–1950*, 179–94. Honolulu: University of Hawai'i Press, 2007.

Houchins, Lee, and Chang-su Houchins. "The Korean Experience in America, 1903–1924." *Pacific Historical Review* 43, no. 4. (1974), 548–75.

Hsu, Madeline Y. *Dreaming of Gold, Dreaming of Home: Transnationalism and Migration Between the United States and South China, 1882–1943.* Stanford, CA: Stanford University Press, 2000.

Hune, Shirley, et al., eds. *Asian Americans: Comparative and Global Perspectives.* Pullman: Washington State University, 1991.

Hunt, Michael H. *Ideology and U.S. Foreign Policy.* New Haven, CT: Yale University Press, 1987.

Hyun, Peter. *In the New World: The Making of a Korean American.* Honolulu: University of Hawai'i Press, 1995.

———. *Man Sei!: The Making of a Korean American.* Honolulu: University of Hawai'i Press, 1986.

Ichioka, Yuji. *The Issei: The World of the First Generation Japanese Immigrants, 1885–1924.* New York: Free Press, 1988.

———. "Japanese Associations and the Japanese Government: A Special Relationship, 1909–1926." *Pacific Historical Review* 46, no. 3 (1977): 409–37.

Iriye, Akira. *Across the Pacific: An Inner History of American-East Asian Relations.* Chicago: Imprint Publications, 1967.

———. *The Globalizing of America, 1913–1945.* Cambridge, UK: Cambridge University Press, 1993.

———. *Pacific Estrangement: Japanese and American Expansion, 1897–1911.* Cambridge, MA: Harvard University Press, 1972.

Jacobsen, Matthew Frye. *Special Sorrows: The Diasporic Imagination of Irish, Polish, and Jewish Immigrants in the United States.* Cambridge, MA: Harvard University Press, 1995.

Jaroszynska-Kirchmann, Anna D. *The Exile Mission: The Polish Political Diaspora and Polish Americans, 1939–1956.* Athens: Ohio University Press, 2004.

Jensen, Joan M. *Passage from India: Asian Indian Immigrants in North America.* New Haven, CT: Yale University Press, 1988.

Joseph, May. *Nomadic Identities: The Performance of Citizenship.* Minneapolis: University of Minnesota Press, 1999.

Juergensmeyer, Mark. "The Ghadar Syndrome: Immigrant Sikhs and Nationalist Pride." In Mark Juergensmeyer and M. Gerald Barrier, eds. *Sikh Studies: Comparative Perspectives on a Changing Tradition*, 173–90. Berkeley, CA: Berkeley Religious Studies Series, Graduate Theological Union, 1979.

Kang, Man-gil. *A History of Contemporary Korea.* Folkstone, Kent, UK: Global Oriental, 2005.

———. "The Nature and Process of the Korean National Liberation Movement during the Japanese Colonial Period." *Korea Journal* 36, no. 1 (1996): 5–19.

———. "The Significance of the Shin'gan-hoe Society Movement in the History of the Korean National Movements." *Korea Journal* 27, no. 9 (September 1987): 4–10.

Kang, Jin Woong. "The Dual National Identity of the Korean Minority in China: The Politics of Nation and Race and the Imagination of Ethnicity." *Studies in Ethnicity and Nationalism* 8, no. 1 (2008): 101–19.

Kantowicz, Edward T. "Voting and Parties." In Michael Walzer, et al., eds. *The Politics of Ethnicity*, 29–68. Cambridge, MA: Belknap Press of Harvard University Press, 1982.

Karl, Barry D. *The Uneasy State: The United States from 1915 to 1945*. Chicago: University of Chicago Press, 1983.

Karpathakis, Anna. "Home Society Politics and Immigrant Political Incorporation: The Case of Greek Immigrants in New York City." *International Migration Review* 33, no. 1 (1999): 55.

Kasai, Jiuji. *The United States and Japan in the Pacific: American Naval Maneuvers and Japan's Pacific Policy*. New York: Arno Press, 1970.

Katkin, Wendy F., Ned Landsman, and Andrea Tyree, eds. *Beyond Pluralism: The Conception of Groups and Group Identities in America*. Urbana: University of Illinois Press, 1998.

Kazal, Russell A. "Revisiting Assimilation: The Rise, Fall, and Reappraisal of a Concept in American Ethnic History." *American Historical Review* 100, no. 2 (1995): 437–71.

Keane, John, ed. *Civil Society and the State: New European Perspectives*. London: Verso, 1988.

———. *Democracy and Civil Society: On the Predicaments of European Socialism, the Prospects for Democracy, and the Problem of Controlling Social and Political Power*. London: Verso, 1988.

Keller, Morton. *Affairs of State: Public Life in Late Nineteenth Century America*. Cambridge, MA: Belknap Press of Harvard University Press, 1977.

Kelley, Robin D.G. *Race Rebels: Culture, Politics, and the Black Working Class*. New York: Free Press, 1994.

Kennedy, David M. *Over Here: The First World War and American Society*. New York: Oxford University Press, 1980.

Keylor, William R. *The Twentieth-Century World: An International History*. New York: Oxford University Press, 1996.

———. *A World of Nations: The International Order Since 1945*. New York: Oxford University Press, 2003.

Kim, C. I. Eugene, and Han-Kyo Kim. *Korea and the Politics of Imperialism, 1876–1910*. Berkeley: University of California Press, 1967.

Kim, Hakjoon. "The Emergence of Siberia and the Russian Far East as a 'New Frontier' for Koreans." In Stephen Kotkin, and David Wolff, eds. *Rediscovering Russia in Asia : Siberia and the Russian Far East*, 302–11. Armonk, NY: M.E. Sharpe, 1995.

Kim, Han-Kyo. "The Declaration of Independence, March 1, 1919: A New Translation." *Korean Studies* 13 (1989): 1–4.

Kim, Hyung-chan. *Tosan Ahn Ch'ang-ho: A Profile of a Prophetic Patriot*. Seoul, Seattle, Los Angeles: Tosan Memorial Foundation, Korean American Historical Society, and Academia Koreana, Keimyung-Baylo University, 1996.

Kim, Hyung-chan, ed. *The Korean Diaspora: Historical and Sociological Studies of Korean Immigration and Assimilation in North America*. Santa Barbara, CA: ABC Clio, 1977.

Kim, Key-Huik. *The Last Phase of the East Asian World Order: Korea, Japan, and the Chinese Empire, 1860–1882*. Berkeley: University of California Press, 1980.

Kim, Ki-Jung. "Theodore Roosevelt's Image of the World and United States Foreign Policy toward Korea, 1901–1905." *Korea Journal* 35, no. 4 (1995): 39–53.
Kim, Ronyoung. *Clay Walls*. Sag Harbor, NY: Permanent Press, 1984.
Kim, Sunhyuk. *The Politics of Democratization in Korea: The Role of Civil Society*. Pittsburgh: University of Pittsburgh Press, 2000.
Kim, Warren Y. *Koreans in America*. Seoul: Po Chin Chai, 1971.
Kim, Won-yong. *Chaemi Hanin 50-yonsa*. Seoul: Hyean, 2004.
King, Ross. "Blagoslovennoe: Korean Village on the Amur, 1871–1937." *The Review of Korean Studies* 4, no. 2 (2001): 133–76.
Knock, Thomas J. *To End All Wars: Woodrow Wilson and the Quest for a New World Order*. New York: Oxford University Press, 1992.
Koh, Songmoo. *Koreans in Soviet Central Asia*. Helsinki: Finnish Oriental Society, 1987.
Kolarz, Walter. *The Peoples of the Soviet Far East*. New York: Frederick A. Praeger, 1954.
Krasner, Stephen D. *Sovereignty: Organized Hypocrisy*. Princeton, NJ: Princeton University Press, 1999.
Ku, Dae-yeol. *Korea Under Colonialism: The March First Movement and Anglo-Japanese Relations*. Seoul: Royal Asiatic Society Korea Branch, 1985.
Ku, Daeyeol. "China's Policy toward Korea during World War II: Restoration of Power and the Korean Question." *Korea Journal* 43, no. 4 (2003): 215–39.
———. "The March First Movement: With Special Reference to its External Implications and Reactions of the United States." *Korea Journal* 42, no. 3 (2002): 219–56.
———. "A Preliminary Study on the World Powers' Appoaches to the Korean Question before 1945: The Role of Perception in International Relations." *Korea Journal* 41, no. 2 (2001): 292–319.
Lauren, Gordon Paul. *Power and Prejudice: The Politics and Diplomacy of Racial Discrimination*. Boulder, CO: Westview, 1988.
Lee, Chae-Jin. *China's Korean Minority: The Politics of Ethnic Education*. Boulder, CO: Westview Press, 1986.
Lee, Chang-soo. "The United States Immigration Policy and the Settlement of Koreans in America." *Korea Observer* 6 (1975): 412–51.
Lee, Chong-sik. *The Korean Workers' Party: A Short History*. Stanford, CA: Hoover Institution Press, 1978.
———. *The Politics of Korean Nationalism*. Berkeley: University of California Press, 1963.
———. *Revolutionary Struggle in Manchuria: Chinese Communism and Soviet Interest, 1922–1945*. Berkeley: University of California Press, 1983.
Lee, Jean-young. "The Korean Minority in China: The Policy of the Chinese Communist Party and the Question of Korean Identity." *The Review of Korean Studies* 4, no. 2 (2001): 87–113.
Lee, Jongsoo. *Paekpŏm ilchi - The Autobiography of Kim Ku*. Lanham, MD: University Press of America, 2000.
Lee, Ki-baik. *A New History of Korea*. Cambridge, MA: Harvard University Press, 1984.
Lee, Kwang-rin. "The Rise of Nationalism in Korea." *Korean Studies* 10 (1986): 1–12.

Lee, Mary Paik. *Quiet Odyssey: A Pioneer Korean Woman in America*. Seattle: University of Washington Press, 1990.

Lee, Robert G. "The Hidden World of Asian Immigrant Radicalism." In Paul Buhle and Dan Georgakas, eds. *The Immigrant Left in the United States*, 256–88. Albany: State University of New York Press, 1996.

Lee, Timothy S. "A Political Factor in the Rise of Protestantism in Korea: Protestantism and the 1919 March First Movement." *Church History* 69, no. 1 (2000): 116–42.

Lee, Yur-bok. *Diplomatic Relations between the United States and Korea, 1861–1887*. New York: Humanities Press, 1970.

LeFeber, Walter. *The American Search for Opportunity, 1865–1913*. Cambridge, UK: Cambridge University Press, 1993.

Leff, Mark H. "Revisioning U.S. Political History." *American Historical Review* 100, no. 3 (1995): 829–53.

Lemelle, Sidney J., and Robin D.G. Kelley, eds. *Imagining Home: Class, Culture, and Nationalism in the African Diaspora*. London: Verso, 1994.

Leuchtenburg, William E. "The Pertinence of Political History: Reflections on the Significance of the State in America." *Journal of American History* 73, no. 3 (1986): 585–600.

Levering, Ralph B. *The Public and American Foreign Policy, 1918–1978*. New York: William Morrow and Company, 1978.

Levitt, Peggy. *The Transnational Villagers*. Berkeley: University of California Press, 2001.

Lewis, Earl. "To Turn as on a Pivot: Writing African Americans into a History of Overlapping Diasporas." *American Historical Review* 100, no. 3 (1995): 765–87.

Liem, Channing. *Philip Jaisohn: The First Korean American, A Forgotten Hero*. Philadelphia: Philip Jaisohn Memorial Foundation, 1984.

Link, Arthur S. *Woodrow Wilson and a Revolutionary World, 1913–1921*. Chapel Hill: University of North Carolina Press, 1982.

Littlefield, Heather C. "Irony of Japanese Imperialism: Korean Resistance Movements in Manchuria and Kando in the 1930." *Overseas Young Chinese Forum* 6, no. 3 (2005): 4–13.

Lowe, Lisa. *Immigrant Acts: On Asian American Cultural Politics*. Durham, NC: Duke University Press, 1996.

Lyu, Kingsley K. "Korean Nationalist Activities in Hawaii and the Continental United States, 1900–1945, Part I (1900–1919)." *Amerasia Journal* 4, no. 1 (1977): 23–90.

———. "Korean Nationalist Activities in Hawaii and the Continental United States, 1919–1945, Part II (1919–1945)." *Amerasia Journal* 4, no. 2 (1977): 53–100.

Ma, L. Eve Armentrout. *Revolutionaries, Monarchists, and Chinatowns: Chinese Politics in the Americas*. Honolulu: University of Hawai'i Press, 1990.

Macmillan, Michael E. "Unwanted Allies: Koreans as Enemy Aliens in World War II." *The Hawaiian Journal of History* 19 (1985): 179–203.

Mahler, Sarah J. "Constructing International Relations: The Role of Transnational Migrants and Other Non-state Actors." *Identity* 7, no. 2 (2000): 197–232.

Manela, Erez. *The Wilsonian Moment: Self-Determination and the International Origins of Anticolonial Nationalism*. New York: Oxford University Press, 2007.

Marr, David G. *Vietnamese Anticolonialism, 1885–1925*. Berkeley: University of California Press, 1971.

———. *Vietnamese Tradition on Trial, 1920–1945*. Berkeley, CA: University of California Press, 1981.

Martin, Bernd. "The Politics of Expansion of the Japanese Empire: Imperialism or Pan-Asiatic Mission?" In Wolfgang J. Mommsen and Jurgen Osterhammel, eds. *Imperialism and After: Continuities and Discontinuities*, 63–82. London: Allen & Unwin, 1986.

Martin, Terry. "The Origins of Soviet Ethnic Cleansing." *Journal of Modern History* 70, no. 4 (1998): 813–61.

Masayuki, Suzuki, "The Korean National Liberation Movement in China and International Response." In Dae-Sook Suh and Edward J. Shultz, eds. *Koreans in China*, 115–43. Honolulu: Center for Korean Studies, University of Hawaiʻi, 1990.

Matsusaka, Yoshihisa Tak. *The Making of Japanese Manchuria, 1904–1932*. Cambridge, MA: Harvard University Asia Center, 2001.

Matthews, Fred. "Paradigm Changes in Interpretations of Ethnicity, 1930–1980: From Process to Structure." In Peter Kivisto and Dag Blanck, eds. *American Immigrants and Their Generations: Studies and Commentaries on the Hansen Thesis after Fifty Years*, 167–88. Urbana: University of Illinois, 1990.

Mayer, Arnold J. *Wilson vs. Lenin: Political Origins of the New Diplomacy, 1917–1918*. Cleveland, OH: Meridian Book, 1963.

Maytray, James Irving. *The Reluctant Crusade: American Foreign Policy in Korea, 1941–1950*. Honolulu: University of Hawaiʻi Press, 1985.

McCormick, Thomas J. *America's Half-Century: United States Foreign Policy in the Cold War*. Baltimore: Johns Hopkins University Press, 1989.

McDonald, Jason. *American Ethnic History: Themes and Perspectives*. New Brunswick, NJ: Rutgers University Press, 2007.

McGrew, Anthony G., and Paul G. Lewis. *Global Politics: Globalization and the Nation-State*. Cambridge, UK: Polity Press, 1992.

McKeown, Adam. *Chinese Migrant Networks and Cultural Change: Peru, Chicago, Hawaii, 1900–1936*. Chicago: University of Chicago Press, 2001.

McLennan, Gregor, David Held, and Stuart Hall, eds. *The Idea of the Modern State*. Milton Keynes, UK: Open University Press, 1984.

McNamara, Dennis L. "Comparative Colonial Response: Korea and Taiwan." *Korean Studies* 10 (1986): 54–68.

Mehta, Uday S. "Liberal Strategies of Exclusion." In Frederick Cooper and Laura Ann Stoler, eds. *Tensions of Empire: Colonial Cultures in a Bourgeois World*, 59–86. Berkeley: University of California Press, 1997.

Melendy, H. Brett. *Asians in America: Filipinos, Koreans, and East Indians*. New York: Hippocrene Books, 1977.

Miller, Kerby. *Emigrants and Exiles: Ireland and the Irish Exodus to North America*. New York: Oxford University Press, 1985.

Mitter, Rana. *The Manchurian Myth: Nationalism, Resistance, and Colloboration in Modern China*. Berkeley: University of California Press, 2000.

Morawska, Ewa. *For Bread and Butter: The Life-Worlds of East Central European in Jamestown, Pennsylvania, 1890–1940.* New York: Cambridge University Press, 1985.

———. "Immigrants, Transnationalism, and Ethnicization: A Comparison of This Great Wave and the Last." In Gary Gerstle and John Mollenkopf, eds. *E Pluribus Unum? Contemporary and Historical Perspectives on Immigrant Political Incorporation*, 175–212. New York: Russell Sage Foundation, 2001.

Morawska, Ewa, and Spohn Willfried. "Moving Europeans in the Globalizing World: Contemporary Migrations in a Historical-Comparative Perspective (1955– 1994 v. 1870–1914)." In Gungwu Wang, ed. *Global History and Migrations*, 23–61. Boulder, CO: Westview Press, 1997.

Myers, Ramon H., and R. Peattie Mark, eds. *The Japanese Colonial Empire, 1895–1945.* Princeton, NJ: Princeton University Press, 1984.

Myers, Robert J. *Korea in the Cross Currents: A Century of Struggle and the Crisis of Reunification.* New York: Palgrave Macmillan, 2001.

Naficy, Hamid. *The Making of Exile Cultures: Iranian Television in Los Angeles.* Minneapolis: University of Minnesota Press, 1993.

Nagel, Joane. "The Political Construction of Ethnicity." In Susan Olzak and Joane Nagel, eds. *Competitive Ethnic Relations*, 93–112. Orlando, FL: Academic Press, 1986.

Nahm, Andrew C. "Durham White Stevens and the Japanese Annexation of Korea." In Andrew C. Nahm, ed. *The United States and Korea: American-Korean Relations, 1866–1976*, 110–136. Kalamazoo: Center for Korean Studies, Western Michigan University, 1979.

Narangoa, Li, and Robert Cribb, eds. *Imperial Japan and National Identities in Asia, 1895–1945.* London: Routledge, 2003.

Nathan, James A., and James K. Oliver. *Foreign Policy Making and the American Political System.* Baltimore: Johns Hopkins University Press, 1983.

Ngai, Mae M. *Impossible Subjects: Illegal Aliens and the Making of Modern America.* Princeton, NJ: Princeton University Press, 2004.

Neill, Stephen. *Colonialism and Christian Missions.* London: Lutterworth Press, 1966.

Nelson, M. Frederick. *Korea and the Old Orders in Eastern Asia.* New York: Russell & Russell, 1945.

Ninkovich, Frank. *The Wilsonian Century: U.S. Foreign Policy since 1900.* Chicago: University of Chicago Press, 1999.

O'Grady, Joseph Patrick. *Irish-Americans and Anglo-American Relations, 1880–1888.* New York: Arno Press, 1976.

Okihiro, Gary. *Cane Fires: The Anti-Japanese Movement in Hawaii, 1865–1945.* Philadelphia: Temple University Press, 1991.

Oliver, Robert T. *Syngman Rhee: The Man Behind the Myth.* New York: Dodd Mead and Company, 1955.

Omi, Michael, and Howard Winant. *Racial Formation in the United States from the 1960s to the 1980s.* New York: Routledge, 1989.

Ong, Paul, Edna Bonacich, and Lucie Cheng, eds. *The New Asian Immigration in Los Angeles and Global Restructuring.* Philadelphia: Temple University Press, 1994.

Osterhammel, Jürgen. *Colonialism: A Theoretical Overview*. Princeton, NJ: Markus Wiener Publishers, 1997.

———. "Semi-Colonialism and Informal Empire in Twentieth-Century China: Towards a Framework of Analysis." In Wolfgang J. Mommsen, and Jürgen Osterhammel, eds. *Imperialism and After: Continuities and Discontinuities*, 290–314. London: Allen & Unwin, 1986.

Osterhammel, Jürgen, and Niels P. Peterson. *Globalization: A Short History*. Princeton, NJ: Princeton University Press, 2003.

Osterhammel, Jürgen. "Semi-Colonialism and Informal Empire in Twentieth-Century China: Towards a Framework of Analysis." In Wolfgang J. Mommsen, and Jürgen Osterhammel, eds. *Imperialism and After: Continuities and Discontinuities*, 290–314. London: Allen & Unwin, 1986.

Pai, Margaret K. *The Dreams of Two Yi-min*. Honolulu: University of Hawai'i Press, 1989.

Pak, Mikhail N. "The Anti-Japanese Korean Independence Movement in Russian Territories: The 1920s and 1930s." *Korea Journal* 30, no. 6 (1990): 37–44.

Palais, James B. *Politics and Policy in Traditional Korea*. Cambridge, MA: Harvard University Press, 1975.

Palumbo-Liu, David. "Theory and the Subject of Asian American Studies." *Amerasia Journal* 21, no. 1/2 (1995): 55–66.

Park, Hong-Kyu. "From Pearl Harbor to Cairo: America's Korean Diplomacy, 1941–43." *Diplomatic History* 13 no. 3 (1989): 343–58.

Park, Hyun Ok. "Korean Manchuria: The Racial Politics of Territorial Osmosis." *South Atlantic Quarterly* 99, no. 1 (2000): 193–217.

———. "Repetition, Comparability, and Indeterminable Nation: Korean Migrants in the 1920s and 1990s." *boundary 2* 32, no. 2 (2005): 227–51.

———. *Two Dreams in One Bed: Empire, Social Life, and the Origins of the North Korean Revolution in Manchuria*. Durham, NC: Duke University Press, 2005.

Parreñas, Rhacel S., and Lok C.D. Siu, eds. *Asian Diasporas: New Formations, New Conceptions*. Palo Alto, CA: Stanford University Press, 2007.

Patterson, Wayne. "Horace Allen and Korean Immigration to Hawaii." In Andrew C. Nahm, ed. *The United States and Korea: American-Korean Relations, 1866–1976*, 137–61. Kalamazoo: Center for Korean Studies, Western Michigan University, 1979.

———. *The Ilse: First-Generation Korean Immigrants in Hawaii, 1903–1973*. Honolulu: University of Hawai'i Press and Center for Korean Studies, University of Hawai'i, 2000.

———. *The Korean Frontier in America: Immigration to Hawaii, 1896–1910*. Honolulu: University of Hawai'i Press, 1988.

———. "Ninety Years of Koreans in America: New Perspectives on Korean-American Relations, 1902–1992." In Donald N. Clark, ed. *U.S.-Korean Relations*. Claremont McKenna College: Keck Center for International and Strategic Studies, 1995.

Peterson, M. J. "Political Use of Recognition: The Influence of the International System." *World Politics* 34, no. 3 (1982): 324–52.

Piao, Changyu. "The History of Koreans in China and the Yanbian Korean Autonomous Prefecture." In Dae-Sook Suh and Edward J. Shultz, eds. *Koreans in China*, 60–84. Honolulu: Center for Korean Studies, University of Hawai'i, 1990.

Plischke, Elmer. *U.S. Department of State: A Reference History*. Westport, CT: Greenwood Press, 1999.

Pohl, J. Otto. *Ethnic Cleansing in the USSR, 1937–1949*. Westport, CT: Greenwood Press, 1999.

Pomerantz, Linda. "The Background of Korean Emigration." In Lucie Cheng, and Edna Bonacich, eds. *Labor Immigration Under Capitalism: Asian Workers in the United States Before World War II*, 277–311. Berkeley: University of California Press, 1984.

Poyo, Gerald E. *"With All, and for the Good of All": The Emergence of Popular Nationalism in the Cuban Communities of the United States, 1848–1898*. Durham, NC: Duke University Press, 1989.

Prakash, Gyan. "Writing Post-Orientalist Histories of the Third World: Perspectives from Indian Historiography." *Society for Comparative Study of Society and History* 32, no. 2 (1990): 383–408.

Puri, Harish K. *Ghadar Movement: Ideology, Organisation, and Strategy*. Amritsar, India: Guru Nanak Dev University, 1993.

Putnam, Robert. *Making Democracy Work: Civic Traditions in Modern Italy*. Princeton, NJ: Princeton University Press, 1993.

Radhakrishnan, R. *Diasporic Meditations: Between Home and Location*. Minneapolis: University of Minnesota Press, 1996.

Reed, James. *The Missionary Mind and American East Asian Policy, 1911–1915*. Cambridge, MA: Council on East Asian Studies, Harvard University Press, 1983.

Rhee, Syngman. *The Spirit of Independence: A Primer of Korean Modernization and Reform*. Honolulu: University of Hawai'i Press, 2001.

Riggs, Fred W. *Pressures on Congress: A Study of the Repeal of Chinese Exclusion*. West port, CT: Greenwood Press, 1950.

Robinson, Michael E. *Korea's Twentieth-Century Odyssey: A Short History*. Honolulu: University of Hawai'i Press, 2007.

Robinson, Michael Edson. *Cultural Nationalism in Colonial Korea, 1920–1925*. Seattle: University of Washington Press, 1988.

Roediger, David, and James Barrett. "Making New Immigrants 'Inbetween': Irish Hosts and White Panethnicity, 1890 to 1930." In Nancy Foner and George M. Frederickson, eds. *Not Just Black and White: Historical and Contemporary Perspectives on Immigration, Race, and Ethnicity in the United States*, 167–96. New York: Russell Sage Foundation, 2004.

Rogers, Reuel R. *Afro-Caribbean Immigrants and the Politics of Incorporation: Ethnicity, Exception, or Exit*. Cambridge, UK: Cambridge University Press, 2006.

Rosenberg, Emily S. *Spreading the American Dream: American Economic and Cultural Expansion, 1890–1945*. New York: Hill and Wang, 1982.

Rosenberg, William G., and Marilyn B. Young. *Transforming Russia and China: Revo lutionary Struggle in the Twentieth Century*. New York: Oxford University Press, 1982.

Roucek, Joseph S., and Bernard Eisenberg, eds. *America's Ethnic Politics*. Westport, CT: Greenwood Press, 1982.

Ryang, Sonia. "Diaspora and Beyond: There is No Home for Koreans in Japan." *The Review of Korean Studies* 4, no. 2 (2001): 55–86.

———. "Historian-Judges of Korean Nationalism." *Ethnic and Racial Studies* 13, no. 4 (1990): 503–26.

Safran, William. "Diasporas in Modern Societies: Myths of Homeland and Return." *Diaspora* 1, no. 1 (1991): 83–99.

Sánchez, George J. *Becoming Mexican Americans: Ethnicity, Culture and Identity in Chicano Los Angeles, 1900–1945*. New York: Oxford University Press, 1993.

Sarna, Jonathan D. "From Immigrants to Ethnics: Toward a New Theory of 'Ethnicization.'" *Ethnicity* 5 (1978): 370–78.

Savage, Timothy L. "The American Response to the Korean Independence Movement, 1910–1945." *Korean Studies* 20 (1996): 189–231.

Saveliev, Igor. "Militant Diaspora: Korean Immigrants and Guerillas in Early Twentieth Century Russia." *Forum of International Development Studies* 26 (March 2004): 147–62.

Scalapino, Robert A., and Lee Chong-sik. *Communism in Korea, Part I, The Movement*. Berkeley: University of California Press, 1972.

———. "The Origins of the Korean Communist Movement (I)." *Journal of Asian Studies* 20, no. 1 (1960): 9–31.

———. "The Origins of the Korean Communist Movement (II)." *Journal of Asian Studies* 20, no. 2 (1961): 149–67.

Schaar, John H. *Loyalty in America*. Berkeley: University of California Press, 1957.

Schmid, Andre. "Looking North Toward Manchuria." *South Atlantic Quarterly* 99, no. 1 (2000): 219–40.

Schultz, April R. *Ethnicity on Parade: Inventing the Norwegian American through Celebration*. Amherst: University of Massachusetts Press, 1994.

Schwabe, Klaus. "The Global Role of the United States and Its Imperial Consequences, 1898–1973." In Wolfgang J. Mommsen, and Jürgen Osterhammel, eds. *Imperialism and After: Continuities and Discontinuities*, 13–33. London: Allen & Unwin, 1986.

Seligman, Adam B. *The Idea of Civil Society*. New York: Free Press, 1992.

Shain, Yossi. *The Frontier of Loyalty: Political Exiles in the Age of the Nation-State*. Middletown, CT: Wesleyan University Press, 1989.

———, ed. *Governments-in-Exile in Contemporary World Politics*. New York: Routledge, 1991.

———. *Marketing the American Creed Abroad: Diasporas in the U.S. and Their Homelands*. Cambridge, UK: Cambridge University Press, 1999.

———. "Marketing the Democratic Creed Abroad: US Diasporic Politics in the Era of Multiculturalism." *Diaspora* 3, no. 1 (1994): 85–111.

Sheffer, Gabriel. *Diaspora Politics: At Home Abroad*. New York: Cambridge University Press, 2003.

———, ed. *Modern Diasporas in International Politics*. London: Croom Helm, 1986.

Shin, Gi-Wook, and Michael Robinson, eds. *Colonial Modernity in Korea*. Cambridge, MA: Harvard University Asia Center, 1999.

Shin, Yong-ha. *Formation and Development of Modern Korean Nationalism*. Seoul: Korea Research Foundation, 1990.

Shin'ichi, Yamamuro. *Manchuria Under Japanese Domination*. Philadelphia: University of Pennsylvania Press, 2006.

Shklar, Judith N. *American Citizenship: The Quest for Inclusion*. Cambridge, MA: Harvard University Press, 1991.

Shukla, Sandhya. *India Abroad: Diasporic Cultures of Postwar America and England*. Princeton, NJ: Princeton University Press, 2003.

Simons, Geoff. *Korea: The Search for Sovereignty*. London: Macmillan, 1995.

Siu, Lok C. D. *Memories of a Future Home: Diasporic Citizenship of Chinese in Panama*. Palo Alto, CA: Stanford University Press, 2005.

Smith, A. D. "States and Homelands: the Social and Geopolitical Implications of National Territory." *Millennium: Journal of International Studies* 10, no. 3 (1981): 187–202.

Smith, Anthony D. "State-Making and Nation-Building." In John Hall, ed. *States in History*, 228–63. Oxford: Basil Blackwell, Ltd., 1986.

Smith, Anthony D. "The Nation: Invented, Imagined, Reconstructed?" In Marjorie Ringrose and J. Lerner Adam, eds. *Reimagining the Nation*, 10–28. Buckingham, UK: Open University Press, 1993.

Smith, M. G. "Ethnicity and Ethnic Groups in America: The View from Harvard." *Ethnic and Racial Studies* 5, no. 1 (1982): 1–22.

Smith, Michael Peter, and Luis Eduardo Guarnizo, eds. *Transnationalism From Below*. New Brunswick, NJ: Transaction Publishers, 1998.

Snow, Jennifer C. *Protestant Missionaries, Asian Immigrants, and Ideologies of Race in America, 1850–1924*. New York: Routledge, 2007.

Sollors, Werner. *Beyond Ethnicity: Consent and Descent in American Culture*. New York: Oxford University Press, 1986.

———. "A Critique of Pure Pluralism." In Sacvan Bercovitch, ed. *Reconstructing American Literary History*, 250–79. Cambridge, MA: Harvard University Press, 1986.

Son, Young Ho. "Early Korean Immigration in America: A Socioeconomic and Demographic Analysis." *Korea Journal* 28, no. 12 (1988): 33–45.

———. "Korean Response to the 'Yellow Peril' and Search for Racial Accommodation in the United States." *Korea Journal* 32, no. 2 (1992): 58–74.

Steigerwald, David. *Wilsonian Idealism in America*. Ithaca, NY: Cornell University Press, 1994.

Suh, Dae-Sook. *The Korean Communist Movement, 1918–1948*. Princeton, NJ: Princeton University Press, 1967.

———, ed. *Koreans in the Soviet Union*. Honolulu: Center for Korean Studies, University of Hawai'i Press, 1987.

Suh, David Kwang-Sun. "American Missionaries and a Hundred Years of Korean Protestantism." In Youngnok Koo and Dae-Sook Suh, eds. *Korea and the United States: A Century of Cooperation*, 319–84. Honolulu: University of Hawai'i Press, 1984.

Sunoo, Sonia Shinn. *Korea Kaleidoscope: Oral Histories*, Vol. 1, *Early Korean Pioneers in USA: 1903–1905*. Sierra Mission, CA: United States Presbyterian Church, 1982.

Takaki, Ronald. *Strangers from a Different: A History of Asian Americans*. New York: Penguin Books, 1989.

Thomson, James C. Jr., Peter W. Stanley, and John Curtis Perry. *Sentimental Imperialists: The American Experience in East Asia*. New York: Harper & Row, 1981.

Tölölyan, Khachig. "Elites and Institutions in the Armenian Transnation." *Diaspora* 9, no. 1 (2000): 107–36.

———. "Rethinking Diaspora(s): Stateless Power in the Transnational Moment." *Diaspora* 5, no. 1 (1996): 3–35.

Trewartha, Glenn T., and Zelinsky Wilbur. "Population Distribution and Change in Korea, 1925–1949." *Geographical Review* 45, no. 1 (1955): 1–26.

Vassady, Bela Jr. "The 'Homeland Cause' as Stimulant to Ethnic Unity: The Hungarian-American Response to Karolyi's 1914 American Tour." *Journal of American Ethnic History* 2, no. 1 (1982): 39–64.

Vecoli, Rudolph J. "Ethnicity and Immigration." In Stanley Kutler, ed. *Encyclopedia of the United States in the Twentieth Century*, 161–93. New York: Simon & Schuster, 1996.

Wada, Haruki. "Koreans in the Soviet Far East, 1917–1937." In Dae-Sook Suh, ed. *Koreans in the Soviet Union*, 1–23. Honolulu: Center for Korean Studies, University of Hawai'i Press, 1987.

Walzer, Michael. "Pluralism in Political Perspective." In Michael Walzer, et al., eds. *The Politics of Ethnicity*, 1–28. Cambridge, MA: Belknap Press of Harvard University Press, 1982.

———. "The Civil Society Argument." In Ronald Beiner, ed. *Theorizing Citizenship*, 153–74. Albany: State University of New York, 1995.

Wang, L. Ling-chi. "The Structure of Dual Domination: Toward a Paradigm for the Study of the Chinese Diaspora in the U.S." *Amerasia Journal* 21, no. 1–2 (1995): 149–70.

Waters, Mary C. *Ethnic Options: Choosing Identities in America*. Berkeley: University of California Press, 1990.

Weber, Max. *From Max Weber: Essays in Sociology*. New York: Oxford University Press, 1946.

Wells, Kenneth M. *New God, New Nation: Protestants and Self-Reconstruction in Korea, 1896–1937*. Honolulu: University of Hawaii Press, 1990.

West, Rachel. *The Department of State on the Eve of the First World War*. Athens: University of Georgia Press, 1978.

Weston, Rubin Francis. *Racism in US Imperialism*. Columbia: University of South Carolina Press, 1972.

Wiebe, Robert. *The Search for Order, 1877–1920*. New York: Hill and Wang, 1967.

Wilson, Rob. "Theory's Imaginary Other: American Encounters with South Korea and Japan." In Masao Miyoshi, and H. D. Harootunian, eds. *Japan in the World*, 316–37. Durham, NC: Duke University Press, 1993.

Wilz, John Edward. "Did the United States Betray Korea in 1905?" *Pacific Historical Review* 54, no. 3 (1985): 243–70.

Wong, Janelle S. *Democracy's Promise: Immigrants & American Civic Institutions*. Ann Arbor: University of Michigan Press, 2006.

Wong, Sau-ling C. "Denationalization Reconsidered: Asian American Cultural Criticism at a Theoretical Crossroads." *Amerasia Journal* 21, no. 1/2 (1995): 1–28.

Yang, Eun Sik. "Korean Revolutionary Nationalism in America: Kim Kang and the Student Circle, 1937–1956." *California Sociologist* 13, no. 1–2 (1990): 173–98.

———. "Korean Women of America: From Subordination to Partnership, 1903–1930." *Amerasia Journal* 11 (1984): 1–28.

Yim, Sun Bin. "The Social Structure of Korean Communities in California, 1903–1920." In Lucie Cheng, and Edna Bonacich, eds. *Labor Immigration Under Capitalism: Asian Workers in the United States Before World War II*, 515–48. Berkeley: University of California Press, 1984.

Young, Iris Marion. *Justice and the Politics of Difference*. Princeton, NJ: Princeton University Press, 1990.

Young, Louise. *Japan's Total Empire: Manchuria and the Culture of Wartime Imperialism*. Berkeley: University of California Press, 1998.

Young, Marilyn Blatt. *The Rhetoric of Empire: American China Policy, 1895–1901*. Cambridge, MA: Harvard University Press, 1968.

Yu, Renqui. *To Save China, To Save Ourselves: The Chinese Hand Laundry Alliance of New York*. Philadelphia: Temple University Press, 1992.

Yuh, Ji-Yeon. *Beyond the Shadow of Camptown: Korean Military Brides in America*. New York: New York University Press, 2002.

Zabrovskaia, Larisa V. "Consequences of Korean Emigration to Jiandao." *Korea Journal* (Spring 1993): 69–73.

Zunz, Oliver. "American History and the Changing Meaning of Assimilation." *Journal of American Ethnic History* 4 (1985): 53–84.

INDEX

Ahn Chang-ho, 51fig., 67, 83
Aigukgum. See Patriotic Fund Drive
Alekseyevsk, 84–5, 91fig.
Alien Land Laws of 1913 and 1923, 3–4, 24
Alien Registration Act, 129, 132
Allen, Horace, 19, 28, 29
American Christian missionaries, 20, 28, 56–57, 60–65
   March First Movement and, 61–65
   "missionary mind" and, 63, 174n51
American group, 9, 83, 159, 160
   American public opinion and, 56, 63–65, 136
   Christianity and, 55–56, 60–63
   American democratic values and, 9, 54–56, 59–60, 139, 163
   diplomatic recognition and, 57, 86, 133, 135, 160
   financial contributions of, 53, 67–80
   international diplomacy and, 9, 50, 53, 56, 86–87, 133, 160–61
   lobbying activities and, 50, 52, 60, 136
   U.S. state power and, 9, 52, 107–8, 133, 135–36, 137, 145, 152, 160–62
   Woodrow Wilson's Fourteen Points and, 52, 160
Amur province, 84
anti-Asian sentiment, 3–4, 7, 12, 22–24, 39, 41, 119, 153, 186n81
Atlantic Charter, 137, 139, 141, 142, 143

Barrett, John, 36, 40
Berle, Adolph, 142, 147
Biddle, Francis, 132–33
Bolsheviks, 48, 52, 80, 85
"Brief for Korea," 86
Breuilly, John, 165n19

Bryan, William Jennings, 4–5, 44
Butler, Kim, 166n20

Cairo Declaration, 133, 135, 152, 156, 190n66
California, 3–6, 23, 36, 64, 68, 77, 128, 131, 147–48
Chan, Sucheng, 166n31
Chang In-whan, 32–41, 34fig., 171n59
Chiang Kai-shek, 115, 116
Chientao, 49, 81–82, 91fig., 168n39
China, 7, 9, 14, 16–17, 43, 46, 47, 60, 61, 86, 87, 111, 113, 115, 116, 126, 128, 133, 135, 137, 140, 153, 156, 157, 159, 167n4 (*see also* Chungking, Manchuria, Shanghai)
   alliance with Koreans and, 124–26
   KPG in, 145, 146, 152
   Nationalist government of, 115, 116, 125, 183n16, 183n27
   suzerainty over Korea and, 17
Ch'ingshan-li Battle, 81
Chita, 83, 91fig.
Chun Myung-won, 26–27, 31–41
Chung, Henry, 54, 55fig., 61, 73fig., 174n48
Chungking, 138fig., 140, 142, 149, 153
Churchill, Winston, 137, 190n66
citizenship, 7, 11–12, 43, 84, 120, 121, 184n47
civic nationalism, 120, 128, 184n47
civil society/state relationship, 66, 75–76, 108, 136, 174n1
Cold War, 158, 162, 163
Comintern, 84–85, 115
Communism, 48, 83–85, 115–16, 157, 163
Communist Party of All Koreans in Russia, 84

Comrade Society. *See* Tongjihoe
Conference of Limitations on Armament,
    86–88
    Korean Mission to, 86–88
Confucianism, 17, 59, 60, 167n4
Constitution (Republic of Korea), 58, 75
Coughlan, Nathan C., 36, 39–40
Cristy, Judge Albert M., 97–98, 100, 101,
    105–8
Cromwell, James H.R., 140–43, 146, 147
Cumings, Bruce, 190n66
Cynn, Hugh C., 35, 36, 37

Dern, George, 112
diaspora (*see also* American group, Korean
    diaspora, Koreans in America, Koreans
    in Hawaii, Siberian-Manchurian
    group)
    consciousness and, 8, 13, 25, 27, 36
    defined, 8, 166n20
    geopolitics and, 16, 25, 52, 133, 160
    nationalism and, 7, 8, 6–14, 27, 46–65,
        67, 85, 135–57, 158–59, 160–62
    transnational practices and, 8–10, 13–14,
        36, 68, 136, 152, 161
Dinuba, 23
diplomatic recognition, 110, 112, 133,
    135–36, 139, 140–43, 147, 153, 160
Dolph, Fred, 86–87
Dunn, Jacob Kyuang, 139, 144, 146, 147,
    150, 151–52, 153, 155

ethnic American, 109–10, 120, 128, 136,
    155, 162–63, 166n27
ethnic consciousness, 6, 10–11, 13–14, 97,
    110, 162
ethnic politics (*see also* ethnicity)
    citizen-based vs. noncitizen-based,
        11–12, 162
    political interest groups and, 10–11, 136,
        162
ethnicity, 6, 10–13, 110
    citizenship and, 11–12, 154–55, 162
    culture vs. race and, 9, 12, 162,
        166n24
    identity formation and, 6–7, 10–11,
        13–14, 110, 162
    political participation and, 6, 10–11, 97,
        155, 162, 166nn25, 27
    pluralism and, 12, 120, 136, 163

state recognition of, 10, 14, 120, 155,
    166n26
Exit, Voice and Loyalty, 120, 184n49

factionalism, 9, 14, 30, 67, 80, 81, 90, 114,
    115, 141, 148, 150
Farrington, Joseph R., 154, 190n61
Ferral, Robert, 36, 40
First Circuit Court of Hawaii, 96–97
Fort Shafter (HI), 116
Free City Incident, 85
Fresno, 23
futei senjin, 81, 82, 177n70

geopolitics, 7, 8, 13, 15, 47, 108, 112,
    169n40
Gerstle, Gary, 184nn44, 47
Gillette, Guy, 125
global-local dialectic, 92–93, 137
Great Britain, 17, 37, 53, 86, 133, 137, 156
Great People's Assembly. *See* Min Joong
    Dai Hoi
Greater Korean Independence Corps, 85

Haan, Kilsoo, 14, 109–34, 137, 146–47,
    150, 151fig., 185n61
    "constructive Americanism" and, 109
    ethnicization of Korean nationalism and,
        109–10
    "Japanization" of Hawaii and, 109, 121–22
    Sino-Korean Peoples League and, 111,
        114, 115, 116, 121, 125, 128, 129, 130,
        131, 136
    "A Survey of Public Opinion," 111–12,
        116–17, 118, 119–20
    U.S. Bureau of Investigation and, 117–19,
        184n44
    as W.K. Lyhan, 111
Hamilton, Maxwell M., 128, 129, 131
Hanin Hopsonghoe, 35
Hawaii, 46, 52, 73, 74, 92–108, 100, 111,
    113, 116, 119, 125, 127–28, 129, 131,
    149, 153, 155 (*see also* Koreans in
    Hawaii *and* KNA of Hawaii)
    Korean immigration to, 7, 13, 14, 15, 16,
        19–22, 74, 150
    plantation labor in, 19–21, 23, 33
    statehood hearings and, 123–24, 186n70
Hawaiian Sugar Planters' Association
    (HSPA), 19–20

Hemet (CA) 1913 incident, 3–8, 44
Hirschman, Albert O., 120, 184n49
Honolulu, 13, 41, 63, 74, 78, 93–96, 102, 105, 110, 117, 131, 136–37, 143–44, 146, 149
Honolulu United Korean Committee. *See* HONUKC
HONUKC (Honolulu United Korean Committee), 136, 137, 140, 143, 144, 146, 148, 149, 150
HSPA. *See* Hawaiian Sugar Planters' Association
Hughes, Charles Evans, 87–88
Hulbert, Homer, 63–64
Hull, Cordell, 122, 123, 124, 125, 126, 128, 140–42, 146–47

independence movement. *See* Korean independence movement
international diplomacy, 4, 9, 50, 53, 56, 86–87, 133, 160–61
Iriye, Akira, 172n2
Irkutsk, 84–85, 91fig.
Ito Hirobumi, 29

Jacobsen, Matthew Frye, 166n19
Jaisohn, Philip, 53–60, 55fig., 139, 173n25
Japan, 36, 47, 60, 86, 114, 135, 139, 140 (*see also* Japanese colonialism in Korea)
  as emerging world power, 18, 21
  emigration to America and, 19
  Gentlemen's Agreement and, 22, 27
  imperialism and, 5–7, 13, 16–17, 18, 28–31, 56, 61, 87, 111–12, 113, 122, 156, 161
  invasion of Manchuria and, 108, 111, 112, 113, 115
  Kangwha Treaty and, 16–17
  Meiji reforms and, 16
  Russo-Japanese War and, 18, 27
  Sino-Japanese War and, 17–18, 113
  Taft-Katsura agreement and, 19, 174n56
  Treaty of Portsmouth and, 18, 64, 174n56
  war with United States and, 114, 117–19, 137, 141, 142, 143, 147, 151–54, 157, 159
Japanese Association of Southern California, 4–6

Japanese colonialism in Korea, 7, 9, 15, 22, 25, 27–28, 31–34, 36–38, 40, 43, 46, 55, 64, 80, 127, 130, 143, 152, 158
  annexation, 5, 13, 15, 19, 26, 44, 47, 61, 87, 174n56
  atrocities, repression and, 26, 29, 33, 36, 38–40, 46, 49, 56, 57, 60, 61–62, 67, 81, 87, 127, 158
  protectorate and, 19, 28–30, 31, 33, 64, 87, 174n56
Japanese Consulate in America, 4–6, 31, 37, 38, 112–13, 122–23, 185n61
Japanese militarism, 48, 56–57, 80–82, 121, 125–26, 127, 128, 130, 157

Khaborovsk, 48, 91fig.
Kim, Bernice, 20
Kim, Charles Ho, 139, 143, 144, 146, 147–48
Kim, Henry (Kim Hyon-gu), 94–95, 97, 98, 101, 103, 104, 105, 106, 118, 150
Kim Hyon-gu. *See* Kim, Henry
Kim Il Sung, 159, 160
Kim Ku, 108, 115, 116, 147, 159
Kim, Warren (Kim Wong-yong), 97, 118, 124–25, 148, 150, 153
Kim Won-bong, 115–16, 183n27
Kim Wong-yong. *See* Kim, Warren
Kim Young-jeung, 150, 153
Kimm, Kiusic, 69fig., 73–78, 83, 111, 115, 116, 178n74
King, Samuel, 123
KNA (Korean National Association), 5–6, 14, 21, 66–68, 70–78, 89, 114, 136, 172n72, 175nn14–17 (*see also* KNA of Hawaii)
  central headquarters of, 41, 44, 70, 74–76, 79, 92
  civil society and, 66, 75, 108, 174n1
  diaspora and, 35–36, 41–45
  formation of, 35–36
  independence movement and, 41–45, 138fig.
  Patriotic Fund drive (*Aigukgum*) and, 68, 70–77
  self-governance and, 44, 66
  Sinhan Minbo and, 26, 42, 43fig.
  supranational state functions, 5, 44–45
  transnational fundraising, 36, 68

Index [217]

KNA of Hawaii, 36, 74, 92–108, 111, 118, 136, 138fig., 148, 179n2
   factions (regular and irregular) and, 93
   First Circuit Court of Hawaii and, 96–97
   Kungminbo and, 42
   Kyomindan (Korean Residents Association) and, 92, 93, 102–3, 108
   U.S. judicial system and, 93, 108
Knight, Samuel, 38–40
Koike Chozo, 31, 37, 38
Kojong, King, 19, 28, 29, 63–64
Kongchaipyo. See Liberty Bonds *and* KORIC
Konglip Association (Kongliphoe), 30, 31, 42
KOPOGO (Korean Provisional Government). *See* KPG
Korea (Korean peninsula)
   bans on emigration from, 16, 21
   China's suzerainty and, 17
   Christianity in, 20, 54, 57, 60, 61
   civil war in, 158, 159, 161
   Confucianism in, 60, 167n4
   division into two states and, 158–163
   foreign competition over, 17, 157
   Korean Communist Party and, 90
   Korean Provisional Government and, 142
   liberation from Japan, 52, 127, 135, 152, 159, 161
   March First movement and, 13, 45–48, 49, 61, 173n32, 177n70
   mass migration from, 16, 19–22
   military dictatorships and, 158, 161
   as modern nation-state, 13, 17, 47, 50, 51–52, 54, 58, 46–65, 158–59, 160
   national sovereignty and, 5, 7–8, 13, 15, 17, 26, 45, 51, 57–58, 64, 87–88, 158
   Patriotic Enlightenment movement in, 48
   post-WWII occupation of, 156–58, 161
   Protestant missionaries in, 20, 27, 60
   Republic of (ROK), 58, 68, 159, 160, 161, 163
   Sin'ganhoe (New Korea Association), 90
   38th parallel and, 157, 158
   trusteeship of, 152, 156–57
   U.S. military and, 158, 161
Korea Review, 61
Korean-American Council, 138fig., 140, 142–43, 145, 146, 147
Korean Anti-Japanese Front Unification League, 116
Korean Commission. *See* KORIC
Korean Communist Party, 90
Korean Congress in Philadelphia. *See* Philadelphia Korean Congress
Korean Consolidated Association. *See* Hanin Hopsonghoe
Korean Declaration of Independence, 47, 55, 57, 140
Korean diaspora
   American group and, 9, 47, 52–65, 67–80, 133, 135–57, 161–63
   anti-Japanese activity of, 48–50, 113–14, 147, 158
   China and, 7, 16, 46, 114, 140, 145
   Cuba and, 7, 16, 138fig.
   Europe and, 7
   factional conflict and, 9, 14, 30, 67–85, 92–108, 159, 161, 163
   ideological camps within, 9, 48, 50–52, 108, 158–59, 161
   independence movement and, 7–14, 25, 37, 42–45, 46–65
   Japan and, 36, 140
   March First movement and, 46–65, 74, 89, 173n32, 177n70
   Mexico and, 7, 16, 36, 42, 44, 138fig., 172n70
   national identity and, 5–14, 26–27, 30–45, 51, 54, 110, 120, 162, 163
   Siberian-Manchurian group and, 9, 48–52, 80–85, 115–16, 159–60, 168nn39–40, 179n98
   and Stevens case mobilization, 35–36, 41
Korean Diplomatic Mission, 155
Korean immigration, 7, 13, 15–16, 19–22, 74, 127, 130, 163, 168n39
Korean Independence League, 136
Korean independence movement, 5–14, 25, 37, 46–65, 109, 110, 111, 125, 133, 134, 136, 138fig., 147, 150, 152, 154, 156, 160, 161, 162 (*see also* nationalism)
   KNA and, 5–6, 14, 21, 41–45, 66–68, 70–78, 89, 114, 136, 175nn14–17
   KPG and, 46–65, 108
Korean Independence Party, 136, 138fig.
Korean Information Bureau, 60–61, 110
Korean Liberty Conference, 139, 140

Korean Methodist Church, 30, 31, 32, 33, 35, 39, 138fig.
Korean National Association. *See* KNA
Korean National Front Federation, 125, 138fig.
Korean National Herald, 63, 103, 138fig., 147, 149, 150, 152, 154
Korean National Revolutionary Party (KNRP), 116, 124, 136
Korean nationalist movement. *See* Korean independence movement *and* nationalism
Korean People's Communist Party, 83–85
Korean Provisional Government. *See* KPG
"Korean Question," 61, 63–64, 86–87, 151, 174n48
Korean Residents Association. *See* Kyomindan
Korean Revolutionary Military Congress, 85
Korean Revolutionary Party, 138fig., 151
Korean Righteous Fighters' Corps. 115, 116
Korean Situation, 62–63
Korean Socialist Party (Hanin Sahoedang), 48, 49, 50, 83
Korean Volunteer Corps, 125, 138fig.
Korean War, 158, 159, 161, 163
Korean Women's Patriotic Society, 136
Korean Women's Relief Society, 136
Koreans in America, 3–14, 46–47, 52–54, 89, 109–10, 130, 136–37, 142, 150, 152, 161 (*see also* American group, Korean diaspora, Koreans in Hawaii)
 American political institutions and, 4–14, 109–34, 162–63
 Christianity and, 5–6, 20, 56–57, 60–64
 community formation and, 8, 10, 13, 15, 22–25, 74, 162–63
 ethnicity and, 6, 9–11, 109–10, 120, 136, 162–63
 fundraising and, 53, 67–80
 homeland orientation of, 8, 10, 26–27, 30–45, 110, 120, 162, 163
 immigration patterns of, 7, 13, 19–25
 independence movement leadership and, 47, 53, 58–59, 74, 142
 McCarran-Walter Act and, 162, 190n7
 national identity as Koreans and, 5–14, 26, 54, 162
 racialized status of, 7, 8, 10, 12, 119, 120, 128, 134, 162
 transnational networks and, 8–10, 13–14, 36, 68, 136, 152, 161
 U.S. state power and, 9, 11–12, 14, 129, 130, 133, 156, 161, 162
Koreans in Hawaii, 7, 15, 16, 19–22, 25, 36, 46, 52, 58, 67–68, 73, 89, 92–108, 119, 123, 128, 132, 136–67, 146, 150, 153, 154, 177n61, 183n16 (*see also* KNA of Hawaii *and* HONUKC)
 Christianity and, 20, 56
 community development and, 25, 74
 as contract plantation labor, 19–22, 33
 as enemy aliens, 109–10, 120, 128, 136, 162–63, 187n93
 HSPA and, 19
 immigration and, 7, 13, 14, 15, 16, 19–22, 56, 58
 migration to U.S. mainland of, 20, 25, 33
 Sino-Korean Peoples League and, 116
KORIC (Korean Commission), 14, 60, 66–79, 86, 89, 92, 93, 131, 137, 138fig., 140, 144–45, 146, 147, 150, 155, 175n17, 177n61
 creation of, 60
 Kiusic Kimm and, 69fig., 73–78, 83
 Liberty Bonds (*Kongchaipyo*) and, 68–72, 74, 76–77, 79
 state power and, 71, 74, 75–76
 Syngman Rhee and, 66–72, 69fig., 131, 137, 144, 149–50, 153
KPG (Korean Provisional Government), 13–14, 46–65, 66–83, 85, 102–3, 108, 114, 124, 133, 135, 137, 138fig., 145, 146, 152, 155, 160–61
 Ahn Chang-ho and, 51fig., 67, 83
 armed resistance groups and, 49
 Chungking and, 138fig., 140, 147, 149, 152, 153
 as democratic republic, 47–48, 58
 diplomatic recognition and, 110, 112, 133, 135–36, 139, 140–43, 147, 153, 160
 founding of, 46–48
 as government in exile, 46, 47, 172n4
 impeachment of Rhee and, 95
 National Congress of, 70
 "New Korea" and, 51–52, 58, 59, 160
 Provisional Legislative Assembly, 88–89
 Republic of Korea and, 50, 55, 68, 69fig., 70, 75, 160

Index [219]

KPG (*Continued*)
  Seoul and, 49, 50
  Shanghai and, 13, 46, 47, 49, 53, 67, 70, 72, 75, 77, 79, 80, 82, 83, 85, 89, 90, 91fig., 92, 102–3, 115, 150
  as sovereign political entity, 58, 67, 88, 139, 160–61
  UKC and, 143, 144, 155
  as united front, 50, 52, 67
  United States and, 47, 64, 86–88, 133, 134, 140–41, 155, 160
  Vladivostok and, 49
  withdrawal of Siberian-Manchurian group from, 83
Kungminhoe. *See* KNA
Kyomindan (Korean Residents Association), 92, 93, 102–3, 108, 179n2 (*see also* KNA of Hawaii)

labor migration, 7, 13, 14, 15, 16, 19–22, 56, 58, 167n18
LAUKC (Los Angeles United Korean Committee), 136, 137, 140, 143, 144, 146, 147, 149
League of Friends of Korea, 60, 61, 62, 87
League of Nations, 63, 108
Lee, Chong-sik, 166n22
Lee, David, 5, 70, 71
Lee Kyung-won (K.W.), 173n25
Lee Won Soon, 143
Lenin, Vladimir, 80–81, 83, 85
Liberty Bonds (*Kongchaipyo*), 68–79
Los Angeles, 13, 22, 24–25, 35, 132, 136, 137, 143, 144, 146, 148, 151, 153, 155
Los Angeles United Korean Committee. *See* LAUKC
Lyhan, W.K. *See* Haan, Kilsoo

MacFarland, James P. 117, 118–19
Manchuria, 7, 9, 16, 18, 36, 42–43, 46–49, 51, 68, 80–82, 84, 89, 91fig., 116, 125, 140, 159, 160, 168n39, 169n40, 177n70, 179n98
  Japanese invasion of, 108, 111, 112, 113, 115, 157
Manela, Erez, 173n19
March First movement, 13, 45–48, 49, 53, 57, 74, 173n32, 177n70
Maritime Province, 48, 50, 51, 82, 84, 89, 91fig., 177n70

McCarran-Walter Act, 162, 190n7
Mexico, 7, 16, 21, 22, 36, 42, 44, 74, 79, 172n70
"middle generation" leaders, 150–54
Min Joong Dai Hoi (Great People's Assembly), 148, 149

Nagel, Joane, 166n25
Nanking, 115, 116
national self-determination, 8, 9, 52, 53, 57, 137, 158, 160, 163
national sovereignty, 5, 7–8, 13, 15, 17, 26, 45, 51, 57–58, 64, 87–88, 158, 160, 165n18
nationalism (*see also* Korean independence movement)
  civic vs. racial, 119–120, 184n47
  Communism and, 48, 84, 115
  diasporic, 7, 8, 13, 27, 85, 35–57, 161
  ethnicization of, 110, 136, 162
  ideological work of, 9, 13, 42, 160
  leadership and, 13, 167n33
  March First movement and, 13, 45–48, 49, 53, 57, 74, 173n32, 177n70
  national identity and, 5–14, 26–27, 30–45, 51, 54, 110, 120, 162, 163
  as state-building, 7, 8, 165n19
nation-state system, 8, 9, 15–16, 17, 58, 80, 160, 165n18
Nebraska, 22, 63
neocolonialism, 160, 161
New Il-han, 150
New Korea. *See Sinhan Minbo*
Norris, George, 63
North Korea (Democratic People's Republic of Korea), 158, 159, 160, 161, 163

O'Brien, Ray J., 98, 101, 106, 107
Office of Naval Intelligence (ONI), 185n61

Pacific War Council, 156
Pai Yil-Chin, 97–98, 100, 101, 104, 105, 106, 107
Paik, Earl, 70, 72
Patriotic Fund drive (*Aigukgum*), 68, 70–77
Patterson, Wayne, 21
Pearl Harbor, 130, 131, 133
Pehle, John W., 130, 131
Perry, Commodore Matthew, 16

[220] *Index*

Phelan, James, 64
Philadelphia Korean Congress of 1919, 53–60, 139
　"Aims and Aspirations" and, 58–59
　"An Appeal to America" and, 56
Philippines, 19, 30, 127, 174n56
picture brides, 15, 22
Portsmouth Treaty, 18, 64, 174n56
Putnam, Robert, 174n1

racial discrimination, 7, 11–12, 120–21, 128, 134, 162, 184n47
"recalcitrant Koreans." See futei senjin
Redlands, 23, 25
Reedley, 23
Rhee, Syngman, 51, 55fig., 61, 66–89, 109–10, 131–32, 139, 140, 142, 153, 155, 159, 175n17
　as head of state, 75, 108, 160
　impeachment from KPG and, 89
　KNA of Hawaii and, 92, 102–4, 106, 107, 108
　Korean Diplomatic Mission and, 155
　KORIC (Korean Commission) and, 66–72, 69fig., 131, 137, 153
　as KPG President, 14, 50, 53, 54, 59, 67–89, 103
　Tongjihoe and, 27, 102–4, 148–50, 155
　United Korean Committee and, 143, 144–45, 146, 147, 148–50
Richardson, Robert C. 133, 153
Righteous Armies, 29, 48–49
Riverside, 3, 5, 23, 25
Robinson, Michael E., 167n1
Roosevelt, Franklin, 124, 125, 126, 137, 156, 190n66
Roosevelt, Theodore, 18, 22, 64
Russia, 9, 17, 18, 43, 80, 83–85, 113 (see also Siberia and Soviet Union)
Russian Far East, 80, 82, 84–85, 91fig., 178n83
Russian Revolution, 80
Russo-Japanese War, 18, 27, 64

sadae kyorin, 167n4
Sánchez, George J., 182n2
San Francisco 5, 13, 22, 23, 24–25, 75–76, 100, 125
　KNA headquarters in, 41, 44, 66–67, 70, 79, 92, 93

Stevens' assassination and trial events in, 27, 29–41
Seoul, 17, 28, 46, 47, 49, 50
Shain, Yossi, 173n31
Shanghai, 13, 46, 47, 49, 53, 67, 70, 72, 75, 77, 79, 80, 82, 83, 85, 89, 90, 91fig., 92, 102–3, 115, 150
Shon, Duk-yin, 94–95, 97, 99–107
Shumiatsky, Boris, 85
Siberia, 7, 9, 16, 36, 39, 42, 46, 47, 48, 49, 52, 68, 80–85, 140, 168nn39–40, 178n83, 179n98 (see also Maritime Province and Russian Far East)
Siberian-Manchurian group, 9, 48–52, 80–85, 115–16, 159–60, 168nn39–40, 179n98 (see also Yi Tong-hwi)
　armed struggle and, 9, 48–50, 80–81, 116, 160
　Ch'ingshan-li Battle and, 81
　émigré communities in, 68, 178n83, 179n98
　Free City Incident and, 85
　guerrilla raids and, 48, 81, 115, 160
　Irkutsk group and, 84–85
　Korean Socialist Party and, 48
　Leninist self-determination and, 9, 52
　military operations and, 53, 80–81, 84, 115–16
　"1920 Massacre" and, 81
　revolutionary vision and, 52, 80, 160
　"Russianized" vs. nonnaturalized foreign Koreans and, 84–85
　Shanghai-Chita group and, 83–84
　socialism and, 9, 48, 52, 160
　Soviet funding and, 80–81
　terrorism and, 49, 115–16
Sinhan Minbo, 26, 42, 43fig., 75, 76, 147
Sino-Japanese War, 17–18, 113
Sino-Korean Peoples League, 111, 114, 115, 116, 121, 125, 128, 129, 130, 136, 138fig.
Smith Act. See Alien Registration Act
So Chae-pil. See Jaisohn, Philip
socialism, 9, 48, 52, 160
South Korea (Republic of Korea), 158, 159, 160, 161, 163
Soviet Union, 50, 52, 156, 157, 158, 159
Spencer, Seldon, 63
Staggers, John, 140
Stalin, Josef, 156, 178n83

state power, 7, 9, 11–12, 13, 14, 52, 66, 68, 74–76, 107–8, 129, 130, 133, 135–36, 137, 145, 152, 156, 160–62
state sovereignty, 5, 7–8, 13, 15, 17, 26, 45, 51, 57–58, 64, 87–88, 158, 160, 161, 165n18
statelessness, 7, 25, 26, 44–45, 84, 162, 169n40
Stevens, Durham White, 27–41, 171n46
   service to Japanese government and, 27–30, 33
   assassination of, 31–32, 37
Stimson Doctrine, 112

Taedong Association, 30, 31, 35
Taft-Katsura agreement, 19, 174n56
Tehran Conference, 156
Tonghak rebellion, 17–18
Tongjihoe (The Comrade Society), 27, 102–4, 136–37, 138fig., 148–50, 155
Tongjipkum. See Korean Independence Funds
transnationalism, 8–10, 13–14, 36, 68, 136, 152, 161 (*see also* diaspora)
Treaty of Amity and Commerce (1882), 17, 28, 57, 64, 86, 126
Truman, Harry S. 157

uibyong. See Righteous Armies
UKC (United Korean Committee), 135–57 (*see also* HONUKC, LAUKC)
   Third Annual UKC Conference in 1944, 153
   in Washington, DC, 150, 152, 153, 155
United Korea (*Konglip Sinbo*), 37, 42
United Korean Committee. See UKC
United Nations, 139, 140, 153
United States, 67, 68, 73, 78, 79, 89, 131
   anti-Asian sentiment in, 3–4, 7, 12, 22–24, 39, 41, 119, 153
   citizenship and, 7, 11, 154, 184n47, 186n81
   civil society and, 66, 136, 174n1
   ethnic pluralism in, 12, 136, 163, 174n1
   ethnicity and race in, 6, 9–12, 14, 109, 110, 119, 120, 128, 136, 155, 162, 163, 164nn24, 27, 174n1, 184n47
   European immigrant groups in, 11, 12, 162

   exclusionary immigration policies of, 7, 16, 19, 21, 162–63
   globalization of power and, 13, 47, 52, 55, 160, 162
   "Korean Question" and, 63–64, 127, 128, 174n48
   naturalization and, 154, 168n26, 186n81
   Neutrality Act of 1935 and, 126, 186n77
   neocolonialism and, 160–61
   support for Korean independence by, 63, 125, 133, 145, 153
U.S. Army, 116, 118, 119, 123, 126, 131, 133
U.S. Bureau of Investigation, 117–19, 184n44
U.S. Congress, 52, 63–64, 124, 126, 154, 174n56, 186n70
U.S. Department of Justice, 4, 117, 119, 130, 131, 132, 133
U.S. global hegemony, 158, 161, 162–63
U.S. House of Representatives, 123, 128, 154, 190n61
U.S. military intelligence, 111, 116–17, 118, 123, 127–28, 131, 184n44, 185n61
U.S. Navy, 114, 126, 185n61
U.S. Senate, 63, 123
U.S. State Department, 4–5, 44, 87–88, 112, 122–23, 125, 128, 129, 131–33, 139–45, 147, 153, 156
U.S. Treasury Department, 129, 130, 131
U.S. War Department, 18, 112, 131

Vladivostok, 48, 49, 50, 91fig.

Washington, D.C., 4, 6, 13, 29, 31, 51fig., 60, 66, 70–72, 74–80, 86, 88–89, 122, 123, 125, 131, 137, 139, 140, 145–47, 149–53, 155
Wells, B. H., 116–17
Western nation-states, 8–9, 17, 80
Westphalian system of states, 8, 165n18
White Russian, 81, 84
Williams, Jay Jerome, 140
Willows, 23
Wilson, Woodrow, 9, 57, 62, 137, 160
   Fourteen Points and, 9, 52, 137, 160
World War I, 11, 13, 24, 47, 52, 68, 160

World War II, 11, 14, 121, 124, 150, 151, 156, 157, 159, 161, 168n26, 187n105

Yalta Conference, 156
Yi Kojong. *See* Kojong
Yi Tong-hwi, 48–49, 50, 51fig., 80–85, 115

    as Korean Socialist Party founder, 48–49
    as KPG premier, 50, 67, 80
    resignation from KPG and, 83
Yo Un-hyong, 159
Yucatan peninsula, 21, 44, 138fig.

www.ingramcontent.com/pod-product-compliance
Ingram Content Group UK Ltd.
Pitfield, Milton Keynes, MK11 3LW, UK
UKHW041306180426
11947UKWH00009B/730